Social Control in Nineteenth Century Britain

EDITED BY A.P. DONAJGRODZKI

CROOM HELM LONDON

ROWMAN AND LITTLEFIELD
Totowa, New Jersey

© 1977 A.P. Donajgrodzki
Croom Helm Ltd., 2-10 St John's Road, London SW11

British Library Cataloguing in Publication Data
Social control in nineteenth century Britain.
   1. Labour and labouring classes − England −
History. 2. Social control − History
   I. Donajgrodzki, A P
   301.44'42'0942   HD8388

   ISBN 0-85664 589-3

First Published in the United States 1977
by Rowman and Littlefield, Totowa, N.J.

ISBN 0-87471-880-5

Printed in Great Britain
by Redwood Burn Ltd, Trowbridge and Esher

CONTENTS

ACKNOWLEDGEMENTS

We are obliged to the Controller of Her Majesty's Stationery Office for permission to make use of Crown-copyright material in the Public Record Office. We are grateful to the libraries mentioned in this book for permission to use and quote from the papers in their care, and to the staff of these institutions for their assistance.

As editor, I should like to thank colleagues in the Department of Adult Education and Extra-mural Studies for help and advice, and especially Mr David Goodway; Mr Gerald Cooper; Ms Jane M. Belson of University College Library, London; Mrs Jean White for her speedy and accurate typing; and finally, Noni, Patrick, Antonia and Stephen.

LIST OF CONTRIBUTORS

John Stevenson, Lecturer in History, University of Sheffield.

Tony Donajgrodzki, Lecturer in the Department of Adult Education and Extra-Mural Studies, University of Leeds.

Richard Johnson, Senior Lecturer in Social History, Centre for Contemporary Cultural Studies, University of Birmingham.

Jennifer Hart, Tutor in Modern History and Fellow of St Anne's College Oxford.

Robert D. Storch Assistant Professor of History, University of Wisconsin – Janesville

Hugh Cunningham, Lecturer in History, University of Kent.

Michael E. Rose, Senior Lecturer in Economic History, University of Manchester.

Judith Fido, Senior Lecturer in Social Policy, Leeds Polytechnic.

Victor Bailey, Research Officer, Centre for Criminological Research, Oxford.

INTRODUCTION

Much recent writing on social history has been characterised by its use of concepts borrowed from sociology. The present volume is concerned to apply one such concept, social control, to the study of relationships between rich and poor in nineteenth-century British society. Its contributors view the concept from sometimes different standpoints, but all share an assumption which lies at its heart; the belief, that is, that social order is maintained not only, or even mainly by legal systems, police forces and prisons, but is expressed through a wide range of social institutions, from religion to family life, and including, for example, leisure and recreation, education, charity and philanthropy, social work and poor relief. A broadened perspective on the question of order in society is not entirely new in historical studies,[1] but the concept of social control will be unfamiliar to many historians, and it has sometimes been misunderstood even by those who have used it. It may be useful then to preface this, the first collection of historical essays to make use of the concept, with a brief description of its sociological development and usages.

I

It will perhaps be best to consider the sociological development of the concept in the light of two kinds of misconception historians may hold about it. The social control approach, it has been suggested, implies a belief that order is the product of many social processes, relationships and institutions. It may be feared, to take the first area of misunderstanding, that the use of the idea commits the social historian to a species of crude reductionism, which doubts the humanity of the humanitarian, sees clergymen, social workers or educators as *only* and *merely* policemen without boots, to an approach which, in short, coarsens our appreciation of the complexity of social relationships and historical processes. But although the concept may have a certain seductive appeal for those who, as Engels expressed it, want to write a materialist history without going to the trouble of doing the history,[2] the concept itself does not necessitate such crudity, as an analysis of the idea itself, and a reading of the studies in this book will show.

The social control perspective has been questioned, secondly, by some radical historians, especially, somewhat surprisingly, by Gareth

Stedman Jones.[3] He suggests that since the concept originated in 'an incompatible sociological tradition', Marxists who use it are 'uncritically eclectic'. He argues that the concept necessitates the acceptance of a consensual social model, even within capitalist society. He points out too, that in the sociology of Durkheim and Parsons it is associated with a description of the transition from agrarian society to capitalism which denies the permanency of class struggle. Now it is true, as Stedman Jones says, that the idea was pioneered within a conservative sociological tradition, but it is more flexible than he allows. It is, in fact, trans-ideological. The use of social control, like the use of the concept of 'socialisation' does not imply adherence to a sociology based on any particular ideology. Thus it should occasion no surprise that the concept has been used in radical as well as conservative sociologies.

The concept of social control was first used by E.A. Ross, whose *Social Control* appeared in 1901. He put forward the central tenet of social control, that social order is the product not only of law, but of a much wider set of phenomena, and in a passage which suggests the applicability of the concept both to conflict-orientated and consensual theories, divided the means of social control into two broad categories:

> Such instruments of control as public opinion, suggestion, personal ideal, social religion, art and social valuation draw much of their strength from the primal moral feelings. They take their shape from sentiment rather than utility. They control men in many things which have little to do with the welfare of society regarded as a corporation. They are aimed to realize not merely a social order but what one might term a *moral* order. These we may call *ethical.*
>
>   On the other hand, law, belief, ceremony, education, and illusion need not spring from ethical feelings at all. They are frequently the means deliberately chosen in order to reach certain ends. They are likely to come under the control of the organised few, and be used, whether for the corporate benefit or for class benefit, as the tools of policy. They may be termed *political* using the word 'political' in its original sense of 'pertaining to policy'.[4]

The preponderance of one category of control measure over the other depended on the 'constitution' of the society.

Ross began a tradition of theory on social control which was carried through to the 1950s. Some sociologists, like Paul Landis, expanded its scope so greatly that, as Buckley has noted, 'social control' and 'sociology' became virtually interchangeable terms. In Landis' hands, too, social control was associated with a conservative social vision very similar to that expressed by some Victorian British social commentators. He suggested that modern industrial society possessed a 'general culture', crossing class and ideological boundaries, which is the foundation of social order. But modern society was considerably less efficient at realising the general culture through its institutions than more primitive and religious societies. The growth of great cities, the decline of religion, and the onslaught of 'disintegrated forces' on the family had weakened social bonds. Thus Landis argued, 'social control is the major problem of our time'. It was a problem for which he attempted to find practical solutions and, predictably, he came to place his faith in education as the best means to ensure the stability of society.

Although Landis pressed the definition of social control beyond reasonable bounds, and harnessed it to the defence of the *status quo* in a manner likely to evoke the suspicion of more mainstream sociologists, he made the important point that many social control mechanisms operate independently of any conscious manipulative process:

> The most deep-seated and important influences in the development of the socialized personality, and in the regulation of human institutions, come from the non-rational, unconscious, all pervasive influences that mold the individual without his knowledge. They are a part of the general culture and become incorporated there without any conscious attempt on the part of any particular group, or even of a society to develop or foster them.[5]

Thus control will not always be overt, and may or may not be recognised as such by controller or controlled.

Landis' view that order in society was the product of a consensus, but a consensus threatened by forces of disintegration, is a manifestation of a tradition of social and political speculation which goes back to Hobbes, and whose most distinguished early sociological exponent was Emile Durkheim. He did not use the concept of social control as such, but his speculations on the conditions for social solidarity have been influential in its development. Durkheim argued that society was sustained by morality, a morality based on solidary ties:

> Law and morality are the totality of ties which bind each of us to society, which make a unitary coherent aggregate of the mass of individuals. Everything which is a source of solidarity is moral, everything which forces man to take account of other men is moral,

everything which forces him to regulate his conduct through something other than the striving of his ego is moral, and morality is as solid as these ties are numerous and strong.[6]

In early societies, whose members possessed virtually identical patterns of relationships, ranges of skills, beliefs and attitudes, such solidarity was 'mechanical'. Social evolution, however, brought greater complexity and a division of labour, and with it the development of an 'organic' solidarity which was the complement of differences in society. But organic solidarity was more fragile than mechanical solidarity, because sectional solidarities to some extent weakened the collective conscience. Durkheim saw 'justice' as the great unifying factor, but it was one about which he had increasing doubts. Towards the end of his life, he advocated the establishment of occupational groups occupying an intermediate position between the state and the family, groups which, bound together by a warm sense of community, would equally discourage egoism and *anomie*.

The most influential modern functionalist sociologist to use the social control concept is Talcott Parsons. Parsons envisages a more minor role for social control than Landis, regarding it as a mechanism which, jointly with socialisation, produces social order. Socialisation, 'mainly through the mechanisms of learning of which generalization, imitation and identification are perhaps particularly important', accounts for the way in which the majority of members of social systems come to conform to social norms. Social control mechanisms counteract deviancy at points where socialisation has failed. He summarises the general characteristics of social control mechanisms as follows:

Every social system has, in addition to the obvious rewards for conformative and punishments for deviant behavior, a complex system of unplanned and largely unconscious mechanisms which serve to counteract deviant tendencies. Very broadly these may be divided into the three classes of a) those which tend to 'nip in the bud' tendencies to development of compulsively deviant motivation before they reach the vicious circle stage, b) those which insulate the bearers of such motivation from influence on others, and c) the 'secondary defences', which are able, to varying degrees, to reverse the vicious cycle process.[7]

In any social system, social control mechanisms are thus inbuilt into the structure of relationships; in a complex society they will be diffused through the institutions of that society. Indeed, in some instances, 'secondary institutions' apparently hostile to established social order, like the American 'youth culture', may paradoxically be mechanisms of social control, since they enable protest both to be expressed and to be contained within socially acceptable limits.

Parsons' early writings assumed a static equilibrium model of society, but more recently he has modified his theory to give it a relativistic dimension. On this view, if the conflict within a social system becomes excessive, socialisation and social control mechanisms may fail:

> Failure of the mechanisms of socialization to motivate conformity with expectations creates tendencies to deviant behavior which, beyond certain critical points, would be disruptive of the social order or equilibrium. It is the function of the mechanisms of social control to maintain the social system in a state of stable or moving equilibrium; and insofar as they fail to do so, as has often happened in history, more drastic disequilibriation will take place before equilibrium is reestablished, that is, there will be changes in the structure of the social system.[8]

Thus he suggests, all social systems necessarily try to devise social control mechanisms, producing an equilibrium if successful, however transitory.

The use of the social control concept has not been restricted to consensualists and functionalists. Gramsci's concept of 'hegemony' is compatible with it, and recently, especially, radical sociologists have used the concept in their explanations of the ways in which in a conflict-ridden society authority is maintained, and in particular, to account for the social management and manipulation of crime, deviance and political protest. One element in the new 'sociology of deviance', Stanley Cohen argues, involves the necessity 'to recognise the problematic nature of social control'. Functionalist theorists, including Parsons, have suggested that deviance produces social control. The sociologists of deviance, following Lemert, have turned this premise on its head:

> ... older sociology tended to rest heavily upon the idea that deviance leads to social control. I have come to believe that the reverse idea, i.e.,that social control leads to deviance, is equally tenable and the potentially richer premise for studying deviance in modern society.[9]

Studies by sociologists of deviance have, for example, explored the ways in which the police, the courts, the 'respectable' public, and the cultural establishment, including the mass media, can not only regulate the amount and kind of deviancy in society, but actually create, shape and sustain it.[10] In the related field of mental illness, Thomas Szasz has suggested that mental disorder is a social creation, used to provide necessary scapegoats on whom the evils of society can be blamed.[11] 'Outsiders', whether religious or racial minorities, the mentally-ill or criminals, are often held to perform a social control function for the community at large, diverting and channelling conflicts inherent in capitalist society away from consideration of its actual source.

Despite their divergences, there is a considerable measure of agreement between radicals and functionalists as to the existence of, and indeed about the nature of social control mechanisms within society. This is true not only of their accounts of social control within society as a whole, but also at the level of the smaller social systems which together make up the larger society. Many users of social control, from Ross to Parsons, have tended to discuss the concept in the context of society as a whole. The most recent British writer on the subject, C.K. Watkins, has suggested, however, that it may aptly be applied to the study of social sub-systems, for example, industrial firms, trade unions or deviant groups.[12] Some studies, especially perhaps by sociologists of deviance, have already done this. Howard Becker's *Outsiders,* for example, extends and enriches our appreciation of the Durkheimian concept of solidarity, and provides important insights into the ways solidary groups are formed, transformed and controlled.[13] Some criminologists in studies of prison communities,[14] have illustrated the complexities of social control processes in ways which have a general applicability to the work of sociologists and historians concerned to study the relationships of the powerful and 'powerless' in society.

There are obvious dangers in summarising a concept which has had a long and varied sociological history, but perhaps enough has been said to show its ideological flexibility. The fact is that it remains, in Richard Johnson's terms, 'a concept in search of a theory':[15] theories perhaps rather than a single theory. It would be unfortunate were the concept to be captured either by left or right. There remains the problem of reductionism. As we have seen, most sociologists place great emphasis on the value and strength of internalised and largely unconscious control mechanisms, deeply embedded in social forms. This has two implications which may answer the difficulty. It suggests, first, that social control may be one only aspect of relationships or institutional forms. To identify social control processes in religion, social work, leisure or even the agitation for public health, (as several essays in this volume do), is not to assert that the control element within each is necessarily its main characteristic, still less its only meaning. Parents undertake control functions with respect to their children, and vice versa, but it would be a cynic indeed who saw this as the true and only meaning of family life. Second, it is important for its use in the study of inter-class relations to recognise that the concept suggests that controllers *and* the controlled are, as it were, trained to their roles. Hence, although in some nineteenth-century instances, the rich made a conscious and cynical use of religion, education and so on to keep the poor down, they were just as likely to have a genuine, even a burning, passion for their cause. Dr Brian Harrison has noted, as one of the sources of impetus to the temperance movement, the psychological condition of its leaders, men like the founder of the Scottish movement, John Dunlop. 'I got no sleep except dozing all night, and dreamed of drunken women and boys, till I overheard myself groaning, so that I was afraid I might disturb those that slept in the room'.[16] The actions of men like Dunlop may properly be considered as contributing to social control, indeed in one of its more aggressive forms. Yet this is not to assert that their description of their motives was false or hypocritical. A similar passion is evident in many humanitarians. Social control seeks to place it in a context, not to explain it away.

The unconscious nature of some social control mechanisms has one more very different implication. It suggests that the absence of overt conflict is not in itself evidence of a consensus. Studies of penal institutions or of 'outsiders' show that, as Becker recognises, a man does not need to be beaten every day to be hag-ridden. An operational consensus, even some sort of reciprocity and harmony, may be discerned between rulers and ruled even in a prison. To distinguish a true consensus from an operational one is a difficult task for the historian as for the sociologist.

What advantages then may historians hope for from the concept of social control? It is clearly not a philosophers' stone, whose discovery will resolve the problems of social history, but it seems reasonable to suggest that it could help to illuminate some hitherto rather dark areas. One general advantage it possesses is its assertion that the cultural forms of the different component parts of social systems are formed in a process of interaction. Sometimes in the past, the history of social policy, or of the middle or working classes has been written from a standpoint which has failed to recognise this. Benefit too, might be derived from an application of the concept to some of the major themes of nineteenth-century labour history. A study of the rise of the trade union movement which took account of the nature and limits of its solidary ties, its methods of controlling its membership, and sanctions against deviants, might have great value in explaining its successes and failures. But it may be anticipated that it will be in the study of the relations between rich and poor that such an approach will have most immediate value, and it is to this subject that the essays in the present volume are addressed.

II

The studies collected here illustrate some of the ways in which police forces and courts, education, religion, charity and social work in nineteenth-century Britain contributed to social order. Despite their coverage of specialised topics and different periods they present a surprisingly consistent picture of a ruling class which was aware of the breadth of the base of social order, and often concerned to articulate and act upon this belief. Magistrates, policemen, employers, philanthropists, clergymen, educators and civil servants often expressed views and attitudes rather like those of Ross or Landis: it is perhaps no coincidence that social control was one of the earliest concepts to be developed by sociologists.

Some nineteenth-century commentators saw order in rather the same way as Durkheim, attainable only through the moralisation of the poor. This might imply, as it did for Tremenheere and Chadwick, the realisation of 'social police': a tutelary control of the working class by their betters, achievable only through a coordinated social policy which would include in addition to police forces and the poor law, the provision of adequate housing and sound sanitation, socially constructive leisure, education and moral supervision. Not every commentator took such a broad view, but even those more narrowly concerned with law and order were, as John Stevenson's essay shows, aware of the utility of subtler means to preserve the peace than police forces or the militia: soup kitchens, for example, price controls and even gestures to assert the psychological solidarity of rich and poor, like reductions in their own consumption in times of dearth.

The belief that social order was intimately linked with morality meant that the church was a crucial agency of social control. Moral instruction, narrowly defined, was essential, but as Jenifer Hart's study reveals, clergymen often used the sermon in a more direct way to

reinforce the social order. They explained and often justified the existence of poverty and inequality in society, preached the merits of due
subordination, discerned a divine basis for wealth and authority in
society, and asserted its harmonious nature. Doubtless the contribution
of some clergymen to social control began and ended with such
exhortations, but for many more, and for Roman Catholic priests and
nonconformist ministers, the pulpit was a platform for expressing
views which in their pastoral work they attempted to enforce. At the
end of the century Durkheim noted, as an important fact in explaining
its stability, that England had the highest number of clergy per church-
goer of any European protestant country.[17] Many were busily engaged
as mediators of 'correct' values to the poor, in a variety of guises. On
the magistrates' bench, as hospital governors, members of poor law
boards, administrators of charities, as educators, as controllers of leisure,
and in the nascent social work profession, they were key figures in
social control throughout the century. If the churches failed to reach
the mass of the working class it was not through want of effort.

The drive to moralise the poor and education were closely associated,
throughout the nineteenth century, and the social control uses of
education have been described elsewhere by Richard Johnson.[18] His
present essay is concerned to explore a different aspect of the same
issue: the sources and nature of the early Victorian 'experts' view of
the educational question, and the political and class implications of
their relatively meagre achievements in 1839. He demonstrates that
'hegemony', in Gramsci's sense, underlay their educational aims, and
suggests too, that there was 'a kind of counter-revolutionary logic',
to their failure, to the truth of which the 'experts' themselves had to
be educated. For although the upper classes might share a hegemonic
aim, their different interests prevented the adoption of a radical plan to
enforce it. The result, a compromise, was one discernible in other areas
of social policy, for example on the police issue, or the poor law, and
a similar conflict shaped the attitudes of philanthropists to state intervention.

Wherever the rich were 'benefactors' of the poor in the nineteenth
century, they were inclined to speculate on the social control aspects of
their actions. Benevolence was often seen as problematic. On the one
hand it was the duty of the rich, as well as a means of ensuring social
stability; on the other, indiscriminate open-handedness might demoralise
the poor. In the Lancashire cotton famine, as Michael Rose's study
shows, skilful administrative innovation enabled charity and poor relief
to be so coordinated that the twin evils of hunger riots and demoralis-

ation were almost completely avoided. A similar aim characterised the work of the Charity Organisation Society which, as Judith Fido's essay shows, gave birth to the social work profession. Her study suggests that ideology and the development of casework were inseparably connected, social casework a vehicle through which the COS could regulate donors, control caseworkers, and paradoxically, in the name of an ideology which stressed economic independence, specify and manage many aspects of the lives of the poor. It was a paradox rather than a contradiction: throughout the century, and perhaps earlier, upper and middle-class efforts to force economic independence on the poor were not taken to imply the right of the poor to adopt life-styles independent of socially or morally 'correct' values. *Laissez-faire*, in so far as it was advanced as a virtue, was not, as it affected the poor, held to extend to morality or the structure of everyday life.

Robert Storch's study illustrates the truth of this at a period, and in an area, the industrial West Riding, which, if not the birthplace of economic *laissez-faire*, was one of its great bastions. Economic *laissez-faire* had led to the growth of a *de facto* working-class independence, and to the insulation of working-class communities from their neighbours. But the middle class refused to accept this situation. Regarding the working class as normless, where not actually prone to adopt a vicious normative system, they launched an assault on independent working-class cultural forms. Leisure was seen, Dr Storch suggests, as a symbol of the anarchic threat represented by working-class independence, and a variety of means were used to create 'conventicles of respectability', self-sustaining 'moralised' working-class groups, separated from the mass by their adherence to 'correct' social values.

Fairs were a traditional and important working-class leisure form in early Victorian England, one which, Hugh Cunningham's account of the metropolitan fairs shows, was generally viewed at that time by the respectable classes with fear and disapproval. But this attitude, which saw fairs as hotbeds of vice and nurseries of crime, was replaced towards the end of the century by a new tolerance. Fairs were, according to the new view, sometimes a nuisance, especially for the police, but integrated into a wider and accepted leisure system, they were no longer a problem. In fact, the fair had been tamed; in due course to become a subject for nostalgia and revival. Dr Cunningham explains this change of attitude in terms of the strengthening position of the forces of law and order, on the one hand, and on the other, of an increasing convergence of norms between showmen and fairgoers and authority.

Moralising movements took many forms, and drew their supporters from a variety of social backgrounds. But if such movements were manifestations of class hegemony, their relationship to the class struggle was often oblique and indirect. Victor Bailey's study of Salvationism and the resistance to it in small south-country townships, illustrates some of the complexities of which the hegemonic view must take account. The Salvation Army, drawing its membership largely from the working class, aimed at a remoralisation of the 'dangerous classes' not dissimilar to that attempted by other more respectable groups of moral reformers. But far from receiving the approval and support of authority, the Army was contained by the development of local solidarities which resisted the intrusion of what was perceived as an alien and threatening religious organisation. Opposition united all classes. Magistrates and town councils stretched or broke the law, police forces colluded with 'skeletons', who harassed the salvationists, and working-class crowds, urged on by their betters from the sidelines, undertook a vigorous and physical defence of community values. It is not only the curious class alignments in this situation which are paradoxical. His essay shows competing systems of social control in action. Community resistance served the purposes of all the communal vested interests and thus, as Dr Bailey notes, disorder might sometimes serve as a form of social control rather than a challenge to it.

III

The present collection of essays is a pioneering venture; it would not claim to give an exhaustive account of social control processes in nineteenth-century Britain. As a whole though, the essays point to certain generalities, and suggest hypotheses and questions which may prove useful as starting points for further study. These may be organised under two main headings. The first concerns the issue of order itself. To what extent and in what ways was social control seen as a problem in the nineteenth century? The second relates to the general nature of social control mechanisms. Did structural changes take place in the general mechanisms of social control during the century, and if so, in what ways? There is neither space here, nor as yet sufficient evidence to answer these questions fully, but it is, perhaps, worthwhile at least to raise them.

The Problem of Social Control

There is no doubt, first, that the ruling classes often saw the control of the poor as a problem. So aware of it were they, that the language of social control came to have a certain polemical value, in the politics both of left and right. It is, nevertheless, important not to regard such concern as universal or undifferentiated. Thus there appear to have been at least two distinguishable but sometimes interrelated kinds of awareness about the problem of the poor in the nineteenth century. One saw the poor as a continuing, a *chronic* problem; the other, related more closely to specific social and economic contexts, as an *acute* problem. The first, which may be termed the moralists' or moralisers' concern, represented perhaps, a contemporary manifestation of a traditional, indeed a classical anxiety about society's morals. Thus some churchmen, philanthropists and educators throughout the century attempted a moralising assault on the vices of the poor: their hedonism, improvidence, cruelty and licentiousness, or irreligion. Such assaults were, perhaps, especially intense in the nineteenth century, but there was nothing new about them. Attacks on working-class leisure were traditional by the nineteenth century.[19] Moral reform campaigns can be traced back at least to the eighteenth century,[20] and it is difficult to believe that the sort of exhortations which Jenifer Hart cites were new to the nineteenth century.

In many cases support for moralistic initiatives or movements came from all classes. This was true, for example, of sabbatarianism and the RSPCA.[21] Equally, resistance crossed class lines. It was not only Salvationists who provoked such opposition. County magistrates protected, so far as they could, traditional sports from the crusading activities of the RSPCA, and militant religion might provoke hostility in any class. It was, after all, Lord Melbourne, scarcely the poor man's friend, who observed: 'Things have come to a pretty pass when religion is allowed to invade the sphere of private life'.[22] The bedrock social conservatism which moral reform often ran against, had strata in all social classes.

Yet there were periods when a concern not unlike that of the moralising minority gained more general currency; when the issue of social control became an acute and immediate reality. At such periods, the conceptualising of the working-class problem usually took a similar turn. The masses were defined as a problem; the 'insulation' of social classes was noted; the city itself was often identified as a source of disorder. Strenuous appeals were made for the establishment of a 'personal influence' over the lives of the poor which would ensure their adoption of a 'correct' value system. Such an aggressive assertion of the harmony of society was not infrequently accompanied by a sharpened distinction between those who were inside society, and its enemies, 'outsiders', groups which, though differently defined, were identified as fit subjects for often drastic means of coercion.

This kind of awareness flared up at least twice, perhaps three times, in the nineteenth century, each time at periods of profound economic and social stress. The urban situation of London at the end of the century provoked such a response,[23] and — if the vision of Patrick Colquhoun was more than personal and idiosyncratic — population growth and the Napoleonic wars may have produced a similar climate of opinion at the beginning of the century.[24] The evidence would suggest, however, that awareness of the problem was most acute in early Victorian Britain, a period at which the vision of the social question in these terms was perfected.

It may be doubted whether even at these points of crisis, the whole ruling order was sensitised, and certainly no concerted front was presented by it. The schemes of educators, police reformers and theorists on social policy were implemented, if at all, in ways which accommodated the different interests of the rulers. The results of compromise were often slight enough. Instead of Colquhoun's preventive police system, London received the comparatively meagre police reforms which Dr Stevenson describes. Fear of Chartism did not produce even a national police force, let alone a scheme of national education. In the 1880s, systematic plans to counter the social threat also failed.[25] In part this was due to the factors which Richard Johnson describes; in part, perhaps to the ephemeral nature of the concern itself. As the threat of social disruption receded, the high price of radical social control measures became discernible.

The Changing Nature of Social Control Mechanisms

It is easier to generalise about the theories and ideas advanced by contemporaries to account for order, or to ensure it, than it is to identify the actual mechanisms of social control. A full account of these mechanisms must wait until we have a more detailed analysis of social institutions (particularly perhaps the working-class family)[26] from the social control standpoint, until we appreciate better the nature and limitations of consensus (however contrived) between classes, and will have to take into consideration, too, the different rates of social change in particular localities. The dark areas are formidable; but it may be possible to discern one general trend, the corollary of the growth of the mass society. At the beginning of the century many control activities seem to have been conducted informally, or if through institutions, in the context of personal relationships. By the end of the century, control was increasingly mediated, at one remove, through institutions. The controlling scope of personal relationships shrank, and, at the same time, formal institutions seem to have acquired a new dimension of impersonality. The trend is discernible in many areas, representing at one level no more than a change from a society whose social control processes were based on paternalism, to one which was, however incompletely, bureaucratised. But the social control perspective helps to explain the urgency of the issue of inter-class relations, especially for the early Victorians, and focuses attention, too, on the still unexplained problem of how and why such a transition proved possible, even easy.

The development of law and order apparatuses illustrates the nature of the change and some of its problematic aspects. The peacekeeping structure which John Stevenson describes left the maintenance of law and order largely in local hands. The personnel who staffed the institutions which countered riot or lawlessness — magistrates, the militia and local volunteers, for example — were often those who in different relationships employed the poor, educated them, or administered poor relief and charity. Chartism was, despite some innovations, met by a similar array of forces. One consequence was that as late as the 1840s, even disorders took place within the context of personal relationships between rich and poor. Neither the 'mob' nor 'authority' were always faceless, and this was the source of the problem of the early Victorians) the peacekeeping apparatus largely depended on such relationships, even where they did not exist. It presupposed that only through 'influence' could order be maintained. In 1842, Graham, the Home Secretary, outlined this in a letter to Lord Balcarres who, alarmed by a large mob which had surrounded his house, had given them food. Balcarres said that he would defend his property in the way he thought best, an opinion which drew an angry and revealing retort from Graham:

> It is the first duty of every subject, even at some personal risk, to uphold the law and to resist open violence. If this firmness is generally evinced by Men of Property exercising influence in their respective neighbourhoods, the public danger from mobs acting in opposition to law and to the constituted authorities is not really formidable, but if Noblemen of high rank and station refuse to defend their own Property, unless military assistance be on the spot, and if they set the example of concession to Threats in the hope of averting the danger of the moment, then indeed the most serious

consequences may be expected to result from such fatal tameness; and no amount of military Force will be found sufficient to protect Property against numbers, when the Owners of Property themselves shall cease to defend it.[27]

The actions of the property owner must be guided by the fact of his membership of a ruling order. He was expected to act out a symbolic role, as the visible embodiment of authority, asserting through his participation in the local drama the wider constitutional and social issues at stake. His authority, reinforced through the breadth of his contacts with the poor, was further strengthened by control of the apparatus of justice, which could, in ways Dr Stevenson describes, be tailored to bring this morality play to its just conclusion.

Change was, nevertheless, taking place: everywhere, by the 1840s, the rulers of society were perceived to be abandoning this traditional and onerous duty. By the 1880s the personal dimension had largely disappeared, replaced by processes involving professional police institutions. A moral drama still took place, but it was confined to the court room, and communicated to the wider society through a professional press. In the process of transition the social meaning attached to personal influence underwent a change. Impersonality, equated with impartiality, became a virtue; 'influence', the distinction between its legitimate and illegitimate forms forgotten, came to be regarded as a sort of corruption.

It is not surprising that the early Victorians regarded the breakdown of social control mechanisms with serious and urgent alarm. They had little experience of social control mechanisms not dependent on personal ties, and what they had was scarcely reassuring: the anarchy of the new industrial areas, or the controlling despotisms of continental states like Prussia. Thus the impetus to devise means to tame industrialism. These efforts, which included social legislation, church building and religious settlements, paternalist companies, and attempts to establish 'conventicles of respectability', may have been greater in scale and influence than has sometimes been allowed, but inevitably they failed.

The transition from one system to another was not always untroubled. Dr Rose notes, for example, an element of precariousness in the institutional structure devised to control unemployed workers during the cotton famine, and the establishment of police forces met with resistance in some places. There were still, in late Victorian Britain, points of anxiety. In charity, especially, impersonality devalued the gift, and the late Victorians were obliged, as Judith Fido shows, to devise a structure, social casework, which institutionalised personal influence. Many early Victorians felt that property could only be preserved if the rich performed their public duties. Goulburn argued, for example, that public service in local government or on the bench was onerous and sometimes unpleasant, but a necessary *quid pro quo* for the ownership of property.[28] To an extent which would have amazed the early Victorians, however, it proved possible for the rich to retain their property and to distance themselves from the poor. So long as they maintained the 'commanding heights' of the new institutional structures on magisterial benches, in watch committees, in the church, and in the civil service, for example, their position proved secure. Direct day-to-day contact with the poor could, for most purposes, be delegated to paid agents, like policemen, teachers, and relieving officers, working in an expanding range of professional institutions. It remains, in Goulburn's sense, an enigma as to why transition was so easily accomplished.

IV

It is hoped that this account of some of the general issues of nineteenth-century social control processes will stimulate further study, and this appeal for more research is far from a routine editorial parting shot. There is an intrinsic interest in such issues, and in others which there is not space here to consider; consensus between classes, for example, or the social control aspects of that hierarchical tendency which permeated Victorian social life. But there are broader interests which further study may serve. It may be, indeed, that until we know much more about the sources of order in nineteenth-century society, we shall not fully appreciate the nature of the political and social transformation which it experienced.

Notes

1.   It is impossible to list them all here. But see H. Perkin in *The Origins of Modern British Society 1780-1880* (London, 1969), pp. 38-56, who uses the concept of 'friendship' to explain eighteenth-century social solidarity, The relationships between order and philanthropy, moral reform and leisure have also been noted. See B. Harrison, 'Philanthropy and the Victorians',*Victorian Studies* IX (1966), pp. 353-4, and 'Religion and Recreation in Nineteenth Century England', *Past and Present* 38 (1967), pp. 108-19; R. Price, 'The Working Men's Club Movement and Victorian Social Reform Ideology', *Victorian Studies* XV (1971), pp. 117-47. The wider relationships of law to social forms and structure are discussed in D. Hay, P. Linebaugh, C. Winslow, J. Rule and E.P. Thompson, *Albion's*

Fatal Tree. Crime and Society in Eighteenth-Century England (London, 1975). None of these works uses the concept of social control, which is however, mentioned by G. Stedman Jones in *Outcast London* (Peregrine edn., 1976), p. 251, in a discussion of the uses and form of charity, p. 241 ff. Two conferences of historians have recently been held on the theme of social control, at Newcastle University in 1972, and by the Society for the Study of Labour History; 'The Working Class and Leisure: Class Expression and/or Social Control', in 1975, which is reported in the *Bulletin of the Society for the Study of Labour History* 32 (1976), pp. 5-18.

2. See Engels' comments, and Thompson's remarks on them in, E.P. Thompson 'The Peculiarities of the English', *Socialist Register* (1965), p.338.

3. This account is taken from the synopsis of his remarks in the Report of the conference 'The Working Class and Leisure: Class Expression and/or Social Control', *Bulletin* p. 17, where he was concerned to discuss the applicability of the concept to the study of working-class leisure. There is not space here to take account of all his criticisms; but those referred to are the most fundamental. D. Hay expresses doubts about the concept, too, noting its (conservative) ideological history, and its use 'often with little critical examination'. Hay *et al., Albion's Fatal Tree*, p. 62 n.l.

4. E.A. Ross, *Social Control: A Survey of the Foundations of Order* (New York, 1929), p. 59.

5. P.A. Landis, *Social Control: Social Organisation and Disorganisation in Process,* revd. edn. (Chicago, 1956), p.7.

6. E. Durkheim, *The Division of Labour in Society,* quoted in R.N. Bellah (ed.),*Emile Durkheim on Morality and Society. Selected Writings* (Chicago, 1973), p. 136. Bellah gives a very useful introduction to Durkheim's life and thought.

7. T. Parsons, *The Social System* (London, 1951), p. 321. See also *The Structure of Social Action* (paperback edn., 1968), pp. 87-94.

8. Parsons, E.A. Shils and J. Olds in T. Parsons and E. Shils (eds.),*Towards a General Theory of Action* (New York, 1965), p.228.

9. Quoted in P. Rock and M. McIntosh (eds), *Deviance and Social Control* (London, 1974), p. 4. On the general development of the sociology of deviance, see, in the same volume, S. Cohen, 'Criminology and the Sociology of Deviance in Britain', pp.1-40

10. See, e.g., J. Young 'The Role of the Police as Amplifiers of Deviancy, etc.', in S. Cohen (ed.), *Images of Deviance* (Harmondsworth, 1971), pp.27-61.

11. T. Szasz, *The Manufacture of Madness* (London, 1971).

12. C.K. Watkins, *Social Control* (London, 1975).

13. H. Becker, *Outsiders* (New York, 1963).

14. See, especially, R. Cloward, D. Cressey, G. Grosser, R. McCleary, L. Ohlin, G. Sykes and S. Messinger, *Theoretical Studies in Social Organisation of the Prison,* Social Science Research Council Pamphlet 15 (New York, 1960).

15. See below, p.78

16. B. Harrison, 'Philanthropy and the Victorians', p. 358.

17. *Suicide: a Study in Sociology.* Quoted in L. Coser and B. Rosenberg, *Sociological Theory: A Book of Readings,* 3rd edn. (London 1969), p.194.

18. R. Johnson, 'Educational Policy and Social Control in Early Victorian England', *Past and Present* 49 (1970), pp. 96-119.

19. R.W. Malcolmson, *Popular Recreations in English Society. 1700-1850* (Cambridge, 1973), pp. 100-9.

20. See, e.g. the account given in L. Radzinowicz, *A History of the Criminal Law and its Administration* (London, 1948-68),III, pp. 141-207.

21. B. Harrison, 'Religion and Recreation', pp. 103-8.

22. Remark on hearing an evangelical sermon, Quoted in *The Concise Oxford Dictionary of Quotations*, p.141.
23. Stedman Jones, *Outcast London*, pp. 281-314.
24. See below, pp.54-6.
25. Stedman Jones, *Outcast London*, pp. 303-12, describes schemes to eradicate the residuum, and their failure.
26. Though see, M.Anderson, *Family Structure in 19th Century Lancashire* (Cambridge, 1971); and for the later period R. Roberts, *The Classic Slum. Salford Life in the First Quarter of the Century* (Manchester, 1971).
27. Draft letter of Graham to Balcarres, 23 Sept. 1842, PRO Home Office Papers, HO 45/249B.
28. C.S. Parker,*The Life and Letters of Sir James Graham* (London, 1907). vol. I, pp. 335-6.

1 SOCIAL CONTROL AND THE PREVENTION OF RIOTS IN ENGLAND, 1789-1829

John Stevenson

Preventive justice is upon every principle of reason, humanity, and of sound policy, preferably in all respects to punishing justice.
Blackstone

Did England face a crisis of public order in the years between the French Revolution and the beginning of the crisis that led to the First Reform Act? An older generation of historians certainly thought so: in a famous passage the Hammonds contrasted the urbane sentiments of Burke about popular discontent in 1770 — 'The people have no interest in disorder. When they do wrong it is their error and not their crime' — with the situation after 1789:

> The poorer classes no longer seemed a passive power: they were dreaded as a Leviathan that was fast learning his strength. Regarded before as naturally contented, they were now regarded as naturally discontented. The art of politics was not the art of keeping the attachment of people who cherished their customs, religion, and the general setting of their lives, by moderation, foresight, and forbearance: it was the art of preserving discipline amongst a vast population destitute of the traditions and restraints of a settled and conservative society, dissatisfied with its inevitable lot and ready for disorder and blind violence. For two revolutions had come together. The French Revolution had transformed the minds of the ruling classes, and the Industrial Revolution had convulsed the world of the working classes.[1]

Few historians would now accept that the contrast between the calm of the eighteenth century and the years which followed the upheaval in France can be depicted quite so starkly. None the less, a recent historian has commented 'that there was a problem was a matter of no doubt amongst contemporaries; nor has it been amongst the historians'.[2] My intention here is to examine the ways in which the authorities maintained public order in the years after 1789 and particularly the survival of traditional forms of social control in the face of the economic and political crises which affected the country in the years

27

before 1829.

The eighteenth century had hardly been one of unruffled calm. Popular disturbances were frequent and occurred on a wide range of issues, including wages, elections, religion, enclosures and recruiting. Undoubtedly the most common were those associated with food prices. A number of waves of food riots have been identified in the latter part of the eighteenth century and persisting into the early years of the nineteenth, for example in 1756-7, 1766-8, 1773-4, 1795-6 and 1800-1. It has been estimated that two out of three disturbances in the eighteenth century were food or price riots, including such activities as stopping the movement of grain, forcible seizure and resale of food, attacks upon mills and warehouses, and various forms of tumultuous assembly. Some of the larger waves of food rioting affected scores of towns and villages, most commonly the market towns and centres of transport or populous centres of trade and industry.[3]

But it was not only 'revolts of the belly' which disturbed public order in eighteenth-century England. Riots were an integral part of the social fabric in which the objects of attack or disapprobation varied endlessly. Distinguished historians, such as George Rudé and Edward Thompson, have stressed the semi-organised and ritualised aspects of popular disturbances, placing them within the context of eighteenth-century life. Rudé, for example, has shown that the typical eighteenth-century 'mob' was usually composed of a cross-section of the local population, asserting its voice on issues which closely affected their everyday lives, rather than the criminal riff-raff so often assumed by contemporary writers.[4] Edward Thompson has argued forcefully that the eighteenth-century crowd acted to resist interference with customary rights. Infringements of the popular 'moral economy' by excise men, recruiting parties, enclosures and middlemen in the food trade could easily spark off crowd activity. At the level of local and isolated communities, this could lead to mob pressure against strangers, such as methodist itinerants for example, or against the moral offender or unconventional, seen in the 'skimmington' or 'skimmity ride' which persisted in some rural areas until the twentieth century.[5]

Almost every study of local communities reveals fresh instances of riots or other disturbances. Many more lie buried in the obscurity of the legal records, often disguised by charges of assault. Still more represent a 'dark number' of disturbances which for one reason or another did not appear in court records, local memoirs or newspaper accounts. Only a small minority were of sufficient seriousness to warrant the attention of central government. Riots were part of the normal experience of most towns and cities in England. But as breaches of public order they were usually minor, causing relatively little damage to persons and property. Serious casualties, though by no means entirely absent, were the exception rather than the rule. So interwoven was crowd activity into the fabric of eighteenth-century life that there were many instances of the 'mob' being 'licensed' to act by local community leaders. Many of the mobs raised against methodists, and later in the century radicals, were operating with the collusion of local magistrates, squires or parsons.[6]

Towards the end of the eighteenth century, however, it was increasingly apparent that the security of some of the larger towns and cities was being undermined by the twin processes of population growth and urbanisation. By 1801 there were more than twenty towns in England and Wales with populations of more than 10,000 inhabitants. Both Manchester and Birmingham were rapidly approaching populations of 100,000 people, while London had become a giant metropolis of almost a million. To deal with these growing communities, the authorities were still dependent upon a structure of local government designed for the world of the rural village and small market town. Many unincorporated industrial towns of the north and midlands were still dependent upon unpaid parochial officials led by the local justice of the peace. The difficulties which this antiquated system of law and order was to have in containing the populations of the new industrial towns was to form one of the central threads of law and order during the Napoleonic Wars and after.

But if the maintenance of public order was a problem in the growing towns and cities of the industrial revolution, these problems were dwarfed in size by those of London. Half as big again as Paris by the end of the eighteenth century, the capital was growing at a rate of 10 per cent per decade, creating problems of public order which were almost unique in scale. Most of the population growth of the capital was concentrated in the out-parishes of Middlesex and Surrey, beyond the jurisdiction of the municipal administration of the cities of London and Westminster. The capital was therefore faced with an acute version of the problem which harassed the manufacturing areas — the growth of virtually unregulated urban populations. The work of George Rudé has shown that the London crowd had a tradition of intervention in the life of the capital and also upon the life of the nation as a whole. His studies of the London 'mob', especially of the Wilkite disturbances, showed that it could play an important role in shaping political developments. Within twenty years, the capital saw disturbances on an

unprecedented scale. The prolonged agitation surrounding John Wilkes
had seen a shrewd demagogue harnessing the socio-economic grievances
of the populace to his own ends. Then in 1780 occurred the most
serious riots of the century when the mob held the streets of London
against the civil and military authorities for almost a week. The death
toll was over 400 people killed or executed for their part in the
disturbances and thousands of pounds worth of damage.[7] This evidence
of the power of the populace to defy the authorities and break free from
traditional restraints prompted many, including Burke, to comment
upon the inadequacy of the peacekeeping forces of the capital. Events
in Paris in 1789 served to confirm the dangers of urban insurrection in
a large capital city, even one which possessed a professional police.

   From the outbreak of the French Revolution, the country was
faced not only with the consequences of urban growth in the capital
and the manufacturing districts, but also with the threat of popular
radicalism. The fear of the 'evil-minded' and 'seditious', acting within
the country to subvert order and assist an attempted French invasion
was a real one to the authorities. The threat of a rising in the manufacturing areas or the capital, or both, remained through the period
from 1789 a spectre to haunt the worst nightmares of government. As a
Home Office correspondent argued in 1794, the country could with-
stand an invasion 'provided there were no tumults or insurrections in
the country to distract the attention of government'.[8] In 1796 the
Home Office itself circulated a memorandum on the danger of disturbances in the capital. A sharp distinction was drawn between 'a sudden
collection of idle and mischievous people without any preconverted
plan or purpose' and 'a riot occasioned by persons disaffected to the
government, long premeditated and its promoters only waiting for a
fit opportunity to embody themselves for the desperate purposes of
promoting French principles. . .'.[9]

   In order to meet the threats posed by social changes and political
developments, the government wielded an apparatus of public order
which had been little altered for centuries. The first line of resistance
to any outbreak of disorder lay with the civil forces under the
command of local justices of the peace. These were at their weakest in
the new manufacturing districts, where law and order had to be
maintained by a handful of magistrates, often living at some distance
from the trouble centres. A correspondent in 1819 described the
district that comprised Oldham, Middleton and Ashton as being
entirely without magistrates. A memorial from the Potteries in 1817
claimed that a district forty miles in circumference, with more than

50,000 inhabitants, had no acting magistrate.[10] Of the 5,000 magistrates who did operate in England and Wales, the majority were land-owners, lay and clerical, many of whom had little or no intimate knowledge of the conditions in the industrial towns. More important the quality of magistrates varied enormously; for every energetic and active justice, there were far more who found the difficulties of the office beyond them. The events of Peterloo showed the inadequacy of the magistracy in one of the most critical centres of political radicalism and industrial growth. As a recent historian has commented of them: 'They did panic, they exercised an ill judgement, they took wrong decisions, and these decisions were ineptly carried out.' Their crime was less conspiracy than incompetence.[11]

In the capital, the situation was as varied. In 1797 it was estimated that 270 magistrates were available for law and order. These were split up between the jurisdictions of the City of London, the City of Westminster, the county of Middlesex, the Liberty of the Tower and the Borough of Southwark. The City magistracy, headed by the Lord Mayor and Alderman, was the most able, having a considerable force of watchmen and beadles under their control, paid for by a rate levied on the City wards. Outside the City, there was a bewildering confusion of provision. Some of the richer parishes had obtained private acts for the setting up of a more efficient Watch and by 1811 these controlled half the constables and watchmen available for the capital. Beyond these well-regulated parishes, however, lay a virtual absence of effective local policing. The 'trading justice' was still in evidence as late as 1816, and even in 1828 it was estimated that there were 186,000 people in parishes in London without any watch or force of efficient constables.[12]

A major initiative had been taken in 1792, however, with the Middlesex Justices' Act. This set up seven public offices in the capital, each manned by three stipendiary magistrates and controlling a force of a dozen constables, so that they functioned both as professional magistrates and as heads of police. Under the direct control of the Home Office, which provided their salaries and directed appointments, they formed a small professional force which the Home Secretary could use to police the capital. As a major departure from the tradition of parochial organisation and unpaid local forces, the public offices marked a significant step towards a professional police force, albeit on an extremely limited scale. The government's principal concern had been to provide a higher standard of justice in the capital and the daily sessions at the seven public offices certainly helped to provide this, but inevitably they came to be used as a general police force. The public offices operated as an important intelligence gathering network for the Home Office, and regular reports were demanded by the Home Office. It was hardly surprising that the system of stipendiary magistrates and professional constables set up in London should attract attention elsewhere. Representations for an efficient police force were received by the Home Office from several manufacturing centres after 1812, including Nottingham, Newcastle and Sunderland. In 1812, the Manchester magistrates actually held a meeting to propose a system modelled upon that of London, but the scheme came to nothing.[13]

In the absence of an efficient parochial system and the failure to create an extensive professional police, public order ultimately depended upon the regular forces of the crown. At regular intervals in the eighteenth century it was the volley fire of the troops, which eventually quelled a disturbance which the local forces could no longer control. For the Hammonds, the army formed the crucial instrument of repression in the years which followed the French Revolution. That and the barrack-building policy of Pitt and Dundas, were seen as the means by which a turbulent proletariat was cowed into submission. In fact, the army's role was hedged around with restrictions. One of the most important lay in the army's inadequacy in terms of numbers. At the outbreak of the war with revolutionary France, the army establishment stood at less than 40,000 men. Once the war started, its numbers quickly rose to a peak of almost a quarter of a million by 1812. When the war was ended the number fell back to just under 100,000 men, remaining at approximately the same level throughout the 1820s.[14] During the war, however, the bulk of the army was engaged either in overseas campaigns or in guarding the coast against possible invasion. Scarcity of troops, rather than abundance was the usual situation. Colonial garrisons, continental expeditions and desertion reduced the Home Army to a fraction of its paper strength. So severe became the shortage of troops that the Guards regiments were stripped from the capital in 1812 and ceremonial duties taken over by the volunteer forces.[15] At no point did the government after 1789 have the forces available to enable it to saturate the country with troops. The oft-quoted remark that the army in the northern districts was as large as that in the Peninsular campaigns, tends to ignore the fact that the armies under Moore and Wellington rarely topped 10,000 men. A force of this size to police the manufacturing districts against the sporadic attacks of the Luddites, before the days of the telegraph, the railway and modern road transport, represented a very small force indeed.

The barrack-building policy highlighted by the Hammonds was less

sinister than it appeared, in some respects, more a sign of potential
weakness than of repressive intent. In 1793 barrack accommodation
existed for only 21,000 troops in forty-three garrison towns. The
remainder were quartered in ale houses. In London, there was a severe
shortage of barracks for the troops which were normally garrisoned
there. For 7,000 men, there existed only 2,000 barrack places in
1804 and 4,000 in 1818. The rest were billeted all over London, some
as far from the City centre as Marylebone and Camden. In the case of
a sudden emergency when larger bodies of troops were required in the
capital, Hyde Park had to be pressed into service as an encampment.
The existing garrisons were designed to protect ports or to provide
depots for troops awaiting shipment overseas, few were situated
conveniently to police the manufacturing districts and some of those
that existed in the capital were hardly equipped to deal with civil
insurrection. One commander complained that the Tower was incapable
of resisting the assault of a gang of determined children, so overgrown
with outbuildings had it become.[16] The major barrack-building
programme undertaken by Pitt and Dundas added 155 barracks, capable
of holding 153,000 troops, but the majority were built on the coasts and
in ports. Only small barracks were built for detachments of troops in the
manufacturing towns. In many ways the barrack-building programme
was defensive in inspiration. The tour of Colonel De Lancy in June 1792
to enquire into the disposition of the troops in the north was undertaken
to find out 'how far they were to be depended upon in any emergency'.
He recommended the barrack-building programme on the grounds that
it was 'a dangerous measure to keep troops in the manufacturing towns
in their present dispersed state, and unless Barracks could be established
for them where they could be kept under the eyes of their officers it
would be prudent to Quarter them in the towns and villages in the
vicinity, from whence in case of emergency they would act with much
more effect'.[17] The fear was that dispersion and contact with sedition
might undermine the discipline of the troops. But barrack-building
was never sufficient to eliminate the dangers of dispersion, ill-discipline
and subversion. Thus as late as 1823, we find a memorandum from the
barrack department complaining that soldiers were exposed to 'the
society of the tap room' and the 'contaminating influence of the very
lowest and most disorderly part of society', such as might 'tempt the
soldier and render him likely to be misled from the path of his duty at
those critical periods when it is of utmost importance to secure his best
and most zealous service'.[18]

The actual instances of overt disloyalty in the army were few. Some troops were involved in the plottings of the United Irishmen and the Despard conspiracy, but general mutinies were conspicuous by their absence. There were tremors of mutiny amongst the artillery at Woolwich arsenal in 1797 because there had been a delay in the award of an increase in pay which was given to the army at the time of the naval mutinies.[19] Again in 1820, one battalion of the Coldstream Guards refused to stand to duty during the Queen Caroline agitation because of discontents about pay and conditions.[20] Both were quickly suppressed. Generally speaking, however, in spite of concern to the contrary, disaffection was far less of a problem than the physical and political difficulties of using the troops as a police force. Harsh discipline, group loyalty, and a low but relatively secure standard of living insulated the troops against the major inroads of subversion.[21]

Far more serious for the government was the general unpopularity of the army. In London and many other towns, the sight of an army uniform was as likely to provoke a riot as to prevent one. Twice in the period 1789 to 1829, the use of the troops led to serious clashes with the populace in London. In April 1810, when the popular champion Sir Francis Burdett was arrested for a libel on the House of Commons, he was escorted by the troops from his house in Piccadilly to the Tower. Although a route had been chosen which avoided the City of London, the troops were attacked when they reached the Tower and in turn opened fire, killing two people. Similarly, in 1821 the funeral of Queen Caroline led to further clashes, when the crowd attacked soldiers guarding the procession with stones. The troops eventually opened fire, again killing two people. The funeral of the two men only occasioned more clashes with the soldiers.[22]

In itself, the hostility shown towards the soldiers by the populace would not have been particularly serious, but the antipathy of the mob towards the army was only part of a wider disapproval of the use of the military which could be used to embarrass the government. The issue of the 'standing army' was one of the political clichés of eighteenth-century politics. During the years of the Revolutionary and Napoleonic Wars it became subtly interfused with what might be called the 'politics of violence'. Instances of government action which seemed to infringe the cherished 'liberties' of Englishmen were likely to be seized upon by a small, but vocal opposition of radical Whigs, and made much of in the radical press. At one time or another, the radicals attacked almost every aspect of the public order apparatus, but their most consistent target was the army with the implied rebuke that the government was arbitrary and tyrannical. In November 1794, the London Corresponding Society accused the magistrates of 'impertinently excluding citizens from the public streets by Martinets armed with fixed bayonets'. During the anti-Corn Law disturbances in London in 1815, when the army had to be called out to prevent a large crowd from mobbing the House of Commons, Lambton protested that the House was being 'menaced by a military force, contrary to the principles of the constitution'.[23] Even in the years which have commonly been regarded as the most threatening for the country as a whole, the army remained an object of criticism. Complaints about the number and cost of the troops were made on a number of occasions after 1816, a subject upon which the Whigs could usually count upon support from a number of 'independents' in the Commons. Some took the view that excessive reliance upon the troops could be dangerous, both to the security of the government and to the liberties of the people.[24] The City of London had brought opposition to the use of the troops to a fine art, in order to extract the maximum political capital. The City retained a prickly concern for its liberties and independence which made any incursion by the troops into a frequent cause of friction between City radicals and the government.[25]

The army was also something of a sledgehammer, the use of which by a local magistrate might lead to great unpopularity, and (even more serious) might lead to him being charged with murder. Widespread confusion about the law of riot led to great hesitancy on the part of some magistrates in authorising the use of troops.[26]

Increasingly after 1815, the radical press was free to conduct a running war with the authorities, condemning occasions of 'praetorian licentiousness'. The events of Peterloo, its very name a product of the radical press, greatly strengthened the case against the use of the soldiers as a police force. Although they had to be used extensively during the Luddite outbreaks, the army frequently opened up the government to attack. In that sense, the army could not be used as lightly as many have supposed. This at least partially accounts for the reluctance of Home Secretaries to despatch troops whenever called upon to do so. In fact the government was frequently in the position of refusing to give military support to worried magistrates. They did this because they often doubted the judgement of the magistrates with which they dealt in the manufacturing districts. They feared too, that the troops would be parcelled out in small detachments and worn out by constant duties – a situation that could easily provoke discontent amongst the troops themselves, besides exposing the army more effectively to the influence of the populace amongst whom they were billeted. Above all, the government urged self-reliance amongst the local population. An often neglected aspect of De Lancey's report in 1792 was that he urged the government to embody the local gentry to preserve public order. It remained an axiom of government policy that the 'respectable' inhabitants and men of property should stand forward and protect their localities. As a recent historian has remarked, policy towards the army remained that they should 'withhold the supply of regular troops and to discourage their use until the very last moment and to withdraw them as soon as possible'.[27]

In addition to the regular army, the government also had available the militia and the volunteers. The militia was organised on a county basis and was under the command of the Lord Lieutenant. It was raised by compulsory ballot on the inhabitants, but as substitutes were allowed these tended to be drawn from the poorest section of the community, the same reservoir as the regular army. Contemporaries held it in low regard and its level of trustworthiness was very poor. Desertion was rife and instances of ill-discipline numerous. In London the militia regiments were almost at half strength through desertion and difficulty of obtaining recruits.[28] Worse still, their unreliability made them virtually useless for police duties, being frequent participants in riots themselves. In April 1795, 400 men from the Oxfordshire Militia marched from their barracks with fixed bayonets, entered Seaford and Newhaven, seized provisions and then returned to barracks. As a result, two of the militia were shot, two hanged and three given three hundred lashes apiece. In the same year militiamen were involved in food riots at Wells, Portsmouth, Chichester and Canterbury.[29] On more than one occasion their duties had to be taken over by local volunteer forces. The fear that if they remained in their original counties the militia would refuse to act against the populace which they had only just left, led to a policy of keeping the county militias away from the home areas. In 1812, Parson Hay wrote from Manchester to urge that any militia regiments used should be from the south of England. Others simply wrote them off as 'useless' for police duties.[30] Perhaps the only exception was the remodelled militia of London which played a significant part in dealing with disturbances in the capital. Even here, however, there was an undercurrent of indiscipline: for example in March 1797 the East Regiment of the City Militia paraded in St George's Fields and refused to move to new quarters in Greenwich because they had not received payment of a 'marching guinea'.[31]

The volunteers were an effective rival to the militia as an aid to the regular army and the civil power. Associations of householders to deal

with specific emergencies had become common in the late eighteenth
century. A magistrate would swear in the 'respectable' inhabitants as
Special Constables and they 'associated' as a body to keep the peace.
Associations of this type had been formed in London during the Gordon
Riots. The reaction to Jacobin ideas in the autumn of 1792 led to the
formation, with ministerial backing, of loyalist associations. Although
the associations were intended primarily as political societies, to
combat the spread of Jacobin ideas, from the beginning a number were
semi-military in character. The St James Westminster Association
requested the magistrate to call the inhabitants together and instruct
them how to deal with riots. The London Association met every week
to drill and exercise in arms, wearing a blue and scarlet uniform. Several
of the London associations had subscriptions for arms and uniforms
and by the spring of 1794 were drawing up plans for united action in
case of 'tumults and disturbances'.[32] Indeed the armed associations
were called out to protect the capital during the anti-crimp house riots
of August 1794 and were used on a number of occasions both to prevent
and suppress disturbances in the years that followed.[33] From 1794
however, the associations became absorbed in the volunteer movement
created as a result of the invasion scare of that year. Their purpose was
primarily to deal with instances of internal insurrection or disorder
while the regular army was engaged overseas or guarding the coast. The
first volunteer act was passed in 1794, empowering the Lords Lieutenant
to accept volunteer companies and attach them to the militia. This act
was quickly followed by others in which exemption from the militia
ballot was one of the major incentives for joining. The result was chaos
in the recruiting system which was not ironed out for some years,
depriving the regular forces and the militia of recruits. Genuine loyalty
and the advantages of escape from militia service soon swelled the ranks
of the volunteers. Far from being a socially exclusive organisation, it
expanded to include all classes and provide a massive guarantee of public
order. By 1798 there were 75 corps of cavalry and 475 of infantry,
comprising almost 40,000 men. The volunteer corps were reformed
after the Peace of Amiens and by 1804 there were 25,000 volunteers
available in the capital and almost half a million in the country as a
whole.[34]

The bulk of the volunteer forces were wound up in 1813, but the
cavalry component, the yeomanry, was maintained and provided one
of the principal arms used to deal with the disturbances in the industrial
districts from 1812 to 1819. Perhaps their most infamous intervention
was at Peterloo, when the Manchester and Salford Yeomanry proved

incapable of dealing with the difficult task set them by the Manchester magistrates. None the less, there was ample testimony that they were an important component of peacekeeping in the country at large and in the capital. The hatred in which they were regarded by radicals such as Cobbett was testimony to their ubiquity in the troubled years around the end of the Napoleonic Wars.[35]

The Home Office was the principal organ of government responsible for law and order. The Secretary of State had two under-secretaries and a small staff of clerks to cope with the business of the office. But public order was not its only function; the Home Office also acted as a channel for petitions for clemency from criminals, supervised transportation and some aspects of penal policy, and acted as magistrate in specific crimes against the state. The Home Office was also given responsibility for supervising the militia, yeomanry and volunteers during the war years. Information about the public order situation in the country was only one part of the correspondence coming into the Home Office. In fact, the Home Office had only very limited executive authority over the conduct of public order in the country. Its main function was as the source of troops should local authorities request aid. Hence the Home Secretary had a coordinating role which grew as the period went on. As the only person who could take an overview of the situation in the country as a whole, the Home Office inevitably became the focus of correspondence from worried magistrates, Lords Lieutenant and army commanders in the country.[36]

The situation in regard to London, however, was different from that in the rest of the country. The Home Secretary had executive authority over the forces created under the Middlesex Justices' Act of 1792. The creation of the Thames Police Office in 1798 added an important point of control in the dockside areas. This control was exercised relentlessly during the war years and afterwards. The Chief Magistrate at Bow Street was generally regarded as the principal magistrate of the metropolis and his duties included daily attendance at the Home Office, assistance at all examinations undertaken at the office, and receiving directions for implementation. In return for this he received a considerable allowance in addition to his stipend as a magistrate. The public offices were also expected to communicate daily with the Home Office and, as there was no formal channel of communication between them, the Home Secretary was the effective head of police in London. Magistrates were frequently disciplined by the Home Office if they failed to produce reports or act correctly. In 1793, the then Home Secretary, Dundas, removed a Bow Street magistrate for making an unauthorised trip to Paris. In 1821, Sir Robert Baker, the Chief Magistrate at Bow Street was removed for his failure to prevent riots at Queen Caroline's funeral, in spite of a distinguished record as an active magistrate in the capital.

Although in theory magistrates could call out the troops to assist them, in practice they rarely did this without obtaining the support of the Home Secretary. Almost imperceptibly the Home Office acquired a vastly expanded range of activities. It tightened its control over the forces in London under its direct command and increased in importance for peacekeeping in the country at large, acting as the clearing house for information, coordinator of forces, and source of military support. It was hardly surprising that Sidmouth should describe the business of the office in 1812 as 'very burdensome' and by 1821 as 'much increased'.[37]

But in some ways the impressiveness of the coordinating functions of the Home Office and the general efficiency of the peacekeeping forces can be exaggerated. Given time, there was no threat to public order which the authorities could not suppress, providing the troops remained loyal. But the lesson of the Gordon Riots had been that once the civil authorities had been overcome, it could take days to mobilise sufficient troops to contain and suppress a large-scale disorder. Even in 1816, when the authorities had fairly large forces available in London and expected some kind of disturbance as a result of the Spa Fields Meeting of 2 December 1816, the Spenceans were still able to lead their small band of several hundred followers the two miles from Spa Fields to the Tower, plundering gun shops and looting food on the way.[38] A more determined insurrectionist would undoubtedly have been able to make considerably more trouble than the Spencean enthusiasts did, but their pathetic attempts illustrated one of the major difficulties of public order in Britain before the era of professional policing, the cumbersome nature of the peacekeeping apparatus, which, while it was sufficient to regain control was always in danger of losing it in the short term.

The difficult years after 1789 forced the authorities to pay greater attention to the means of preventing disturbances. Not only might this avoid the danger of the disaffected turning disorder to their own advantage, but it might enable the authorities to avoid the political pitfalls which the exercise of the troops might cause. In spite of their troubled history, the years between the French Revolution and the Reform Bill of 1832 can in some ways be regarded as surprisingly quiescent. For every disturbance that broke out, there were countless occasions when discontent was allayed or channelled into other forms. A concentration upon the instances of actual disorder, perhaps tends to distort the general picture. Social control was exerted in this period by a variety of means, including the mobilisation of the strong ties of deference and respect which still bound many members of rural and urban society.

Two strands of policy can be distinguished. That which tended to the general elimination of the conditions which might provoke disturbances and that which sought to deal with specific emergencies. The former included the various means by which the authorities tried to contain the spread of what they saw as the occasions of riot and disorder. This usually went hand in hand with the development of more effective forms of policing. For example in March 1811 Nottingham Corporation enrolled special constables and set up a nightly watch of six special and six regular constables. In January 1812, the town was divided into five districts with a nightly watch of troops and constables. The system was used to good effect for a number of months in 1812, and put into operation again in 1814 and 1816. Others, such as Huddersfield and Halifax, put into operation a compulsory system of Watch and Ward.[39] Although the Luddite outbreaks continued to demand the presence of the soldiers in order to disperse disturbances and patrol the countryside, the experiments in more efficient policing in a number of towns provided the beginnings of the move to secure an adequate force of civil officers to deal with disorder.

In London matters went a stage further. In the City of London, the desire to avoid calling on the troops led to the reform of the City's force of constables. An effort was made to secure a disciplined and reputable force by issuing them with uniforms, which was done in 1791, and paying them the considerable rate of 4s. 6d. per day, raised to 5s. 0d. in 1812. A City foot patrol was set up as early as 1784 and by 1822 it consisted of 23 men on day patrol and 16 on night. Each patrol was broken down into smaller groups and assembly points were given in case of riot. Ambitious proposals for 400 patrols under the command of 40 supervisors were, however, frustrated by opposition within the Court of Aldermen. None the less, the City of London possessed a relatively effective force of constables who were active in putting down disturbances in the capital on a number of occasions. Their most important action came in December 1816, when the leaders of the mob which had progressed from Spa Fields were arrested by the Lord Mayor and the City constables at the Royal Exchange.[40]

Elsewhere in London, the professional forces at the public offices provided the key to the break up and policing of events which the authorities considered dangerous. A campaign was waged against disorderly public houses, fairs, bullock hunts, cock fights and other assemblies of the lower classes from which the authorities feared disorder. Francis Place recorded that the annual Guy Fawkes celebrations in London had been almost entirely suppressed by 1823.[41] More important, the constables from the public offices were used to police the series of mass meetings called in the capital by the London Corresponding Society in 1794-5. Though troops were held in readiness at the Tower, Whitehall and the Savoy Palace, the primary task of policing was taken over by constables. The role they had to play was indicated by the instructions given to the magistrates at the Union Hall Office in Southwark to attend a meeting on 29 June. They were to maintain 'a prudent, discreet, and firm but temperate conduct in every exigency which may occur'. A number of commentators attributed the orderly conduct of the meeting to the populace not being 'irritated by an unnecessary display of military force'.[42] By the end of the post-war period the police, now numbering almost 200 men, were being used extensively for duties where a degree of flexibility and prevention could be used to advantage. A pamphlet of 1821 paid this force the tribute that before their inception 'we had riots and every species of incidents'. Robbery and general crime was considered by two leading writers on the subject in 1821 to be now the principal policing problem in the capital.[43]

These general movements towards the better regulation of everyday life have often been missed amidst the greater upheavals of food rioting and Luddism. But the authorities also had considerable reserves of traditional deference which they could utilise to contain disorder. Indeed, periods of shortage and distress actually gave the authorities the opportunity to renew and refurbish just those bonds which they feared were being threatened by political subversion. The mobilisation of charity played an important part in cementing social bonds in a period of tension. The attempts made to relieve the poor were often impressive in their scale. It should be remembered that the decision of the Berkshire magistrates of Speenhamland to subsidise wages on a regular basis was taken early in 1795, a year of severe shortage and high prices. The initiative of the authorities there was copied in several other parishes until the Speenhamland system became fairly general in the years of the Napoleonic Wars. In itself, this policy merely marked the introduction on a regular basis of more casual and irregular attempts to supplement the wages of the poor in times of scarcity.

But even with the adoption of a more generous poor law, there remained great scope for private acts of philanthropy. Two of the principal benefactors of the populace of Oxford in 1795 were the Duke of Marlborough and Lord Harcourt who ploughed up part of their parks to provide extra land for corn growing. A subscription was opened in the city to relieve the poor and the Vice-Chancellor of the University and heads of houses entered into an agreement to reduce their own consumption and that of their families by a third. The continuance of high prices into 1796 prompted the Duke of Marlborough to award to the poor of the district 500 stone of beef and 1,000 loaves. When corn prices again reached high levels in 1800, the City subscription was raised to buy 300 quarters of foreign wheat and sell it to the poor at reduced prices. At Gloucester and Sheffield an agreement was entered into by the prominent citizens not to buy provisions at inflated prices. Near Nottingham a manufacturer presented some villagers with a piece of land on which they could build their mill in order to grind corn at reduced prices.[44] In Cornwall, a subscription in 1795 led to the importation of 3,597 bushels of barley, 172 barrels of flour and 3,000 pounds of biscuit to supply the inhabitants of Wendron, Crowan, Breage and Germoe. In 1800 1,170 people at Breage received corn at a reduced rate.[45]

Subscriptions to provide relief for distress and agreements amongst the wealthy to reduce consumption were a common feature of years of shortage in this period. Though their contribution to relieving distress is questionable, these manifestations of upper-class concern had an important psychological function. The programme of reduced consumption in 1795-6 was well-publicised, the Royal Family giving a prominent lead. Lists of subscribers to relief funds were regularly posted in handbills and given prominence in the newspapers. The Privy Council joined in the exercise and pledges were given by both houses of parliament to reduce consumption. The Home Office circulated resolutions for a reduction of one third in consumption which were read out to congregations in churches.[46] Thus social bonds which might have been threatened were being strengthened in many areas by the relief activities occasioned by the shortages. Often attention was focused upon popular scapegoats, the middlemen and dealers in the corn trade. In 1795-6 they were accused of profiteering and even exporting corn out of the country in a time of shortage. Rumours of corn being smuggled out of the country and of hoarding, became commonplace, even though very little evidence of either could be produced. In the shortage of 1800-1, the attack upon the middlemen became something of a witch hunt, which the authorities did little to discourage. Sir Samuel Romilly commented that 'great pains have been taken by persons in high authority to persuade [the people] that what they suffer is not to be ascribed to those natural causes which were obvious to their senses, but to the frauds and rapaciousness of the dealers in provisions'.[47] This view of the shortage as engineered by the dealers was echoed by Lord Kenyon, the Lord Chief Justice, who proclaimed that: 'Private individuals are plundering at the expense of public happiness. . . when the sword of justice is drawn, it shall not be sheathed until the full vengeance of the law is inflicted on them; neither purse or person shall prevent it'.[48]

The shortages of wartime and the post-war years were also met by a massive mobilisation of public charity in the capital. Cheaper and coarser bread was made available, which though generally unpopular with the consumer, at least meant that a basic subsistence was available. A number of wealthy parishes undertook to supply the bread, but far more important were the inauguration of soup kitchens to provide for the poorest areas. The first were set up in the winter of 1795-6 with the backing of Patrick Colquhoun and the aid of money from the Society of Friends. They provided meals of soup or stew for ½ d. and by the time of the scarcity of 1800-1 had developed into a large-scale operation supplying hundreds of thousands of meals in the poorer districts of Spitalfields and Clerkenwell. New soup kitchens were opened with the aid of money from the Lloyd's Coffee House Committee, offering relief to an estimated 50,000 people by 1801. Three thousand Spitalfields weavers were said to be in receipt of soup or soup tickets out of a population of 15,000. In the renewed distress of 1816, 6,000 quarts of soup daily were made available to the weavers.[49] Several witnesses recorded their role in preserving the peace. In 1800 the American ambassador Mr King expressed the opinion that were it not for the soup kitchens 'the vigour of government would be scarcely able to prevent extensive and serious popular commotions'.[50] Similar schemes were extended to the provinces. In Norwich, a United Friars Society was engaged in the annual distribution of bread and soup, giving out over 28,000 tickets for a penny loaf and a quart of broth in the winter of 1799-1800. In March the Mayor raised a fresh subscription of more than £1,100 and used it to open six soup shops where poor families could buy soup at ½d a pint, a pint per head being allowed to families. By April 1800 it was recorded that 16,000 poor were being relieved from the Soup Institution. Other places, including the manufacturing towns adopted the soup relief system in the years that followed.[51]

The years of dearth also saw local authorities reimpose the old paternalistic legislation which regulated markets against monopolistic offences. Prosecutions were taken in hand against practices which in many markets had become a commonplace as the trade in food became more sophisticated in the course of the late eighteenth century. A number of cases were brought to trial in 1795-6 and 1800-1 as the local authorities sought to assuage the ill feeling of the consumers. In 1800 the most important trial was that in London of John Rusby before Lord Kenyon. But elsewhere, as at Oxford, prosecutions were put in hand against a number of dealers. Significantly, they were dropped once the high prices fell.[52] Other practices which had fallen out of use were also revived, such as banning retail dealers from the markets for specific periods. Elsewhere JPs took the initiative in arranging a reduction of prices with the food dealers, as at Banbury in 1800. At Brandon in 1816, the magistrates agreed to press the corn dealers for a reduction in prices or sometimes prohibited outside dealers from coming into their area.[53] Others took the initiative of going to larger markets to obtain grain for the locality. In some places, including London, the medieval instrument of the Assize was put into operation, often when it had virtually been abandoned. Its primary impact was also psychological — often bakers ignored it or refused to abide by it for more than a short period. But as an eighteenth-century writer had commented, 'in large towns and cities it will always be necessary to set the Assize, in order to satisfy the people that the price which the bakers demand is no more than what is thought reasonable by the magistrates'. Even detractors of the Assize admitted its utility in times of scarcity: in 1814, one feared the removal of a control which 'in times of scarcity. . . had preserved internal tranquillity'.[54]

Local authorities depended heavily upon the efficiency of the local magistracy to preserve public order. An active magistrate was worth many squadrons of troops. Time and again riots were averted by the direct intervention of magistrates. In reports from the localities it is surprising how often one comes across the phrase 'the symptoms of a disturbance'. Magistrates were frequently to be found arguing with angry crowds, urging them to disperse, and assuring them that their grievances could be met without the need to resort to violence. Hence at Norwich in May 1800 the Mayor, Sheriffs and Aldermen visited the market place and reasoned with the crowd assembled there. In September, they had to do the same with crowds assembled around the New Mills.[55] In London, magistrates became adept at dealing with disturbances. If the magistrates could be backed up by a show of force, so much the better, but instances abounded of magistrates turning up at dangerous incidents with a force of constables to dissuade an assembled crowd from turning to violence. In 1801, Sir Robert Baker was able to defuse a dangerous confrontation between the authorities and a crowd on Barnes Common by a 'spirited and conciliating speech'.[56] The famous Riot Act was used probably rather less than has been imagined. One detailed study we have is for London between 1791 and 1821, where the Riot Act was used twenty times. On many other occasions the magistrates preferred to warn the crowd, verbally, or by placards or notices that the Riot Act might be read. Like the troops it was something of a legal sledgehammer with its threat of capital conviction. Warnings that riotous proceedings would be vigorously dealt with were not a cliché. In the face-to-face world of a smaller town or village, it meant that magistrates were serious in their intention to prosecute and that riotous proceedings would not be passed off lightly.

A picture of the dialogue that could exist even between soldiers and rioters is given in the testimony of a participant of the riots in East Lancashire in 1826:

> That morning we set off to the loom-breaking. When we had got on the road we saw horse soldiers coming towards us. There was a stop then. The soldiers came forward, their drawn swords glittering in the air. The people opened out to let the soldiers get through. Some threw their pikes over the dyke and some did not. When the soldiers had come into the midst of the people, the officers called out, 'Halt!'. All expected that the soldiers were going to charge, but the officers made a speech to the mob and told them what the consequences would be if they persisted in what they were going to do. Some of the old fellows from the mob spoke. They said, 'What are we to do? We're starving. Are we to starve to death?' The soldiers were fully equipped with haversacks and they emptied their sandwiches amongst the crowd. Then the soldiers left and there was another meeting. Were the power-looms to be broken or not? Yes, it was decided, they must be broken at all costs.[57]

As the above quote shows, conciliation frequently failed. Nevertheless, it is important to see the activities in the Luddite areas and elsewhere as part of a general social process, in which the outbreak of violence was a last resort when other means had failed. For the authorities too, there were available a range of options to maintain public order. Philanthropy and warnings provided the first line of defence, but even when disturbances did break out, the authorities sought to repair the breaches in the social order by a mixture of terror and mercy. The processes of law, the availability of pardon, and ultimately the use of exemplary capital punishment were usually sufficient to repair the damage caused by the outbreak of disorder.[58] Most eighteenth-century commentators accepted that a certain amount of disorder was inevitable especially in times of dearth. There came, however, a point at which punishment became necessary. An interesting letter from Essex illustrates the point:

> I am very much rejoiced to hear your mobility continue quiet, for I have been under a thousand apprehensions, as I heard they had again assembled and done a great deal of mischief in several parts of Essex, particularly in Chelmsford, but surely your subscription must put an entire stop to all riots in your part, for if they prove refractory after such kindness and attention, it must be clear they are not actuated by real want and of course everyone will join in punishing them with the utmost rigour.[59]

'The utmost rigour' was usually reserved for a few cases. Following riots in London in 1794, the Lord Mayor assured the Home Office that: 'I have been tender about committing, thinking that the best thing for the public service was to reserve a few strong cases such as a jury could not in conscience overlook . . .'[60] In 1802, after a riot amongst Shipwrights at Deptford, the magistrate in charge proceeded against three of the men on a capital charge, reporting to the Home Office: 'I hope the vigorous measures taken against these rioters will produce more good effects than a thousand prosecutions':[61] Those selected for punishment stood a much higher chance of being executed than the general run of felons. In the period 1776 to 1800, over half of all rioters capitally convicted were executed, against an average for all offences of only a third. This policy of 'exemplary punishment' was also adhered to in the executions which flowed from the Luddite outbreaks. The recourse to proceedings of High Treason against the Spa Fields and Pentridge rioters in 1816 and 1817 sprang from the same spirit.

But mercy could also be manipulated to refurbish the authority of the magistrate. In 1800, a Fulham magistrate reported to the Home Office that a number of men had been indicted for a riotous assembly, but 'in consequence of them having begged pardon in the public manner the prosecution stopped'.[62] Public admission of wrong, admonitions from magistrates, and written pledges of good conduct played an important part in the process of preventing renewed outbreaks of disorder. Just how effective the threat of the full rigour of

the law could be, was illustrated in Lancashire in 1826, when twenty
ringleaders in the machine-breaking were arrested in the middle of the
night. The effect was devastating upon the local community. It was
reported that: 'The method of arresting them and taking them away
at once completely put an end to the breaking of power looms. . . The
rioters were so frightened that many durst not go to be in their own
houses. Some left the country; others hid themselves for weeks, some in
one place, some in another, some in coal pits and some, who few, if
any, would have thought would have been guilty of such a crime.'[63]
A similar picture of the effects of heavy punishment upon a small
community is given in the aftermath of the agricultural disturbances
in Essex, where three men from the village of Great Holland were
transported. A local witness affirmed that 'The prompt measures taken
to suppress the disturbance frightened the labourers alarmingly.'[64]

Historians who have been puzzled by the failure to establish a fully
fledged professional police in England before 1829 have perhaps tended
to exaggerate the weakness of the authorities in the period prior to the
Metropolitan Police Act. Here it is important to bear in mind the
comments of F.O. Darvell about the Luddite disturbances: 'The
astonishing thing about all the early Regency disturbances was not that
they should have provoked anxiety on the part of the authorities and
terror on the part of some manufacturers and members of the public
but that this anxiety and terror should have been so restrained.' The
source of this equanimity, according to Darvell, was an assurance on
the part of the authorities that it was within their power 'to restore
and maintain order, once their arrangements had been completed'.[65]
Similarly, in the other great potential source of danger, London, the
authorities had equipped themselves with more flexible and efficient
forces even before 1829. In the rural areas and the older market towns
the traditional apparatus of public order, combined with the time-
honoured processes of social control, was sufficient to maintain public
order well into the nineteenth century.

Moments of particular crisis could be partly allayed by a massive
mobilisation of private philanthropy. However, if this failed, the
authorities had an effective means of repressing any disturbances that
occurred. Retribution might not be swift, but it was virtually certain.
A large-scale police force was not created in England before 1829
because the authorities were confident that they could maintain public
order using the old system, with *ad hoc* modifications. In this they were
more justified than has often been allowed. In a period often characterised as peculiarly violent, one of the most significant lines of enquiry

remains not why there were so many disturbances, but why there were fewer than might have been expected.

Notes

1. J.L. and B. Hammond, *The Town Labourer*, 4th edn. (London, 1966), p.101.
2. M.I. Thomis, *The Town Labourer and the Industrial Revolution* (London, 1974), p.18.
3. See G. Rudé, *The Crowd in History* (New York, 1964), pp.33-45; R.B. Rose, 'Eighteenth Century Price Riots and Public Policy in England', *International Review of Social History*, VI (1961), pp.277-82; J. Stevenson, 'Food Riots in England, 1792-1818', in J. Stevenson and R. Quinault, (eds), *Popular Protest and Public Order* (London, 1974), pp.33-74.
4. G. Rudé, op.cit., pp.195-212.
5. See E.P. Thompson, *The Making of the English Working Class*, 2nd edn. (Harmondsworth, 1968), pp.66-83 and 'The Moral Economy of the English Crowd in the Eighteenth Century', *Past and Present*, *50* (1971), pp.76-136.
6. For a general view of the variety of popular disturbances, though only a fraction of the total number, see R.F. Wearmouth, *Methodism and the Common People of the Eighteenth Century* (London, 1945), pp.19-50.
7. See G. Rudé, op.cit., pp.47-64 and *Wilkes and Liberty* (Oxford, 1962).
8. Public Record Office, Home Office papers (hereafter HO), Series 42, bundle 29: W. Agiloe to HO (undated), March 1794.
9. HO 42/37: Memorandum on riots in the Metropolis (undated), 1796.
10. J.L. and B. Hammond, op.cit., p.90.
11. M.I. Thomis, op.cit., p.24.
12. See P. Colquhoun, *A Treatise on the Police of the Metropolis*, 4th edn. (London, 1797), pp.218-19; L. Radzinowicz, *A History of English Criminal Law* (London, 1956), II; *Parliamentary Papers, 1834*, xvi (600), p.468: Report on the State of the Police.
13. For the public offices and the Middlesex Justices' Act, see my study, 'Disturbances and Public Order in London, 1790-1821' (Univ. of Oxford, D. Phil thesis 1973), pp.37-9.
14. *PP.1868-9*, xxv, pp.697-703.
15. R.J. Hills, *The Life Guards* (London, 1971), p.46.
16. War Office Papers, series 1, vol.880; General return of barracks, 1 May 1804; HO 42/107: Memorandum relative to the Tower and Military stations in the vicinity of the Metropolis, May 1810; HO 50/443; Memorandum upon the Barrack Department of Great Britain, 31 Dec.1823.
17. HO42/20 : Col. de Lancey to Dundas, 13 June 1792.
18. HO 50/443: Memorandum upon the Barrack Department of Great Britain, 31 Dec. 1823.
19. See C. Emsley, 'Political disaffection and the British Army in 1792', *Bulletin of the Institute of Historical Research*, XLVII, no. 118 (1975); F. Duncan, *History of the Royal Regiment of Artillery* (London, 1893), pp.71-2; *London Chronicle*, 25-27 May 1797.
20. See *Gentleman's Magazine*, XC (1820), I. p.559; *The Croker Papers: the correspondence and diaries of J.W.C. Croker*, ed. L.J. Jennings (London, 1884), I, pp.175-6

21. The wages of the troops in this period were complicated by the various allowances and deductions made for food and lodging. In 1792 and 1797 pay rises were granted, bringing pay to 11½d per day above food and allowances. Extra pay was given for active duty and some soldiers in London even worked in off-duty hours in other trades.

22. See J. Stevenson, 'The Queen Caroline Affair', in J. Stevenson (ed.), *London in the Age of Reform* (Oxford, 1977).

23. For the L.C.S. comment, see *Letter of Thanks to the Lord Mayor from the London Corresponding Society* (London, 1794), p.2; *Hansard,* 1815, lxvi, 27-38, 150-7.

24. Demands for a reduction in the numbers of troops took place in 1816, 1820 and 1821.

25. See J. Stevenson. 'The Queen Caroline Affair'.

26. W. Belsham, *Memoirs of the Reign of George III* (London, 1795), III, p.22.

27. M.I. Thomis, op.cit., pp.29-30.

28. J.W. Fortescue, *The County Lieutenancies and the Army, 1803-14* (London, 1909), pp.46-7.

29. See J. Stevenson, 'Food Riots in England, 1792-1818', pp.47-8.

30. J.L. and B. Hammond,op.cit., pp.93-5.

31. *London Chronicle,* 14 March 1797. The 'marching guinea' derived from army usage where soldiers were given a sum of money when they were embodied for active service. See J.R. Western, *The English Militia in the Eighteenth Century* (London, 1965), pp. 345, 348.

32. British Museum, Addit. MSS., 16928 (Reeves Papers), f. 13. Resolutions of the St James' Association. See also A. Mitchell, 'The Association Movement of 1792-3', *Historical Journal,* IV (1961), pp.56-77

33. See J. Stevenson, 'Disturbances and Public Order in London 1790-1821', pp. 186-8, 208-9.

34. Figures from J.W. Fortescue, op.cit., and G. Cousins, *The Defenders* (London, 1968).

35. See O. Teichman, 'The Yeomanry as an aid to the Civil Power', *Journal of the Society for Army Historical Research,* XIX (1940) pp.75-91 and G.R. Codrington, 'Yeomanry Cavalry', *Journal of the Society for Army Historical Research,* X (1930), pp.134-42.

36. On the Home Office, see R.R. Nelson, *The Home Office, 1782-1801* (Durham, N.C., 1969) and J. Sainty, *Home Office Officials, 1782-1870* (London, 1975), pp.1-10. The Home Office possessed ten clerks in 1789, rising to fourteen in 1821.

37. Devonshire County Record Office, Sidmouth Papers, Hobhouse to Lushington, 26 Nov. 1821.

38. For the Spa Fields disturbances, see E.P. Thompson, *The Making of the English Working Class,* pp.694-6 and T.M. Parsinnen, 'The Revolutionary Party in London', *Bulletin of the Institute of Historical Research,* XLV (1972), pp. 266-82.

39. F.O. Darvell, *Public Order in Regency England,* 2nd edn. (Oxford, 1969), pp. 268-73.

40. For the City police, see D. Rumbelow, *I Spy Blue* (London, 1971), pp.98-110.

41. See J. Stevenson, 'Disturbances and Public Order in London 1790-1821', pp. 176-80. For Place's evidence, see M. Thale (ed.), *The Autobiography of Francis Place* (Cambridge, 1972), pp.67-8.

42. HO 65/1: King to Union Hall, 29 June 1795; *Morning Chronicle,* 30 June 1795.

43.   G.B. Mainwaring, *Observations on the present state of the Police in the Metropolis* (London, 1821), p. 135.
44.   *Neale's collections of Oxford,* pp. 490-4, 502.
45.   A.K. Hamilton Jenkin, *The Cornish Miner,* 4th edn. (Newton Abbot, 1972), pp. 90-7.
46.   W.M. Stern, 'The Bread Crisis in Britain, 1795-96' *Economica,* new series, XXXI (1964), pp. 182-3.
47.   S. Romilly, *Memoirs of Sir Samuel Romilly* (London, 1840), I, pp. 73-5.
48.   *Annals of Agriculture,* XXV (1795), p.3.
49.   See HO 42/66: An account of the public services of Patrick Colquhoun, 1804; *Society for Bettering the Condition of the Poor, The Economy of an Institution* (London, 1799); *Morning Chronicle,* 2 Dec. 1816.
50.   R. King, *The Life and Correspondence of Rufus King,* ed. C.A. King (New York, 1894-1900), III, p. 198.
51.   C.B. Jewson, *The Jacobin City* (Glasgow, 1975), p. 99. For their use in other cities, see R.F. Wearmouth, op.cit., pp.74-6.
52.   See J. Stevenson, 'Food Riots in England, 1792-1818', p. 61.
53.   Ibid.
54.   C. Smith, *Three Tracts on the Corn Trade and Corn Laws,* 2nd edn. (London, 1766), p. 30; *Hansard,* Old series 1814, XXIX, 637.
55.   C.B. Jewson, op.cit., pp. 99-100.
56.   *London Chronicle,* 23-25 July 1801.
57.   C. Aspin, *Lancashire, the First Industrial Society.* (Helmshore, 1969), pp.45-9
58.   There is an excellent discussion of the role of the law in the preservation of public order in eighteenth-century England in D. Hay, 'Property Authority and the Criminal Law', in D. Hay, P. Linebaugh, J.G. Rule, E.P. Thompson, and C. Winslow, *Albion's Fatal Tree* (Harmondsworth, 1975).
59.   A.F.J. Brown (ed.), *Essex People, 1750-1900* (Chelmsford, 1972), p. 65.
60.   HO42/33: Le Mesurier to King, 24 Aug. 1794
61.   HO42/66 : Harriott to King, 21 Aug. 1802.
62.   HO 42/52: Mayrick to HO, 28 Oct.1800.
63.   C. Aspin, op.cit., p.45.
64.   A.F.J. Brown, op.cit., p.75.
65.   F.O. Darvell, op.cit., pp.325-7.

2 'SOCIAL POLICE' AND THE BUREAUCRATIC ELITE: A VISION OF ORDER IN THE AGE OF REFORM

A.P. Donajgrodzki

The early Victorians, threatened by industrialism, urbanisation and mass working-class protest, were almost obsessively interested in discovering the bases of social order. This phenomenon has been explored by historians from a number of standpoints, but discussion of the problem as seen by the bureaucratic elite has almost uniformly centred around the issue of state intervention and the revolution in government.[1] Recent research has tended to move away from Dicey's over-simple view that there was a sharp and impermeable division between Benthamites and traditionalists on the issue, to a recognition of the fact that, in Lubenow's phrase, 'early Victorian growth occurred in the context of traditional institutions and values'.[2] The question of values is important, for despite the progressive blurring of other distinctions between the two groups, it is still perhaps assumed that membership of one camp or the other implied acceptance of entirely distinct systems of social values. Thus Benthamites, even in the 1830s and 1840s, have sometimes been portrayed as possessing that commitment to an aggressive liberalism and individualism found in the later writings of J.S. Mill. Conversely, since paternalism and deference were *political* weapons of the old order, the tendency has been to suppose that they, and they alone, appreciated its *social* uses. Thus, even where they acted together, for example, to restrict child labour, it is assumed that their social aim was different. Ashley took up the subject for the wrong (paternalist) reasons; men like Chadwick because it would help to produce a healthier and in the end more independent labour force, and thus would benefit capitalism.

This distinction is not altogether unfounded, but it can obscure the often near-identical presuppositions and social values of some Benthamites and traditionalists. In the 1830s and 1840s, at least, a common frame of mind about what social policy should aim to achieve may sometimes be discerned in their thought. This essay is concerned to explore this common frame of mind in the thought of Hugh Tremenheere, a traditionalist, and Edwin Chadwick, Bentham's amanuensis and devoted, though not slavish, adherent. The approach of both men to the problems of social policy was characterised by an outlook which I have termed 'social police'. The concept may have a further value. It may help to reconcile the apparently inconsistent impulses in early Victorian social reform, which was sometimes 'benevolent', as in the case of the public health movement and at others coercive, as with police forces and the poor law. In fact, as we shall see, far from being inconsistent, benevolent and coercive phases of social policy were regarded as equally important and mutually supportive phases in the control of the poor.

I

The frame of mind which I have called social police was characterised by two sets of assumptions. It was believed, first, that social order was the product of a common morality, which was sustained and expressed by its general diffusion throughout the institutions of society. Thus a social policy which aimed at the preservation of order must include not only consideration of legal systems, police forces and prisons, but of religion and morality, and of those factors which supported or propagated them — education, socially constructive leisure, even housing and public health. This was an assumption which, fifty years later, was to lead sociologists to develop the concept of social control.

Unlike social control theory in general, however, social police, although assuming the mutuality and harmony of different social classes, was a set of attitudes especially evoked when control of the poor was under discussion. It was characterised, to take the second set of pre-suppositions, by a belief that a strong tutelary grasp should be maintained over the poor, whom it was assumed, were normless, or at least insufficient if left to themselves; liable to be led astray by agitators or to form 'perverted' social systems. For Tremenheere, as for many early Victorians, 'personal contact' between classes was essential to prevent such an outcome. A similar belief led Chadwick, I shall suggest, to devise an institutional structure for the same purpose. Such an outlook had an obvious political convenience to theorists from an upper class threatened with working-class political protest, but it was not, as such, a belief designed to 'keep down' the poor. In a society regarded as harmonious, with a common morality as its root, such tutelage was conceived as a duty of the rich, and not always a comfortable one. It was also, as Carlyle suggested, the right of the poor:

> Surely of all 'rights of man', this right of the ignorant man to be guided by the wiser, to be, gently or forcibly, held in the true course by him, is the indisputablest. Nature herself ordains it from the first;

Society struggles towards perfection by enforcing and accomplishing it more and more. . . . It is a sacred right and duty, on both sides; and the summary of all social duties whatsoever between the two.[3]

Tremenheere and Chadwick were particularly well placed to express this frame of mind, and to spell out its implications for social policy but, as Carlyle's observation would suggest, they were not alone in sharing such presuppositions. It is probable that many early Victorians also held them, and it may be that their frame of mind was, in turn, derived from the 'Old Society'. Thus very similar assumptions may be discerned in the writings of Carlyle,[4] among the social novelists,[5] and politically, in 'Young England', and in the paternalism of High Tories like Ashley.[6] The 'model' industrial communities of 'enlightened' employers, too, gave organisational expression to social police. It may also have had a more general currency within the civil service at this time. Many civil servants, especially the itinerant ones, displayed a social concern which went far beyond their immediate brief, a tendency towards the belief that social policy was wide in scope and indivisible in the contribution it made to social order. Thus the Assistant Poor Law Commissioners investigated the housing of the poor,[7] prison inspectors wrote on labour conditions,[8] and almost everybody on education.[9]

Social police perhaps represented an adaptation of, and if so almost certainly an intensification of beliefs about the relations appropriate between classes, and control of the poor, derived from pre-industrial society. In the eighteenth century, for example, civil authority was matched, at least in some parts of the country, by an ecclesiastical authority which permitted an intense and extensive scrutiny of the lives of the poor. Dr McClatchey has shown, for example, that in Oxfordshire the clergy (who were themselves sometimes land-owners and magistrates) were often administrators of local charities, educators, members of hospital management committees and medical advisers, as well as preachers to and visitors of the poor.[10] They were able, through these generalised contacts not only to teach a common morality, which specified, for example, appropriate attitudes to family life or civil authority, but sometimes to enforce it. Thus, Dr Warne notes that in eighteenth-century Devonshire, the ecclesiastical courts regularly tried mothers and fathers of illegitimate children, and dealt with cases of fornication, swearing, or even non-attendance at church.[11] The possibility that obduracy might result in excommunication, and the excommunicate at death be 'pitted' rather than given Christian burial[12] was no doubt itself a formidable instrument of social control.

In such areas order was perhaps ensured by an alliance of gentry and clergy, through the use of a wide range of social contacts, formal and informal, benevolent and coercive, and it is probable that it was from such a tradition that social police arose.

This much is speculative, a hypothesis which can only be tested by further research, but it is certain that at the end of the century, Patrick Colquhoun, in search of a solution to the unique policing problems of London, anticipated in many respects the analysis of Tremenheere and Chadwick. Colquhoun has frequently been seen as a police 'pioneer', a writer who, despite oddities, and a persistent tendency to extremes, may be regarded as the father of the British police, and a great exponent of the 'preventive' principle.[13] But the lip service paid by every modern police organisation to prevention, and the tendency to discount as extreme some portions of his theory, have to some extent disguised the breadth and originality of his thought and its integrated and coherent nature. Colquhoun's search for an efficient police system led him to the wider question of the source of order and thence to morality. 'The only means of securing the peace of society', he wrote in 1806, 'is, by enforcing the observance of religious and moral principles.'[14] Order could only be assured if the police objective were expressed through a general and interrelated network of provision which would both sustain *and* control the poor. Hence the breadth of his prescription. The police and poor law should be jointly managed, interrelated arms of coercion and control.[15] Charity should be used especially in times of dearth, to support law and order;[16] working-class leisure should be supervised. Anticipating later reformers he saw education as a preventive measure. Moral training should be the primary educational aim; the duty of the rich and the right of the poor:

> An immoral man can never be a good citizen. Yet, true it is, that we should have little reason to complain of the inferior ranks of the community, if more attention were bestowed to form proper regulations for their support and improvement in society. If we suffer them to be ill-educated, and then punish them for those very crimes to which their bad education and miserable condition exposed them, the result is, that by such an oversight we make delinquents, and then punish them.[17]

Teachers, clergymen, poor law officials and distributors of charity were to some extent policemen. It followed that even the 'specialised' police function was indeterminate; the policeman a moral guide, lay

preacher and social worker as well as thief-taker. Thus as part of the
effort to moralise the poor, the police should distribute songs which
conveyed 'moral lessons. . . shewing in language familiar to their habits,
the advantages of *Industry and Frugality* . . . and the glory and happiness of *a good Husband, a good Father* and an honest Man'.[18] Similarly
the *Police Gazette* should be used 'to excite in the minds of the labouring people a strong sense of moral virtue, loyalty and love of their
country; to forewarn the unwary, and to arrest the hands of evil-doers'.[19]
Some of his headings for the popular essays he thought the *Gazette*
should carry must have been familiar to the occupants of vicarages and
the homes they visited: on breaches of the Lord's day and regular
attendance at church, on industry, honesty and truth, on the duties of
a good husband or wife, or on the duty of providing for a family.[20] Thus
a well organised police would, in Professor Radzinowicz's words, 'promote the moral improvement of the labouring classes by the exercise of
supervision and restraint.'[21]

Supervision and restraint of course were to take more concrete
forms than moral exhortation. There was no question of the poor being
left to themselves in a state of social *laissez-faire*. Public houses were to
be licensed and watched, their landlords to lose their licences if they
permitted meetings of trade unionists, of political clubs with 'seditious
or traitorous' designs, or merely for allowing the playing of 'idle and
sedentary' games.[22] A number of occupational groups, including
servants, were to be brought under direct supervision.[23] Perhaps the
most powerful instrument of surveillance, however, lay in his proposed
fusion of the poor law and police functions, to be accompanied by a
systematic tabulation and classification of the whole labouring population. Social control mechanisms in rural communities had often
provided subtle means for evaluating the 'worthiness' of the poor. Thus,
for example, Professor Chambers notes that in most Nottinghamshire
parishes the resident poor, unlike strangers, 'seem to have been treated
fairly gently'.[24] Warne suggests that in Devonshire relief and charitable
aid were tailored in a very personal way to the 'needs' of those in
distress, an outcome only possible through considerable personal
knowledge.[25] So, too, outcasts and rebels could be identified. Many
girls in Devonshire preferred to abscond rather than perform humiliating
public penance for bastardy or fornication, thereby joining the
persecuted caste of vagrants.[26] Colquhoun's pauper police establishment
was a means of exercising this discrimination through a formal institution. The pauper police institution was to supervise poor relief, to keep
detailed records of individual indigents, and more generally, to monitor

'the general state of morals in the parish; whether the inferior classes are generally sober and industrious or the reverse, or in what degree and proportion'.[27] Thus it would be able to dispose correctly of individual cases, to *relieve the indigent requiring assistance, to prop up the industrious poor ready to descend into indigence* from sickness or other casualties'.[28] The sheep could be separated efficiently from the goats. Liaison with the detective branch of the police would enable criminals and idlers to be identified and disposed of. Sick beggars and homeless or orphaned children could be despatched to appropriate institutions,[29] wilful vagrants and mendicants employed on public works or in Villages of Industry,[30] and the worst class of the unimprisoned poor, the idle, unemployed, semi-criminal residuum, could be compulsorily enlisted in the army and sent to serve abroad.[31]

Thus by a judicious use of benevolence and coercion, an institutional framework for social order would be established. It looks, from a modern standpoint, authoritarian, and so it was, but it was not intended to be repressive. Pessimist though he was, Colquhoun assumed that society was a harmonious structure and that it possessed a unitary moral system. The honest poor would not be oppressed; only evil-doers need be afraid. This attitude links him with the early Victorians, and there is a further point of similarity. Colquhoun thought his theory — which was, in effect, a plan to institutionalise paternalism — was one which would benefit commercial and industrial society.[32] In the thought of Tremenheere and Chadwick the same discrimination between moral and social, and economic *laissez-faire* is to be found.

II

By the late 1830s many of the problems which Colquhoun had perceived in London a quarter of a century earlier were discernible in the manufacturing districts. In the interval, the economic doctrine of *laissez-faire* had grown to prominence, but it produced no dramatic change in presuppositions as to the constituents of social stability. On the question of order and the correct relations between rich and poor disagreements were more often about *means* than *ends*. The new poor law, for example, divided respectable opinion sharply, but it is important to recognise that its aims, although expressed through new machinery, were traditional: poor laws since the time of Elizabeth I had attempted, as they still do, to ensure that men earned their own livings. But economic independence, for the poor especially, did not carry with it the right to an individualism which would destroy society. On the contrary, the belief continued that such independence was incompatible

with social order. Indeed as we shall see, contemplation of the social
consequences of industrialism tended to intensify this feeling, to
produce anxious expressions of the need for a tutelary control of the
poor, and speculations as to how it might be achieved.

Hugh Seymour Tremenheere, the first mines inspector, developed
this view from a traditionalist starting point. It was his official duty to
report not only on technical aspects of the act and its enforcement, but
more generally, to enquire 'into the state of the population in the
mining districts', a task which he made his main concern.[33] It was not
a responsibility he defined narrowly: his annual reports often contained
the results of his speculations on the principles which should underly a
healthy industrial society, and the relations appropriate between
masters and men, rich and poor. His outlook was Whiggish and
traditionalist;[34] as an individual, he was, his writings suggest, a warm,
humane and benevolent man. Unlike Colquhoun, or for that matter
Chadwick, police forces were never very prominent in his mind, nor
did he tend to look for order in state-regulated institutions. His
language was that of moral persuasion, obligation and improvement.
But he shared their preoccupation with order and like them, came to
see it as attainable only if diffused through a wide range of social
institutions. Colquhoun, starting as it were from a narrow police standpoint, had been driven in his search for order to education and beyond.
Tremenheere, starting from a consideration of moral criteria, was
brought, through a route which saw order as even more diffuse,
eventually to police forces. He expressed, too, more clearly than either
Colquhoun or Chadwick, the necessity for a tutelary control over the
lives of the poor, especially in his descriptions of the works of model
employers, and in his reflections on the needs of the raw new industrial
districts.

Tremenheere wrote detailed accounts of model industrial communities with a specific educational aim. He thought that the most natural
way in which the evils of industrialism could be cured was through the
fostering of harmony between employers and employees, an outcome
which could be realised only if employers exercised their responsibilities
to their workforces. Thus he described the practices of enlightened firms
to encourage emulation by the less responsible.[35] This gave a certain
shape to such reports. He took great care to spell out the moral, social
and financial implications of each aspect of such communities, and
extrapolated the police element within paternalism. The thrust of his
argument was to suggest that order lay in a totally controlling and
sustaining environment, to which even apparently trifling details, like

the provision of gardens, made their contribution. His assertion of this interplay of moral and material factors may be be illustrated by reference to his account of one such ideal industrial community.

In his 1846 report he described the extensive new Cwm Avon Works of the English Copper Company. What characterised the Cwm Avon Works, he suggested, was the extent to which 'the wise moral government of a large assemblage of work-people engages so much careful consideration'.[36] The first element in such 'moral government' concerned the material condition of the poor. The company provided, therefore, well-sited, roomy and properly drained houses for its workforce, at moderate rent. Tremenheere noted with approval gardens 'full of flowers, fruit, and vegetables'. He was pleased to find 'in several cottages papered rooms, as well as excellent furniture and books'. The areas around the cottages were kept clear. Wages were paid in a satisfactory way, and the company shop was a useful facility, unobjectionable, since no credit was allowed and there was no truck system. These were in themselves measures of moral care, Tremenheere said, but he described, too, 'those arrangements which have a more direct and immediate reference to the religious and moral improvement of the people'. Foremost among these was provision for religious worship. The nearby parish church had been enlarged by the company, which had also built a clergy house. It had constructed several dissenting chapels, schools had been set up, and there was an evening class for young men. Facilities had been provided for socially constructive leisure. Lecturers gave talks 'on useful and entertaining subjects', there were singing lessons, a band, a cricket club and sea fishing using the company's drag net. The sale of alcohol was strictly regulated: only two public houses were allowed on the company-owned site, and both closed at 10 p.m.

Tremenheere cited with approval measures taken to supervise the demeanour of the men and to encourage the development of 'character'. 'Fines are imposed for improprieties of conduct, or neglect of duty; for drunkenness, swearing, misconduct towards a fellow workman, smoking during the hours of work, etc. The fines are added to the sick fund. . . The least liberty taken with any of the females employed. . . is punished with discharge.' The company also took action to reinforce family life and to prevent the 'evil' of the early independence of children. 'The Sunday is kept with much propriety', he observed, 'no assemblages of children idling about, are allowed; they are expected to be either with their parents, or at the Sunday School.' The wages of youths were paid to their parents until they were about to marry, a measure taken, he said to avoid 'the total loss of all domestic discipline and the disruption of all family ties'. The consequence of this system of moral government was, he concluded, 'the satisfaction and advantage of the employers, and the comfort, quiet, health, good morals, respectability and intelligence of the work-people'.

Tremenheere's descriptions of other such firms followed similar lines.[37] Order was, to some extent, a commodity which might appear financially expensive; but its provision was not only a moral but a prudential necessity. He wrote of Cwm Avon:

If the bringing together a large mass of people, earning high wages, has not been accompanied in this case by their demoralisation, the cause is clear; many wise precautions have been taken that it should not. These are to a certain extent costly to the Company; but they have this advantage over the contrary plan of laying out nothing upon moral safeguards, and trusting to chance for the result, that the cost is known; it may be included in accounts as 200*l* or 300*l* per annum, as a guarantee-fund against disorder. . . Whatever may be the theory, as to the duties of employers towards their work-people, (and I am happy to say I have met with very few who avowedly hold that they have none, except that of paying them fair wages,) the fact, according to my observation, is nearly universal; that where these responsibilities are neglected, the result is, moral injury to the people, and pecuniary loss to their employers.[38]

Employers had a moral obligation to their workforces, and if wise, would aim 'to contribute in every practicable manner to their intellectual and moral development'.[39] Tremenheere's theory was, as this would suggest, permeated by the language of reciprocal obligation, and by the belief that society was a harmonious structure, the interests of masters and men identical. He had no fear of the 'intellectual and moral development' of the people, regarding it, on the contrary as a means to promote stability. The poor would come to see their true community of interest with the rich, a truth hidden from them when they were surrounded by filth, immersed in drunkenness and 'sensuality', ill-educated, ignorant of religion and deprived of a proper family life. So his appeal was positive and humanitarian: a call for better housing, sanitation, social welfare, pastoral care and education, all provided in a spirit of Christian benevolence. But if duty would not influence employers, prudence ought. Where they failed to do so, the consequences for law and order were serious and far-reaching: working-class drunkenness, and its attendant crimes, incest, disorderliness, property crimes, stoppages, strikes, political riots and disturbances. He approached the issue of social order from the other end to Colquhoun, but they were talking about the same problem. Humanitarianism was, in this sense, the other face of coercion.

Tremenheere would perhaps have liked to see a nationwide structure of industrial concerns which, organised according to his principles, would have fitted easily into the existing structure of deferential interest-based communities: wealthier and larger than their agricultural neighbours, and superior to them in some respects, but similar in character. He was only too aware, however, that new industrial communities were not developing in this way and so he gave much attention to the problems of social organisation in districts where the rich were not fulfilling their responsibilities, and especially to areas like Monmouth and Lanarkshire, where there were large tracts of newly industrialised country, with 'vast populations left without any adequate means of moral and religious superintendence and control'.[40] What he saw in such places did nothing either to minimise his belief in the truly harmonious nature of society, or his opinion that solidary structures should be created to redress the 'social disorganisation and moral degradation',[41] discernible in their working-class populations. Instead, Tremenheere thought the ill effects of the absence of a 'true' community could be mitigated if the family were strengthened and preserved. Control would necessarily be less direct than in model industrial communities, but church and state might, through skilful innovation, assert a control over the poor sufficient to preserve society.

In 1844, for example, he devoted part of his report to a description of the Airdrie and Coatbridge region of Lanarkshire,[42] and proposed measures to combat the anarchy latent in its almost wholly unsupervised 40,000 strong, working-class population. He argued that 'A healthy state of society can spring from no other source than the family life of the people.' Family life was the first among the elements of natural morality since it encouraged parents to self-sacrifice, and because it produced in the children 'affection, respect, deference and obedience', reciprocal sentiments and duties which lay 'at the very foundation of social order and well-being'. Children learnt first, to love and obey their parents, and thence in later life showed the same duty 'to others, equally their superiors, though standing in a different relation'. Thus, through the reciprocal fulfilment of duties, Tremenheere argued, 'society is softened and harmonized'. He continued:

The feeling, founded on a true principle, and operating generally upon the manners, is directed naturally with especial force, in the case of a labourer, towards his employer and master. It gives rise to mutual confidence, which in due time warms into attachment, and confirms the bond of mutual interest and sympathy. Hence it spreads into a wider circle, and. . . to 'those higher and more enlarged regards' which lead to a veneration and love for the institutions of our country.[43]

Sentiment and opinion, then, formed through personal relationships within the family, were the true basis of personal contentment *and* social order. But, given the failure of many employers to exercise their legitimate influence, how could such a system be brought about? Tremenheere suggested a number of means, some to be undertaken by the state, others by the church. The state should provide the outward framework for a healthy family life. A police force should be established and the sale of spirits regulated. These were the entitlement of immigrants to the district who had 'elsewhere been accustomed to live under the protection of a well-regulated state of society' and even more of their children. Alcohol was particularly destructive of family life, since the taste for it spread from men to women and children, and the husband drank away his excess earnings 'instead of bracing up his energies to do his duty to his family, by economising his additional earnings, paying for the schooling of his children, providing more furniture or more clothing, and giving to his habitation the appearance of being the home of a rational man'.[44]

Measures were necessary, too, to eliminate the socially destructive malpractices of employers. Excessive fines on miners, unfair weighing, and the truck system (despite some arguments in its favour) should be eliminated, and the law on the arrestment of wages reformed, since in addition to other disadvantages they gave credence of the view of 'agitators' that they were designed to 'curb and repress' the men. Equally, however, Tremenheere noted that the repeal of the combination laws had not had the consequences that Parliament had expected; and he hinted, no more, that it might be useful to modify the laws relating to trade unions. He recognised, too, as we should expect from his description of Cwm Avon, that something needed to be done to remedy 'the corrupting influences arising from the manner in which the people are collected together and lodged', but although he blamed the masters for abdicating this responsibility, he was not specific about solutions.

The state had a role to play then, although rather a circumscribed one, in correcting the ills of the district. It should also, despite the religious difficulty, increase the number of schools, and staff them with men of a class capable 'by their person and acquirements of really discharging the high duties of education in its widest sense; of forming the mind and character, as well as imparting mere knowledge'. But an augmented clergy was to be the main agency through which society should act. Clergymen should penetrate the homes and minds of the poor, exercising the inseparable roles of moral guide and 'preventive' police, asserting, and to some extent enforcing the proper interpretation by the poor, of the reality of their situation. In a passage which also shows why he gave such prominence to church extension at Cwm Avon, he outlines this role:

> To fulfil the part of moral guide and true friend to a people living under every temptation to sensuality . . . requires the devotion of a life passed in perpetual contact with such a people in their hours of leisure and at their fire-sides. It is only thus that their particular errors can be understood and combated, right reasoning set before them, and right feelings substituted for wrong ones. The mind and heart of the uninstructed expand themselves under such intercourse, in obedience to the natural craving of the human understanding for communion with an intelligence superior to its own. It is the clergy alone, whose position and qualifications inspire the confidence that enables them to discharge this difficult duty.[45]

If there had been sufficient numbers of clergy at the beginning of the region's industrial development:

> How much prejudice might they not have removed from the minds of the people; how much ignorance might they not have cleared away; how many of its injurious results prevented; how much light could they not have thrown upon the many social and economical problems that perplex the partially instructed; how much vanity and presumption, 'the certain attendants upon all those who have never experienced a wisdom greater than their own' might they not have reasoned down; how much improvidence restrained; how many of the virtues most valuable to the labouring man, — honesty, prudence, forethought, temperance, frugality, self-denial, steady industry, just obedience, — might they not have inculcated![46]

The employers too were not without faults. Clergymen might have
pointed out instances of selfishness and neglect of Christian duty to
them, acted as mediators and helped to remove the real grievances of
their men. In this way the clergy would (Tremenheere switched tense
here) establish a healthy society, bringing into harmony parties whose
real interests were identical.

III

It is important to recognise the limits of Tremenheere's appeal for new
means to control the poor. Desperate circumstances demanded extreme
measures. Indeed, perhaps it is indicative of a certain toughness that,
confronted with Coatbridge or Airdrie, Tremenheere was brought only
to a hesitant and circumscribed appreciation of the merits of state
intervention. He saw industrialism as producing a new, almost a neo-
colonial situation, which necessitated urgent action. He noted, and was
pleased to see it, that even some mining communities were respectable,
orderly and moral, since the classes were harmoniously related to one
another. Nor was he concerned to restrict social mobility: one of his
chief objections to the truck system was that it inhibited the growth of
a middle class. But if he did not advocate the extensive restructuring of
social policy it was because he believed that social control structures
normally achieved social police: the system was self-regulating. Action
was required in the new areas to bring them into conformity with the
rest of the country.

Tremenheere's diagnosis of the problem and the solutions he posed
were deeply informed by a faith in paternalism. Chadwick approached
the issue from a Benthamite standpoint. His early career has been fully
and ably described elsewhere[47] and it is not my intention to describe
it again here, except in so far as it illustrates the common frame of
mind he shared with Tremenheere. For despite his different social and
intellectual background, Chadwick's presuppositions on the aims of
social policy in the 1830s and 1840s show a degree of similarity to
Tremenheere's which is remarkable on a traditional reading of
Benthamism. He, like Tremenheere, saw order as the product of diffuse
social processes, and thought it attainable only if the poor were both
watched over and supported. To secure this end, humanitarian and
benevolent provision, decent housing, good sanitation and education
were as important (and as much the moral duty of the rich to provide)
as harsh and coercive measures. There was thus no incongruity between
Chadwick's equally impassioned defences of the poor law and, for
example, sanitary reform. Their agreement as to the means through

which these ends could be achieved was often surprising: Chadwick was, for example, a vigorous advocate of industrial paternalism. Unlike Tremenheere, however, Chadwick looked to the state to realise the common morality. Thus, far from envisaging intervention as a means to promote individualism or liberalism, Chadwick looked to the state to produce a more systematic, humane and efficient system of social police.

Chadwick, like Tremenheere, was convinced of the direct relationship between the material state of the poor and their morals.[48] Equally, he often asserted that bad housing, poor sanitation[49] and lack of education led to crime and unrest.[50] To counter the social threat represented by districts like Coatbridge and Airdrie, he agreed with Tremenheere that a response was required which would provide an interlinked system of support and control, but he proposed slightly different and rather broader solutions. Thus, in a letter giving his reactions to Tremenheere's draft 1844 report, which he thought 'on the whole a very satisfactory paper', Chadwick wrote of the proposals for Coatbridge and Airdrie:

> I think you give undue prominence to church extension. The remedies first in order are: infant schools: juvenile schools for the young: police force: better organised fiscals: restraints on the sale of fermented liquors, remedies against strikes. . . and lastly better religious teachers, after the prevention of immorality by the prevention of overcrowding.[51]

No sound family life was possible without decent housing:

> You should I think have traced out and presented prominently the moral and physical evils of overcrowding adults of both sexes into the same sleeping rooms. Of what use will be your appointment of clergymen to preach on morality, the restraint of the passions, decency, propriety, self-respect whilst you herd all like pigs in nakedness together under circumstances to annihilate these virtues? You appoint a preacher to enforce the precept 'honour thy father and thy mother', whilst you allow the young to be placed under circumstances in which the dishonour of both is inevitable. The double crowding of old cottage tenements in the neighbourhoods of new works presents everywhere an abundant crop of crimes of passion.[52]

Order could not be bought cheaply: an elaborate network of provision was necessary to achieve it. Education and housing were necessary to sustain the poor, police forces and measures against trade unions necessary to control corrupt or dissatisfied elements within the working class. Thus Chadwick thought that Tremenheere had been over-indulgent to 'those rascals' the trade union 'agitators'. It was a demanding programme, and one which Chadwick felt needed to be presented to the public and Parliament as a coherent whole.[53]

Chadwick is mainly remembered, and rightly, as an advocate of state intervention, yet it is often forgotten that at this time, he was as keen an enthusiast for paternalism among employers as Tremenheere himself, and for much the same reasons. In the Sanitary Report, for example, he was insistent that 'the labourer gains by his connexion with large capital',[54] and he suggested, where employers took the trouble to interest themselves in their employees, the advantage was reciprocal. The employer:

> will find that whilst an unhealthy and vicious population is an expensive as well as a dangerous one, all improvements in the condition of the population have their compensation. In one instance, of a large outlay on improved tenements, and in provision for the moral improvement of the rising generation of workpeople, by an expensive provision for schools, the proprietor acknowledged to me that although he made the improvements from motives of a desire to improve the condition of his workpeople, or what might be termed the satisfaction derived from the improvements as a 'hobby', he was surprised by a pecuniary gain.[55]

The employer might regulate the housing and sanitary condition of his workforce, and through the exercise of his legitimate influence promote 'neatness and cleanliness', orderliness, temperance, education and innocent leisure.[56]

On a traditional reading of the aims of Benthamism, such a recital of the benefits of paternalism comes oddly from Chadwick. Odder still, he was prepared to go even further than Tremenheere to promote such paternalism. In condemning truck, Chadwick said, Tremenheere had 'given in to mere vulgar shout'.

> If I were setting to work as a Capitalist to improve the condition of the workpeople, I would insist upon payments in kind, on the truck much more extensively. I would supply them not only with food, bu

with clothes and with houses and would beat every other improver. Depend upon it, that it is to the interest of the labouring classes that the profits of retail distribution should go to those who provide them with capital and labour.[57]

When it came to discussing the value of industrial paternalism, or solutions to the problems of specific industrial areas then Tremenheere and Chadwick were in general agreement. It is not so much that, in Professor Webb's phrase, 'the Benthamite lion lay down with the whiggish lamb',[58] as that it is often difficult to tell the two animals apart. In Chadwick's broader thought on social policy, similar pre-occupations can often be discovered.

His experience at the Poor Law Commission led Chadwick steadily to broaden his view of the constituents of social policy. The poor law led him to education and police and from there he went on to housing and sanitation until, by the mid-1840s, he held the views outlined in his letter to Tremenheere. He came, at the same time, to perceive that it was as an interrelated system that such a social policy would ensure stability. Good housing and sanitation, or education, desirable in them-selves were also means of police. Equally, 'preventive' police, in its narrower sense, was to accomplish broad objectives. Thus the Constabulary Commission Report was as much concerned to counter offences against the common morality — vagrancy, mendicancy and trade union activities, for example — as crime narrowly defined.[59] Similarly, his definition of 'prevention' was extremely broad, and illustrates the tendency in his thought for different categories of social activity to merge with one another.

In a memorandum written in 1837, for example, he subdivided 'prevention' into three phases, each requiring a different order of measure for its implementation. The first concerned personality training and character formation. Obstacles should be interposed to the occurrence of 'any conception in the mind which can lead to the commission of a criminal act'. This subject was to form part of a Report of the Constabulary Commission which was never written. The second and third phases of prevention were derived from his formulation of 1829; means for keeping 'tempting objects' from 'weak or indisciplined minds' and means to induce such people to 'withhold from gratification in the prospect of the infliction of pain of some sort'. Police forces were to be mainly concerned with this last phase. But to secure the first, he argued, moral and educational means were required. 'This class of measures', he wrote, 'comprehends those which relate to education in its widest sense, the precepts and circumstances which so fortify the mind as to render it proof against the influences of tempting opportunities.'[60] Teachers were to achieve the results which Tremenheere hoped for from the clergy. The police could assist by regulating public leisure, and by removing from the streets those, like orphaned children, who were in moral danger, or other groups which represented a social risk.

In the role he proposed for policemen, indeed, Chadwick enshrined his belief in the generality and indivisibility of social policy. In addition to apprehending criminals, the police were to supervise public leisure, enforce measures of public health, and, in a proposal which would have coordinated their work with that of the poor law unions, he recommended that policemen should be employed as assistant relieving officers, a merging of roles which would have gone some way towards establishing that general supervision of the poor advocated by Colquhoun.[61] He was eager, too, that policemen should undertake humanitarian and benevolent activities to offset their coercive functions. Thus he suggested that the rural police should act as firemen, removers of nuisances and obstructions and generally as agents against 'calamities' of any description including destitution. Such actions would, he suggested,

> exercise a beneficial influence on the labouring classes by teaching them to respect and trust the administration of the law and the law itself; by showing them that they are cared for by the authorities, and are not, as they must but too commonly suppose, merely and exclusively the subjects of coercion.[62]

Chadwick baulked at giving local control of police forces to poor law unions,[63] and in general, favoured the establishment of distinct agencies to supervise particular areas of social policy.[64] However, *coordination* was a different matter, and in 1841, prompted by the Home Secretary, Lord Normanby, he drew up a plan for organising the activities of governmental agencies dealing with important aspects of social policy, into a coherent system.[65] Inevitably, he proposed that he should have charge of the system, under the Home Secretary, and equally inevitably he claimed that its implementation would save money. But neither fact detracts from the significance of his proposal.

Chadwick began by noting the trend to establish government agencies to control particular social evils, a phenomenon which showed no signs of abating. But although the trend was irresistible, the manner in which agencies had been established and were developing was profoundly unsatisfactory:

> From haste and want of due consideration: from ignorance as to the
> evils and the importance of the remedial measures, from an
> indifference as to their success and the absence of any care except
> to meet the cry of the day the organisation and action of some of
> these agencies has been such, as not to satisfy the friends of the
> particular measures: to create much discontent amongst the parties
> immediately affected by them and justify the prevalent distrust of
> such agencies in the abstract.[66]

If the work of such agencies were combined, he argued, not only
would this problem be eradicated, but recognition would be given to
the interdependency of much of their work, and 'light and aid' shared
by them. Combination would avoid the prevailing evil of 'the separation
of business of the same nature into such fragments as prevents the
perception of the common principle which should govern its execution'.[67]
In his memorandum on administrative control, he outlined the elements
common to the work of the prison and factory inspectors, and the
Assistant Poor Law Commissioners. Some of their common interests
were in technical matters. Thus all were concerned with ventilation,
whether in factories, prisons or workhouses, and the prison inspectors
and Assistant Poor Law Commissioners had a common interest in the
details of diet, clothing and heating of large groups of persons.[68]

But there were wider areas of common interest. The prison inspectors
and Assistant Poor Law Commissioners were alike confronted with the
problems of improvidence, destitution and crime, and both they and the
factory inspectors had an interest in education, one which, however, was
executed in a dangerously fragmented fashion:

> the prison inspectors have as an incident of their office a portion of
> the functions of the Education inspector. . . the Factory Inspector
> has his portion of the same function as an *incident* in the super-
> intendence of the arrangements for the schooling of the factory
> children: the Assistant Commissioner of poor laws also has as an
> incident his portion of the same field.

The consequence was that:

> the education of the special children of the state, the orphans, the
> deserted and neglected children of the country, on whose correct

training depends whether they shall grow up into armies of vagrants, trampers and delinquents to burthen the land, or whether they shall be added to the stock of honest and productive labour is split up into fragments, divided as incidents of the duties of officers acting separately.[69]

Chadwick stressed the extent to which a generalised experience of social policy enriched considerations of any of its component parts. 'I can myself speak from experience', he wrote, 'when I state that the information gained in one course of enquiry has been found useful in another.' Information acquired as a factory commissioner had been useful in considering administration of relief in industrial districts. 'So the information gained by the enquiries under the Constabulary Force Commission have [sic] enabled me to advise on measures for the prevention of vagrancy.'[70] Specialised expertise was valuable, and he did not propose merging the three agencies completely, but, he suggested, an analysis of the functions of each would prove that they could often act for one another, only calling in the 'specialist' when confronted with a difficult problem.

In the same memorandum Chadwick outlined a number of further advantages. It would be possible, he argued, to reduce the number of minor, locally appointed, subordinate officials, and thus to ensure that the government service was conducted by men of an appropriate educational and social background.[71] More important, he suggested that the consolidated service should provide the membership of commissions of enquiry on social matters in the future. Experience had shown, he argued, that the employment of laymen on such investigations had serious disadvantages. If the three agencies were consolidated, and placed in the control of the Secretary of State, 'a more powerful corps' of social investigators than had 'perhaps ever before been available' would be created.[72]

Chadwick's letter to Normanby took a slightly different, but in some ways even broader ground. He proposed that the work of the prison inspectors, factory inspectors and Assistant Poor Law Commissioners should be combined under his charge. He offered to act as Counsel for the Home Office, taking charge, in addition, of any duties proposed by the Children's Employment Commission and to act as adviser on police matters where, his memorandum anticipated 'an agency will probably be required to superintend the formation and combination of a paid police'.[73] This was, of course, personal empire building on a truly Chadwickian scale, but it does not lessen the grandeur or comprehensiveness of the vision. The interrelatedness of social policy was to be recognised in its organisation at governmental level; the whole placed under the scrutiny of the Home Secretary.

The tutelary element in Chadwick's thought might still be questioned. After all, has not Britain, often at the prompting of social democrats, provided cheap housing for the poor, education, measures of sanitation and public health, and adopted social welfare policies? It is tempting to see Chadwick as a pioneer in this process, albeit a somewhat unwilling one, given his individualism. But this is to confuse means and ends. Chadwick was a great and prolific inventor of bureaucratic processes and institutions, but the end for which he devised them was neither liberal and individualistic, and even less, collectivist in a socialist sense. For him, as for some other reformers, new institutional means were a way of curing the ills of the old order, and a prime necessity at a time of acute social change was to assert a tutelary control over the working class.

Occasionally he expressed such a view explicitly. His thought, for example, about the new industrial districts sometimes took a colonial turn:

> A vast increase of population in some of the manufacturing districts is we submit to be regarded in respect of new arrangements in the same point of view as an actual increase of new territory. Much indeed of the Population in the manufacturing districts is not a native population brought up in the habits of obedience to the laws of that part of the empire in which they residé.[74]

At other times, as in the Sanitary Report, he expressed the view that tutelage of the poor was necessary both in the interests of humanitarianism (and the genuineness of Chadwick's ferocious humanitarianism is beyond question) and utility. Workmen must be forced to take precautions to protect their own health:

> The prevalent impression. . . would be expressed by such phrases as, 'If men will be so careless, there is no help for it: they must take the consequences': but they only take a part of the consequences — the sickness; the main part of the consequences are taken by others, especially if they are married, when the premature widowhood and orphanage are sustained by the wife and children, who are maintained at the expense of the relations or of the public. This recklessness is however the result of neglected education, of which

the workmen are the victims, and for measures of beneficence such workmen are to be regarded and treated as children, for they are children in intellect.[75]

Such statements are rare, though revealing. A better guide lies in the analysis of the theory itself. The very comprehensiveness of his proposed social policy was itself a means for securing a tutelary control over the poor, especially since it advocated a merciless assault on a very widely defined range of deviant activity. The industrious poor, educated and moralised in the schools and lodged in scientifically approved dwellings, were to be watched over by police and overseers as they lived their lives. Thus, his argument ran, they would lead healthier, longer and happier lives than in their present unstructured and often squalid circumstances. But such beneficence justified harsh action against those who, despite such treatment, failed or refused to maintain their economic independence, or who became agitators. Trade union activity should be curbed; vagrants, beggars and travelling people harassed out of existence. Convicted criminals should lose their status as freemen, be supervised by the police, and subjected to a curfew in some cases. Thus, he proposed:

a convicted pick-pocket should be prohibited appearing or might be warned away from any public procession or assemblage wherever, at any market fairs, or theatres where the people congregate in crowds; — Thus also a convicted housebreaker might be prohibited appearing after nightfall.

Similarly, it should be made an offence for any convict to be found in the company of another convict 'and the punishment attached to the offence should be increased in proportion to the number of convicts found together'.[76]

There is no evidence that Chadwick was advocating a police state, since he felt that if society were properly organised, deviance would be minimal. Liberty was not problematic. 'To one sort of liberty; the liberty of doing mischief [sic] it would be destructive',[77] he wrote of his police plans. Control of the poor required enumeration and classification and systematic surveillance by the police. A preventive police force on his lines was never established on a wide scale, but some early chief constables made experiments. Thus police forces made successful attacks on 'outsiders'. Samuel Redgrave noted in 1841 the Chief Constable of Durham's chilling observation that 'Of the general

Results I may mention the almost entire extirpation of Gipsies, Campers and Vagrants.'[78] In 1840, Redgrave sent Chadwick details of the official report of Colonel Oakes, Chief Constable of Norfolk, observing that Oakes 'would seem to have profited by some of your ideas of what a Police might accomplish'. Oakes had enclosed two returns for a division of the county. The first was a return of convicted and suspected persons, classified under the following headings:

Parishes
Names of suspected Person
Offences of which they were Convicted
                                Suspected
Punishment
Remarks on Present Conduct

Under these headings are arranged 41 Parishes and the names of 126 bad characters — of these 126 eight are stated to have been 'good since' having prison.

The second return considered public houses and beer shops, listed under the headings:

Parishes
Names of Landlords
Signs
Public House or Beer shop
If landlord ever convicted
His offence
Punishment
Remarks and present conduct of House.[79]

Such information clearly represented one aspect of an attempt to classify all the poor of the division in question, through personal acquaintance with their habits and presumed characters and to establish an intense invigilation over the most important of their meeting places. Admittedly any police force is likely in the course of its work to identify 'problem' individuals and locales, but this effort to systematise such processes, to produce, as it were, an index of the behaviour of the whole labouring community, constantly kept up to date, is symptomatic of the breadth of a Chadwickian preventive police role.

IV

It would be wrong to suggest that social police was the only frame of mind which contributed to Benthamite thinking on social policy; but it was one element competing with others. During the 1850s and 1860s the social unrest which had led Tremenheere and Chadwick to their aggressive assertions of social solidarity, declined sharply, and with it the frame of mind itself passed away: so completely, indeed, that it was forgotten. As for their concrete proposals, it should occasion no surprise that they remained largely unimplemented, even in the alarmed 1830s and 1840s. True, in the end better housing, sanitation and more education were provided and professional police forces were established, but according to no coherent plan, and often not to serve the needs of social police. The common view they shared of the problem may have had a wider currency, but the political and social differences expressed even in the solutions of Tremenheere and Chadwick, prevented the implementation of a coherent plan of action to tame industrialism. In the end, society rather than industrialism was transformed. It was not feasible, as Chadwick would have liked, to establish a planned society in an unplanned economy. Divisions among the rulers were not in any case the only problem. Working-class movements and their sympathisers would not have tolerated the implementation of such a regime. It was not only Lord John Russell who noticed the Prussian element in the thought of men like Chadwick.[80] Recognition of its tutelary nature may account, in part, for the tenacity of liberalism in the mid-Victorian working class, and the intense suspicion of the state evinced by many working men even in late Victorian Britain.[81] Before the state could be used by the labour movement it had to be tamed.

Notes

1.   The literature on this subject is extensive. For a useful recent survey, see D. Fraser, *The Evolution of the British Welfare State* (London, 1973), pp. 101-14.
2.   W.C. Lubenow, *The Politics of Government Growth: Early Victorian Attitudes to State Interventions* (Newton Abbot, 1971), p.188.
3.   *Chartism.* Printed with *Sartor Resartus, Heroes and Hero Worship* and *Past and Present* (Chapman Hall edn., 1895), p.33.
4.   See, especially, *Chartism* and *Past and Present.*
5.   For a discussion of the social novelists' views, Cazamian is still useful. See, especially chs. II-VII in L. Cazamian, *Le Roman Social en Angleterre* (Paris, 1903). There is an English translation, *The Social Novel in England, 1830-50*

(London, 1973), trans. and with a foreword by M. Fido.

6. See R. Blake,*Disraeli* (London, 1966), pp. 167-89, and for Ashley, G. Best *Shaftesbury* (London, 1964), pp.80-105.

7. See, e.g. C. Mott to E. Chadwick, 20 Nov. 1839; University College, London, Chadwick Papers, 1449. Similar evidence was cited in the Sanitary Report. E. Chadwick, *Report to Her Majesty's Principal Secretary of State for the Home Department, from the Poor Law Commissioners on an Inquiry into the Sanitary Condition of the Labouring Population of Great Britain* (London, 1842); reprinted, edited and introduction by M.E. Flinn (Edinburgh, 1965), *passim.* (Hereafter *Sanitary Report.*)

8. See, e.g. F. Hill to Home Office, 15 May 1846. Public Record Office, Home Office Papers, HO 45/1568.

9. See Richard Johnson's essay, below.

10. D. McClatchey, *Oxfordshire Clergy, 1777-1869* (Oxford, 1960), pp.80-228.

11. A. Warne, *Church and Society in Eighteenth Century Devon* (Newton Abbot, 1969), pp.74-80.

12. Warne, *Church and Society*, p.20.

13. The Webbs called him 'the inventor of the modern police system'. See B. and S. Webb, *A History of English Local Government from the Revolution to the Municipal Corporations Act* (London, 1906-29), *The English Poor Law,* part I (1927), p.403. The best account of Colquhoun's writings, despite its tendency to point to 'extremes' is in L. Radzinowicz, *A History of the English Criminal Law* (London, 1948-68),III, pp.211-312.

14. P. Colquhoun, *A New and Appropriate System of Education for the Labouring People, etc.*(London, 1806), p.70.

15. Radzinowicz, *English Criminal Law*, III, p.275.

16. See his pamphlet *An Account of a Meat and Soup Charity, Established in the Metropolis, in the Year 1797, etc.* (London, 1797).

17. *A New and Appropriate System of Education*, p.69.

18. P. Colquhoun, *A Treatise on the Police of the Metropolis, etc.* (London, 1806), p.348.

19. P. Colquhoun, *A Treatise on Indigence, etc.* (London, 1806), p.97.

20. Ibid. p.99

21. Radzinowicz, *English Criminal Law,* III, p.234.

22. Ibid., p. 266.

23. They are outlined in Radzinowicz, ibid., pp.269-80.

24. J.D. Chambers, *Nottinghamshire in the Eighteenth Century: A Study of Life and Labour under the Squirearchy,*2nd edn. (London, 1966), p.223.

25. Warne, *Church and Society*, p.156.

26. Ibid., p.79

27. *Treatise on Indigence*, p.79.

28. Ibid. p.94

29. Ibid. p.77.

30. Ibid.

31. Ibid.

32. He stated, for example, of education, and the efforts of philanthropic individuals who might support it, 'It is scarcely possible to conceive a mode whereby a greater benefit can be conferred on the state, or on the community at large. It embraces almost every object that is useful and important in political economy.' *A New System of Education,* pp.64-5.

33. O. MacDonagh, 'Coal Mines Regulation: the First Decade',in R. Robson (ed.), *Ideas and Institutions of Victorian Britain: Essays in Honour of George Kitson Clark* (London, 1967), p.63. On Tremenheere, see also E.L. and O.P. Edmonds, *I Was There: the Memoirs of H.S. Tremenheere*

(Eton, 1965); and R.K. Webb, 'A Whig Inspector', *Journal of Modern History,* 27 (1955), pp.352-64.

34. Webb, 'A Whig Inspector', *passim.*
35. E.L. and O.P. Edmonds, *Memoirs,* p.61
36. Report of the Commissioner Appointed under the Provisions of Act 5 and 6 Vict. c. 99, to Inquire into the Operation of that Act, and into the State of the Population in the Mining Districts (hereafter Report), *PP* 1846 (737) XXIV, p. 428. The description on which this account is based is at pp. 423-8.
37. See, e.g., his descriptions of conditions at Flockton, Report, *PP* 1845 (670) XXVII, pp. 218-21; Killingworth and Burraton, and Consett, Report 1846, pp.415-16, and 410-11; Weardale Iron Co., Report, *PP* 1847 (844) XVI, p.421.
38. Report 1846, p.427.
39. Ibid.
40. Report 1846, p.414.
41. Report, *PP* 1844 (592) XVI, p.19.
42. The description on which this account is based is in Report 1844, pp.18-49.
43. Report 1844, p.44.
44. Report 1844, p.23.
45. Report 1844, p.45.
46. Ibid.
47. See S.E. Finer, *The Life and Times of Sir Edwin Chadwick* (London, 1952), and R.A. Lewis, *Edwin Chadwick and the Public Health Movement* (London, 1952).
48. See e.g. *Sanitary Report,* p.194.
49. See *Sanitary Report,* pp.266-7.
50. For an outline of his educational views, see Finer, *Chadwick,* pp.150-3.
51. Chadwick to Tremenheere, 4 Sept. 1844. Chadwick Papers 2181/4.
52. Ibid.
53. 'It is due to the subject, to the public and the labours of other', he wrote, urging Tremenheere to strengthen what he had said about Lanarks by reference to the Constabulary Commission and the Health of Towns Reports, 'that such investigations, whenever they may, should be so combined, as to strengthen each other'. Thus the 'principles of social and political economy' could be properly traced out. Ibid.
54. *Sanitary Report,* p.298.
55. *Sanitary Report.* pp.300-1.
56. *Sanitary Report,* p.298 *et seq.*
57. Loc cit.
58. Webb, 'A Whig Inspector', p.352.
59. *First Report of the Commissioners appointed to inquire as to the best means of establishing an efficient Constabulary Force in the counties of England and Wales* (London, 1839), secns. 1-98, *passim.*
60. Memorandum on Prevention, 1837, Chadwick Papers, 5.
61. Kay thought such a scheme would be difficult to implement, since policemen were 'generally poor scholars'. Kay to Chadwick, 24 Jan.1836. Chadwick Papers, 1130.
62. *Constabulary Report,* secn. 227.
63. *Constabulary Report,* secns. 27809.
64. Chadwick to Tremenheere, 4 Sept. 1844. Chadwick Papers, 2181/4.
65. Chadwick drew up the scheme in response to Normanby's wish that he would propose a post for himself *outside* the Poor Law Commission, where, as usual, Chadwick was at loggerheads with the Commissioners.

The account given here is based on Chadwick's letter to Normanby, 12 May 1841 (Chadwick Papers, 1577) and the undated [1840-2] Memorandum on Administrative Control (hereafter 'Administrative Control'), which develops the theme of his letter at greater length. (Chadwick Papers, 71). The wording, as well as the theme of each is often identical. I hope to discuss the implications of Chadwick's proposals in greater detail in a book, in preparation, on the Home Office in the age of reform.

66.   'Administrative Control', 3-4 ff.
67.   Ibid., f. 25.
68.   Ibid., f. 27 and diagram.
69.   Ibid., 25-6 ff.
70.   Ibid., 26-7 ff.
71.   Ibid., f. 46. The thrust of the memorandum was to suggest that the appointment of small numbers of highly qualified government servants, provided the cheapest and best means of promoting the public service.
72.   'Administrative Control', 28-9 ff.
73.   Loc.cit.
74.   Incomplete, undated (watermark 1836) Memorandum on police. Chadwick Papers, 5.
75.   *Sanitary Report,* p. 320. In this instance, 'moral' and 'social' reform, in Dr Brian Harrison's sense, came together, as, my argument suggests, they usually did in Chadwick's and Tremenheere's minds. See B. Harrison, 'State Intervention and Moral Reform', in P. Hollis (ed.), *Pressure from Without in early Victorian England* (London, 1974), pp. 289-322.
76.   Memorandum on Secondary Punishments, undated, 2-3 ff: Chadwick Papers, 2. The same point was made later in the unpublished Second Report of the Constabulary Commission: see Finer, *Chadwick,* p.165.
77.   Undated Notes on police: Chadwick Papers, 5.
78.   Redgrave to Chadwick, 12 Jan. 1841: Chadwick Papers, 1657.
79.   Redgrave to Chadwick, 6 June 1840: Chadwick Papers, 1657.
80.   See Lord John Russell's comments in Russell to Chadwick, 9 Oct. 1836. Chadwick Papers, 1733.
81.   See, H. Pelling, 'The Working Class and the Origins of the Welfare State', in his *Popular Politics and Society in Late Victorian Britain* (London, 1968).

3 EDUCATING THE EDUCATORS: 'EXPERTS' AND THE STATE 1833-9*

Richard Johnson

I

This essay is about a particular conception of education and its attempted realisation through the state. It focuses on a loosely affiliated group of educationalists (forerunners of a familiar category) who are dubbed, for convenience, 'experts'. It concerns too the outcome of their efforts: the founding of the Education Department and of its 'legislative' arm the Committee of Council on Education in 1839. But first it is useful to consider some contexts. What perspectives suggest the most penetrating or fertile questions about this episode? Or, putting it differently, how can a study of the specific instance serve some wider understandings?

It is tempting to slip inside the problematics of two bodies of historical writing that bear upon the theme: the study of 'administrative history' (or of 'the growth of government') or of 'educational history' as it is usually defined. Historians of both kinds continue to produce thorough and ingenious work, but the questions they ask remain severely limited. Governmental or educational matters (the latter too often resembling the former) are closely examined; the vision of what surrounds them is often blurred. Nor is this myopia simply a missing of contexts or of some peripheral and external relations. It carries the risk of totally misconstruing what is most sharply in focus. Both traditions, moreover, are constructed on assumptions which modern debates about the state or education may call in question: the assumption particularly that the development of state educational systems has been an unambiguously progressive process consisting of the provision, in stages, of a self-evidently necessary service. This belief was serviceable in its own day. In its more generous versions it has informed twentieth-century social-democratic practice, but it tends now to produce a stereotyped history (as well as a deadlocked politics). Within this problematic, the creation of a department of government for 'the education of the people' was a small beginning to a long and difficult progression. Or it was one means of correcting, through 'social policy', the more evident malfunctions of early 'industrialisation'. Correspondingly the early state educators have often been presented as 'pioneers of popular education'. Educational history in Britain still lags behind its transatlantic counterpart, even in the re-evaluation of its pantheon.

A more complete revision, beyond a juggling with historical reputations, requires a redefinition, a reconceptualisation of the field. The concept 'social control' is a helpful point of departure, despite its very heterogeneous origins and the range of current usages. It brings a consideration of authority relations back into the study of school or of knowledge as a whole. It helps to free interpretation from the self-evaluations of educators themselves, yet may encompass their avowed aims within a wider context. Yet it remains a relatively under-developed and persistently ambiguous concept. In many of its current usages it remains a concept in search of a theory.

One way of developing the concept further is to place it within the modern debate about the state and its ideological functions.[1] The critique of established frameworks, implicit in the viewpoint of 'social control', may then be extended. The shift from 'government' to 'state' is especially crucial. 'Government' (provided we forget the *governed*) permits us to think of state administration as a separate object of enquiry with a separate history and even a separate 'science'. 'State', however, forces us to think of government within the context of the social formation as a whole, with its own specific history of course, but always in the relation expressed in Marx's couplet 'State and Civil Society'. From this position histories of government with no perception of the state as an agency of social domination are fundamentally flawed, myopic in the sense discussed above. Histories of public education may similarly trivialise or misrecognise their content for lack of a wider view of the processes they partially describe: the continual work, for instance, of creating conformities between the cultures of a social formation and the necessities of production.

Theorists of the state from Marx onwards have also been concerned with the diversity of forms of state power, not only from one historical epoch to another but also between coeval capitalist societies.[2] Marx himself was familiar, of course, with European differences, writing copiously on England, France and Germany especially, in those moments of defeat, in the middle decades of the century. He was concerned, as a professional revolutionary, with what Edward Thompson has called 'the peculiarities of the English'.[3] One such peculiarity, noted also by Max Weber after him, was the relatively decentralised nature of the British state. Writing of France, Marx stressed the enormous accumulated power of executive government, sedimented in successive class struggles:

Every *common* interest was immediately detached from society, opposed to it as a higher, *general* interest, torn away from the self-activity of the individual members of society and made a subject for governmental activity, whether it was a bridge, a schoolhouse, the communal property of a village community, or the railways, the national wealth and the national university of.France.[4]

Marx was here describing a most un-English situation, even if English chauvinism sometimes exaggerated the differences. Even during the 'revolution in government' of the 1830s and 1840s polycentricity of power and its dispersal through the provinces remained English characteristics.[5] Weber, more interested in the guiding spirit of domination and its organisational forms, later reached similar conclusions. Seeking to match his ideal type of bureaucracy to particular histories, he always had difficulty with Britain. He noted the weakness there of the general Western movement towards bureaucratic forms. 'England', he wrote, early in this century, 'was the slowest of all countries to succumb to bureaucratization, or, indeed, is still only partly in the process of doing so.'[6] The section on bureaucracy in *Wirtschaft und Gesellschaft* twice contains the phrase 'even, today, in England'.[7]

It is important for a later part of the argument that neither Marx nor Weber saw decentralisation or unbureaucratic forms in terms of weakness or failure. Weber thought that the British remained rather unbureaucratic because they had adapted earlier forms, especially rule by 'notables', instead.[8] Marx saw the nature of English politics as a source of strength — strength, that is, for a capitalist ruling class. Executive weakness, the mystifications of 'the British Constitution', the amateurishness of Whig politicians and the concessionary politics of the industrial bourgeoisie formed an opaque camouflage over the real (class) relations of domination.[9] It followed that he devoutly hoped for some radical simplication, and his point has great explanatory power. For if English arrangements served capital peculiarly well, 'continental' centralising solutions might be 'dangerous' as well as illiberal, disturbing delicate political equilibria.

We return, then, to the historical instance. For education (or the schooling of working-class children) was indeed an example of the preference for decentralised administration and amateur agencies. As is well known, legislation before 1870 was limited to groups of children deemed exceptional in some way (though often quite large): the children of paupers, children who had (or might be expected to)

commit offences against the law, children in certain places of labour.
England was the last of the major European powers to acquire a state
system of elementary schools. There was, of course, the Education
Department which, growing alarmingly by the mid-1850s, was a leading
sector of state bureaucracy.[10] Yet this department shared educational
responsibilities with others (Poor Law Board, Home Office, Department
of Science and Art) in a totally pragmatic manner, and was itself a
very English piece of *ad hoc*ery, with a confused chain of internal
command and an unclear relation to Parliament, Cabinet and statutory
authority. The Committee of Council was a constitutional curiosity
even for Britain: not a Board, not a Ministry, but a committee of
ministers in their capacity as Privy Councillors. Arrangements further
removed from Weber's idea can scarcely be imagined. And this structure
grew up alongside a system of schooling in which initiation, control and
management were mainly local, reliant, like the administration of
justice, on voluntary agencies. Voluntary efforts were increasingly artic-
ulated through state finance and supervision, but the Anglican church
was as important here as the Education Department itself. If, as has
been argued elsewhere,[11] the provision and management of schools was
a form of social or class control it was control *diffused through* and
indigenous to civil society, not concentrated in a metropolis, in the
hands of state functionaries, and delegated thence.

We need to know not merely why 'government grew', but why the
educational apparatuses took the form they did. Why was there so
large a difference with continental solutions? Why was so much left to
'private' agencies? What was the logic, in terms of control, of such an
adaptation?

There are, perhaps, two main modes of explanation. The first might
examine those structures that set the limits of the politically possible:
the nature of the political system and the English political culture;
the particular configuration of classes and class fractions in the society
of the 1830s, and their dispositions towards educational questions;
above all, the determining English condition of the coexistence of two
modes of production, both generically capitalist, yet differing in their
local and cultural features — the older agrarian capitalism of the landed
estates and the newer productive modes of capitalist industry. In this
characteristic Victorian dichotomy can be found the deeper explanations of the broad patterns of politics and of competing educational
ideas and practices.[12] Any adequate account of the history of the
British state would have to dig that deep. But it is also necessary to
unravel day-to-day moves in the theatre of politics. For the issues raised

generally above were, at one level, fought out consciously in these years. There *were* protagonists who agitated for a state-enhancing 'continental' push towards 'national education', *and* there were those who opposed them from more conservative positions. At a deeper level of determination, in the outcome, events revealed a logic of their own, but this outcome was only secured through the conscious pursuit of strategies by the groups and the social individuals involved. In what follows, an attempt is made to occupy both these levels of analysis, at the risk of doing justice to neither.

II

The leading actors in the story, agitators for a state educational system, were the 'experts' of the 1830s. Expertise is best described through a kind of composite biography, focusing on central or symptomatic individuals, but 'placing' them socially. Since to be effective, experts had to force a passage into formal politics, we must start with the politicians.

Of leading politicians of the 1830s, likely spokesmen for an educational lobby, Henry Brougham was the most obvious example of one possessing educational expertise.[13] He had been the most visible educational entrepreneur of the first thirty years of the century. His career forms a prehistory of educational liberalism. Founder member of the Royal Lancastrian Association, he sought to generalise the utilitarian cry of 'schools for all' through his Select Committee of 1816-18.[14] He gave to this committee something of the scope of a Royal Commission, attempting the first nationwide count of schools, and using statistics, in what was to become a typical 'expert' manner, as a lever for change. Thereafter projects multiplied: infant schools, the mechanics' institutes, the Society for the Diffusion of Useful Knowledge (SDUK). He anticipated the educationalists' revulsion from monitorialism and was the first Englishman to visit the continental reformers. He was an early convert to less mechanical pedagogies, espousing the training of teachers and other 1830s enthusiasms.[15] He was not the only Whig politician who sought to make an historical reputation on educational issues, but he was the only one who mastered a specialist educational debate. It was for this reason that so many of those mentioned below corresponded with him, as friends, allies or supplicants for places or influence.[16]

Yet as elder statesman of educational politics, twice the age of younger zealots, he suffered serious handicaps. As Whig Lord Chancellor he sat in the House of Lords, a Tory-Anglican stronghold that offered, as he discovered, little chance of legislative successes. His bitter experience of past educational battles, especially the failure of his Bill of 1820, made him very cautious about legislative measures. He was a less important focus of activity than several other MPs.

Several members of the reformed House of Commons made the education issue their own, supported by a wider circle. Three names stand out: R.A. Slaney, Whig MP for Shrewsbury; Sir Thomas Wyse, MP for Waterford; J.A. Roebuck, Radical MP for Bath. Of the three Slaney was the most conventional figure,[17] Born into the Shropshire gentry, he remained in private life very much the country gentleman, indulging in rural pursuits but with a persistently guilty conscience. Two main impulses, recorded in a confessional diary which he kept for most of his life, spurred him into hectic bouts of public activity: an intense religious conviction of a primarily ethical kind, and an anxious perception, out of a rural experience and values, of the situation of the urban working class. As early as 1829, he resolved 'to become acquainted with the causes that depress and degrade the artisans and manufacturers', to devise remedies and to publicise them.[18] With increasing energy through the 1830s, he 'gathered facts' by contacting leading business-men, became involved in the statistical movement and spoke at length on urban problems in the House of Commons.[19] As chairman of the Select Committee on Education of 1838, he played a significant part in marshalling expert opinion and giving it political weight.

Wyse was a more aristocratic and cosmopolitan figure, the son of an Irish land-owner and, unusually, a Catholic.[20] He, if anyone, inaugurated the Irish educational settlement of 1831, but he was also very active in English educational politics. He was founder, chairman and main driving force of the Central Society for Education, a Whig-Radical pressure group of the late 1830s. He served on Slaney's committee, and was closely allied to the Edinburgh phrenologists, James Simpson and George Combe, and with liberal educationalists and businessmen in Liverpool and Manchester. In 1836 he published *Education Reform,* the most ambitious tome in the expert genre, complete with an evaluation of rival educational theories, a discussion of social pathologies and a review of continental models. His motto — Lord Strafford's 'Less than Thorough will not do' — might apply to the 'experts' as a whole.[21]

Roebuck was the most marginal of the three to the world of English politics.[22] Brought up in Canada, he found an intellectual home among the London utilitarians and a constituency by representing the *petit bourgeois* radicals of Bath.[23] Heavily influenced by his friendship with the younger Mill, he belonged, with Francis Place, to the more intransigently anti-Whig wing of London middle-class radicalism. He expressed utilitarian educational principles in their purest form, urging an educational system modelled on the Prussian state.[24]

Roebuck was a philosophic radical of the second generation; Brougham was a life-long friend of James Mill.[25] It is tempting to take these relations as typical of expertise as a whole. Perhaps it was but one more manifestation of 'the growth of philosophic radicalism'. There is some truth in this view. There *were* convergences both in timing and doctrine. Utilitarianism was nurtured in the 1820s and assiduously propagated, in ways revealed by Professor Finer, in the following decade.[26] Scratch a Benthamite or a political economist and one quickly uncovers an educationalist. From Malthus' *Second Essay on Population* onwards, economists heavily endorsed educational solutions. In James McCulloch and still more in Thomas Chalmers they acquired a primacy.[27] Similarly, James Mill's political ideas rested on a psychology that required (for 'utility') a general 'rational' education.[28] As the modern reappraisal of Benthamism has shown, it carried a very positive conception of the state's tutelary role.[29] It is not surprising that many of the innovations that broke with conservative attitudes arose, in part, from this London intellectual milieu – SDUK, mechanics' institutes, the middle-class end of the attack on the Taxes on Knowledge. All the advanced liberal papers of the metropolis gave much space to educational questions and were supplemented by specialist journals like the *Quarterly Journal of Education.*[30] Direct Benthamite influence was waning by the late 1830s, especially in the House of Commons, but it is arguable that its contribution to middle-class common sense was already very deep.

It will not do, however, to identify 'expertise' with Benthamism or even with London intellectuals. What was missing from metropolitan discourse was an encounter with the industrial revolution and the labouring population of its cities, towns and rural townships. The precipitating moment of 'expertise' was the contradictory juxtaposition of liberal theories and the observation, out of a bourgeois culture, of working-class behaviour. As Joseph Parkes of Birmingham remarked, there was a world of difference between Mill's abstraction 'the People' and 'the masses' as he 'knew' them. Only provincial men could gauge the gulf between political improvement and the actual state of the class.[31]

So, more important than intellectuals and radical politicians, were men who shared their philosophies but also had to wrestle a little with obstinate social realities. The typical mediating moment in urban class relations was 'social enquiry', whether conducted under state auspices or as a private venture. Working people were typically encountered as a 'problem', often in a policy-making context. But it is also incorrect to see London as the only source of theory. Scotland, for the educationalists at least, was quite as important. The salient influences seem often to flow along an Edinburgh-London axis.

Educational 'experts' conformed to a type already discerned by historians of the 1830s: Kitson Clark's 'heroic' generation of civil servants, Parris' 'zealots', MacGregor's 'social researchers', Cullen's statisticians, Lucy Brown's men of the Board of Trade.[32] In the groupings of such men who were concerned with education it is useful to distinguish two generations. The older men, aged between thirty-eight and forty-five in 1830, already, by 1835, occupied positions within government: Edwin Chadwick within the Poor Law Commission: Leonard Horner as inspector of factories; G.R. Porter as head of the Statistical Department of the Board of Trade; Nassau Senior, the prototypical government economist, as a personal adviser to Whig ministers since January 1831.

All four moved in London intellectual circles but had also acquired knowledge of the industrial north: Porter as a kind of Director-General of Statistics for the Free Trade Lobby and generous contributor to the debate on education and crime;[33] Chadwick as a polymathic social investigator;[34] Horner in his day-to-day work as inspector.[35] Their 'knowledge' of the north should not be reduced, however, to their official capacities; personal networks were also significant. The whole pattern can be seen especially clearly in Senior's ease.

A gregarious man, he occupied a central place in London society. 'Mr Senior dined at home, *for a wonder*', recorded his long-suffering wife in 1839.[36] Sidney Smith called their house 'the chapel of ease to Lansdowne House', testifying to its comfort, but also to its closeness to power. On the outward-facing side of the relation, Senior did not rely on official information for his knowledge of the working class: 'I like Blue Books', he wrote, 'but distrust knowledge so acquired.'[37] Perhaps he knew too well how Blue Books were compiled! His solution, however was to tour the north with well-connected business friends.[38] Porter and Horner had similar contacts with the big bourgeoisie of the provincial centres, especially with the Manchester men who founded the Statistical Society and the Manchester Mechanics' Institute.[39]

Of these four older men, Horner's was the most significant presence in the educational sphere. Senior and Chadwick were important mainly as patrons of younger men and as organisers of their activities.

Educated in Edinburgh and, like Brougham and James Mill, drawn to London, Horner also personifies the London-Edinburgh link. What was its significance? First, a university education at Edinburgh in the 1790s still bore the stamp of the Scottish Enlightenment.[40] An emphasis on 'conjectural history' — the study of the successive epochs of human society — preserved a notion of social evolution. This was especially important since Bentham's adaptation of eighteenth-century thought was so ahistorical and abstract. A concern with evolutionary themes can certainly be traced in the early *Edinburgh Review* (to which Brougham was a prolific contributor) and in the writings of other Edinburgh-trained educationalists like James Kay.[41] Second, Scotland does appear to have permitted some distancing from English religious entanglements, and an unwillingness to polarise in favour of either Church or Dissent.[42] Third, schooling was more highly valued in Scotland even, it was always said, among the 'peasantry'.[43] Scottish educational egalitarianism was not utterly mythical compared with the hierarchical South. More recent models were also to be found across the border: Robert Owen's New Lanark, the early proto-mechanics' institutes (including Horner's own School of Arts) and the experimental elementary schools of Stowe and Wood at Glasgow and Edinburgh. Edinburgh itself was also one the main centres of phrenology, the educational implications of which were a significant strand in expert thinking, providing a different starting point to utilitarian psychology or the solving of social problems.[44]

The younger experts were all aged between seventeen and twenty-eight in 1830. Some, like H.S. Tremenheere, B.F. Duppa, J.C. Symons and E.C. Tufnell, came from gentry or clerical families, were trained in law, and then became involved in philanthropy or social enquiry.[45] Duppa died young while still secretary to the Central Society for Education (CSE); the others entered government service through the Poor Law Commission or the Education Department. Others, like W.E. Hickson or Frederick Hill, belonged to the urban fraction of their class. Hickson was a London boot-manufacturer who was affluent enough to 'retire' to philanthropy at the age of twenty-seven. He became a free-lance agitator for educational causes, visiting prisons, schools and workhouses, specialising in interviewing children about their school experiences. Sharing the politics of Roebuck and Place, he wrote anonymous and polemical articles for the CSE and a long report, exclusively on education, for the Handloom Weaving Commission.[46] Hill, youngest member of a famous Birmingham Dissenting family, was appointed inspector of prisons for Scotland, joined Edinburgh's intelligentsia, and was impressed by the 'practical' implications of phrenology. His *National Education,* mainly a critical examination of educational statistics, was published in 1836.[47]

Finally, it is worth noting what James Phillips Kay, future secretary to the Education Department, brought uniquely to the education question. In some ways the pattern was the familiar 'expert' one: commercial origins, an Edinburgh education, statistical enquiry, contacts with Chadwick and Senior, appointment as an assistant poor law commissioner.[48] Yet his experience of the North was unusually immediate. Most experts had or acquired contacts there, but he was actually formed in this milieu. The family's capital was in cotton, calico printing and banking. His politics were learnt in the reform bill struggle and in the opposition to the Factory Movement. He allied himself with the merchants, bankers and mill-owners of Cottonopolis.[49] His encounters with working people were traumatic and intense, and portrayed in a pamphlet, written in the aftermath of the cholera epidemic, through which he worked as a doctor. It is rightly regarded (though sometimes for the wrong reasons) as an early industrial classic.[50] Of all the people we have discussed, he came nearest to being an 'organic' intellectual for the big industrial bourgeoisie. He expressed the ideology of the Manchester men, faced with the class which their accumulation of capital had created and was daily reproducing.

A more complete portrayal of expertise would include a much wider circle of influence. It would embrace, for example, many of the fifty-six MPs who joined the Central Society for Education, almost all of them Whigs or Radicals, with a strong Irish contingent.[51] It would include many burgesses from the industrial towns and cities — Kay's Manchester friends, the Liverpool liberals, Slaney's contacts in the midlands, and innumerable statistical experts, like Joseph Fletcher of the London Statistical Society, James Riddall Wood of Manchester, and William Felkin of Nottingham.[52] In the world of religion, if membership of the CSE is any guide, expertise and religious heterodoxy were closely associated. Of the eleven clergymen-subscribers, seven were prominent Unitarians and none distinguished churchmen.

As the biographies suggest, there were also certain nodal points where experts met and discussed their enthusiasms: London salons, the London and provincial statistical societies, the annual meetings of the Statistical Section of the British Association for the Advancement of Science, the provincial networks of organisations like the Society for the Diffusion of Knowledge, caucuses around particular government enquiries or departments, especially the Poor Law Commission, and the

friendships and contacts tying Edinburgh to London. Experts did not
form a 'group' in the classic sociological sense, nor even, united by a
single organisation, a 'movement'. But personal links *were* quite dense,
and expertise *did* have a definite social character and a real ideological
coherence. At its heart was a coalition of liberal intellectuals with strong
personal or ideological links with industrial capital. The apparent
exceptions to this — men from landed or clerical backgrounds — none
the less adopted the viewpoint of capital as a perspective and city or
industrial populations as an object of concern. For an account of this
ideological unity, however, we must turn to an analysis of their
writings.

III

Defining features of the ideology of expertise were the advocacy of
education as a solution and of the state as a means. How were these
positions reached?

The starting point was usually a judgement about the direction of
society as a whole, about what they called 'commercial society' or 'the
manufacturing system' or 'civilisation' — a judgement, in short, about
the whole uneven shift into machinofacture and a developed industrial
capitalism. Though not without reservations, they were on the side of
progress, without nostalgia for a golden age, and conscious of living
through great changes (a 'revolution' even) that marked an epoch.[53]
They participated in the early-Victorian romance of steam and
machinery, and charted the 'progress of the nation'.[54] They underpinned
this faith by comparing 'backward' with 'advanced' regions (agriculture
with industry or domestic industry with the factory) and by showing
the superiority of the latter, even on points of the 'morality' and
'intellect' of their populations.[55]

Yet a concern with 'social problems' 'evils' or 'diseases' was also a
hallmark. Progress was paradoxical. Kay's *Manchester*, for instance, can
be read as an indictment of industrialisation, far though this was from
his intent.[56] The paradox (but not the real underlying contradictions)
was always resolved. Certain evils were irremovable, 'providential',
ultimate limitations on progress, and therefore, strictly, not problems
at all. The danger lay in their remoter effects, since, misconstrued by
the ignorant, they were pretexts for discontent.[57] Periodic crises of
capital accumulation, for instance, were described in analogies drawn
from nature: 'storms', 'seasons' or 'tides'. They had simply to be
borne.[58] The gross inequalities attendant upon class were similarly
tolerated as something quite eternal: 'the working class who labour to
subsist, and the affluent, to whom labour is unnessary'.[59]

This did not prevent discussion of the degrees of 'comfort' possible for working people of 'frugal and steady habits', but a more than moral equalisation was conceivable only as a nightmare.[60] Thus, though expertise was essentially a creed for activitists, it retained much of the fatalism of conservatism.

Evils that could *not* be traced to providence or nature were seen as unconnected with the newer modes of production. This 'evils-extrinsic' argument was classically expressed in Kay's *Manchester* and the auto-review that followed it.[61] It was argued explicitly throughout and was also present in pervasive metaphors of *invasion* and *disease.* Cholera and the Irish, sources of these figures of speech, actually *were* invasions of a body (Manchester) that was fundamentally healthy. This structure of feeling was very common. The main exceptions were Horner, Wyse and the phrenologists who shared a hostility to 'over-labour', especially of children, and pointed to the irrationality, injustice and unnaturalness of this destructive consumption of labour power.[62] Roebuck's analysis, identifying causes as *external* to industry, was, however, more common:

> Of the evils which the members of a community suffer, some may result from the mal-administration of the government; some from their own negligence or error. . . The remedies, therefore, for certain evils, may lie in reforming government abuses; the remedies for certain other evils, may rest wholly with the people themselves acting as individuals. . . We may make the following suppositions: a government. . . puts a tax on bread, thereby diminishing the resources of the country. . . The remedy to this mischief is, reforming the government. . . But suppose the mass of the labouring population utterly careless of their own well-being. . . The remedy will not be reforming the government, but in changing and improving the people.[63]

Clearly, this contains the possibilities of two kinds of politics – a populist, anti-aristocratic radicalism or an alliance with 'reforming' politicians to 'change the people'. In practice the two kinds were not mutually exclusive, as the whole history of English popular liberalism testifies. They contain, indeed, a common element – the deflection of responsibility from the industrial capitalist in his own locale. Though several experts shared a personal history of radical liberal politics (in its utilitarian or Manchester School forms),[64] they tended to lean towards the other pole. 'Reforming the government' and 'changing and improving the people' did not appear in their writings as contradictory prescriptions, but in the relation of means to ends. The end — 'changing the people' — required a kind of moral engineering. This in turn evoked the means — persuading the (aristocratic) politicians to act. The typical charge against aristocracy was therefore neglect; the typical aims were to energise, and to supply the appropriate policies.

Policies were of different kinds depending on the problem. But we must stress, once more, the emphasis laid on transforming working-class belief and behaviour. All expert prescriptions were educative in the broad Gramscian meaning of the word. The state was to educate and 'civilise' (a typical expert word). Schooling always played a part in this policy, but usually in some combination with the educative force of law — with 'police' in its wider nineteenth-century meaning.

Policies for poverty and crime exemplify one such combination. Problems were defined moralistically: poverty appeared as 'pauperism'; offences against property or persons as various species of vice or turpitude.[65] Primary solutions concerned the law and its enforcement; the reform of the poor law and of the penal code; improved poor law administration and the professionalisation of civilian police. Since, however, prevention was cheaper and more humane than cure, mass schooling should follow — hence the importance of the Poor Law Commission as a matrix of educational thinking after 1836 and the long dogmatic debate about the relation between crime and education.[66]

In a second combination, reliance, as educator, was placed on the 'laws' of the economic system itself. A necessarily painful process of trial and error would itself inculcate rationality. This was sometimes called 'the education of circumstance' or 'indirect education'.[67] Free rein should therefore be allowed to market forces, uninhibited by bad law or obsolete custom. This necessarily involved transforming the social and cultural contexts of labour or not intervening to save them. Yet it was also recognised (how could it be ignored?) that working people rarely made the same kind of sense of their experience as did economists or philanthropists. They remained obstinately 'superstitious', 'sensuous' or prone to perverted doctrines. So, as Thomas Chalmers put it, 'the education of circumstance' was impotent without 'the education of principle'.[68] Schooling and other direct influences should reinforce the everyday lessons. The report of the Handloom Weaving Commission is a good example of this combination, recommending free trade, non-intervention in the wages bargain, and a national system of education.[69]

Sometimes, however, it was schooling that was given a primacy. Without it, other changes might be dangerous. Universal suffrage, for example, was dangerous without national education.[70] The limitation of hours of labour would be worthless without an education which would make of leisure a useful pursuit, something to compensate for the entrenchment on capital.[71] Again Horner and the phrenologists stood apart, stressing the social and physiological need for recreation and play.[72] Their arguments prefigure the predominantly environmentalist perspective of the public health debate of the 1840s, though even this sphere was not exempt from moral considerations.[73]

Moral interventionism arose, subjectively, from the contrast between the lived culture of the middle class and what was observed of working people. Here is Roebuck, for example, reflecting on his political career: 'My object has been. . .to make the working man as exhalted and civilized a creature as I could make him. I wanted to place before his mind a picture of civilized life such as I see in my own life. . . *I wanted to make the working man like me. . .*[74] Roebuck's version was that of the philosopher-politician, not that of, say capitalist or cleric, but we will not go far wrong if, in the whole genre, we read for 'civilised' — 'like me'.

Take, for example, the cross-class perception of the complex of relations, wife to husband, and parents to children. Compared with the bourgeois home, the squalid, anarchic no-homes of weavers or factory workers seemed to lack all that 'family' was supposed to be, especially the virtues of authority, decency and order. Ingenious adaptations to crushing exigencies were not understood, and the advice that was so freely given was often to a high standard of inappropriateness.[75] In sexual relations it is not surprising that middle-class men, dependent on the sanctuary of home and the ministrations of their wives, transferred the same needs onto working-class men and disproportionate burdens onto their women.[76]

Middle-class experience also informed theory. The moralism of the religious frame of reference requires no more emphasis. Less often stressed is the same element in the dominant secular systems. Out of Malthus' 'prudential restraint', a tiny bolt-hole from his pessimism, a whole behavioural emphasis within political economy developed. This threatened to swamp, in vulgar versions, the scientific elements of theory. Educationalists, particularly, followed the lead of Chalmers' Malthusianism in stressing 'the ascendency of the moral over the material part of our constitution'.[77] The notion of economic law and of the felicific calculus coexisted quite happily with the ideas of 'providence' and even of 'sin'.[78]

But all this constitutes an explanation of the moral emphasis only in a very limited sense. By reducing it to 'moralism' merely, it may even trivialise. For, though mediated by a bourgeois culture, and expressed in worked-up ideological forms, moralism was based in the cultural necessities of progress — those forms of belief and behaviour, above all an economic rationality, appropriate to labour under capitalism. By commenting on 'indirect education' and noting the whole cultural ferment, experts recognised that capitalist production possessed an educative force of its own: the power to reproduce, in adequate forms, the human means to expansion.[79] In a longer view this was often seen as sufficient. As Thomas Wyse put it: 'Time, indeed, and the compensation of larger benefits will finally reconcile the community to the change.' Meanwhile energetic intervention was necessary, outside production itself, to secure the cultural conformities.[80]

The need for an organic moral reorientation of labour was reinforced by more conjunctural determinations. Much expert literature was concerned not with inertia or resistance to change but with the overtly oppositional challenge mounted by working-class organisation.[81] Expertise was, in large part, a response to the urban radicalisms of 1830-42. The synchronisation between the demand for state education and the growth of Chartism was exact. All the educationalists were hostile to Chartism, Owenism and trade unions even where, like Hickson or Roebuck, they can be called democratic liberals.[82] The challenge was all the more threatening for being possessed of a cultural and educational politics of its own. Working people were not merely ignorant but increasingly had their own kinds of knowledge. Supplying what was absent was no longer enough; intervention must correct what was present already. As Wyse put it, writing of the general growth of the means of education: '*Give* what otherwise will be *taken.* By giving you acquire the means and right of purifying, regulating, and directing: you become master of the new power, instead of the new power becoming yours.'[83]

Educational expertise, in its *internal* dimensions and also in its *external* determinations, does fit the description 'social control'; especially if, for 'social', we read 'class', and, for 'control', 'transformation'. But of all the available theorisations, not excluding Althusser's 'reproduction', it is Gramsci's concept 'hegemony' that provides the greatest insight, especially in relation to 'state':

In my opinion, the most reasonable and concrete thing that can be said about the ethical State, the cultural State, is this: every State is ethical in as much as one of its most important functions is to raise the great mass of the population to a particular cultural and moral level, a level (or type) which corresponds to the needs of the productive forces for development, and hence to the interests of the ruling classes. The school as a positive educative function, and the courts as a repressive and negative educative function, are the most important State activities in this sense.[84]

Expertise, then, was about building the 'ethical state'. But why the state?

IV

Experts generally urged a 'national system of education' but differed on what this meant. Differences were mainly determined by tactical considerations. As we shall see later, the educationalists' campaign did not assume the dimensions of a popular movement marshalled under a single programme and capable of shifting the political relations of force. They worked, instead, within the limits of a pre-existing politics of education, heavily dominated by religious and ecclesiastical parties. They offered a range of programmes from the most ideal to the most pragmatic, sometimes canvassing maximum and minimum versions.[85] Maximum proposals, drawing overtly on continental and especially French or Prussian models, envisaged a complete state system requiring legislation: a Ministry of Public Instruction with large powers over the curriculum, the content of schoolbooks and the training, certification, selection and conditions of service of schoolteachers; the extension of compulsory attendance; the statutory levying of school rates; the creation of a structure of local administration; and a separation of religious and secular education. Full-blown proposals like these came most often from the more theoretical wing of expertise – the London utilitarians and the Scottish phrenologists and their allies.[86] Other experts, like Kay or Joseph Fletcher, favoured municipal solutions under enabling legislation.[87] But the commonest form of programme envisaged, as the key priority, the founding of a government department (a Board, Ministry or 'Commission') with a few limited but strategic functions.[88] The model of government action was 'incremental', persuasive, directive – a matter of educating the educators. There was wide agreement on what these functions should be: the establishment of state 'normal schools' for the training of a new generation of teachers, and powers of inspecting schools. Government should thus supply, in Wyse's words, 'the great element of all state organizations – a central, controlling and directing power'.[89]

The arguments in favour of such measures were of two main kinds: deductions from 'the principles of political economy', and the massive, accumulative exposure of the inadequacies of existing provision.

As Professor West has shown, political economists of this period had few of Adam Smith's original doubts about interference in the educational market.[90] Experts explicitly attacked the application of the principle of *laissez-faire* to schooling.[91] But the interest of their position lies less in its relation to correct economic principles, more in the confirmation it provides concerning their attitudes to the working class. Education, so the argument went, was unlike any other commodity. Supply could not be left to the satisfaction of indigenous demand. It was a taste that required cultivation, or even a duty that might require enforcement, where parents were neglectful. As Wyse put it: 'The very want of means is concomitant not only with a want of education but with a clear sense of its utility. Such sense cannot be communicated by any other means than experience..."L' appetit vient en mangeant".'[92] In other words, no faith could be placed in the labourer's own judgement which required itself to be cultivated. Trusting to supply and demand meant leaving the matter to a generation already corrupted by 'neglect' or, the ultimate pathology, leaving it to Socialist and Chartist agitators. The child must be rescued through a school and schoolmaster equipped to anticipate an antagonistic adult culture.[93]

In one of its moments, then, expertise stood on one side in a class struggle which was conducted cn an educational or cultural terrain. This already carried certain imperatives about the nature and control of education: that is, that it should be public or private, *provided* not *generated within the class.* But experts were also involved in another kind of struggle, this time internal to the bourgeoisie. A new order, of the kind they envisaged, required the modification of ruling ideas. They sought to transform educational practices too. They were critics, therefore, of philanthropy.

This critique was partly quantitative and organisational. The whole development of educational statistics, which as Dr Cullen has shown loomed so large in the statistical movement,[94] must be viewed as an expert strategy within this internal politics. The political use of facts about schooling was, indeed, a defining feature of expertise. The lead was taken by Kay's Manchester Statistical Society and followed by the Education Committee of the London Society whose membership and purposes overlapped with those of the Central Society for Education.[95] The counts that were produced remain, quantitatively, the most reliable of their time, and it was not difficult for experts to show the inadequacies of other contemporary series. It was also clear, by the late 1830s, that philanthropy (as opposed to the private schoolmaster and the sunday school) had scarcely begun to cover the ground.[96]

More relevant here, however, are the broader conclusions drawn from 'the facts'. They were held to demonstrate not merely the quantitative insufficiency of 'public' day-schooling and the qualitative worthlessness of private schools, but also the intrinsic organisational deficiencies of philanthropy. By its very nature — reliance on the fluctuating interest of local benefactors — philanthropy was flawed. It could not raise sufficient resources to maintain the schools, let alone extend and improve them. It could not exercise continual supervision. It was petty, parochial, sectarian, wasteful and inefficient, lacking combined effort and overall coordination. Only the state could bring direction to its 'zig-zag course', coherence to its 'education in sections', and regular supervision and guaranteed support to its intrinsic impermanence.[97]

But a qualitative critique was also launched. Existing forms of school were seen as belonging to 'a past age'; education should be extended but also reformed — the 'third great reform', according to Wyse.[98] The demand for modernisation applied to every aspect of schooling and was especially directed against eighteenth-century forms (endowed or charity schools) and the whole Anglican effort. Educational endowments were criticised as wasteful and liable to maladministration or misappropriation. The ethos of charity also bred pauperism and dependence.[99] Experts attacked the limitation of the curriculum to religious formularies and the 'three Rs', noting that these too, were often poorly taught.[100] They advocated an extended curriculum, including natural science, a knowledge of everyday or common things and, of course, political economy.[101] Individuals pressed for further additions: phrenologists for a knowledge of physiology and the principals of health;[102] others for 'vocal music' as a powerful civilising influence.[103] Though the central emphasis was upon shaping the child as a rational and moral being, there was much interest too in ways of combining literary education with an induction into labour for boys and into domestic duties for girls.

Experts had strong views on method as well. They heavily criticised the monitorial method, the dominant pedagogy of the first phase of mass schooling. At best it taught a knowledge of 'words' but failed to develop the child's understanding. According to Hickson, reading and writing were imperfectly taught in most national and British and Foreign schools. At worst, the monitors formed a kind of mafia extorting petty favours — apples, cakes, toys and even money — from smaller children.[104] Against the monitorial machine, experts advocated a teacher-centred pedagogy, in which adult encountered child more directly, acting as a surrogate parent, or as a civilising example of what home did not provide. For rather similar reasons, and because they were a leading sector of more personalised methods, infant schools were generally favoured.

This range of objections to existing schools was often pressed with a polemical sharpness reminiscent of the language of the radical press, especially on those (rather rare) occasions when working-class audiences were addressed.[105] It is not possible to do justice here to the specifically pedagogic ideas of expertise and especially the borrowings from the continental and Scottish reformers, but it is clear that the conflicts of the 1830s pushed liberal educational ambitions into one of those peaks of progressive enthusiasm which have been a recurrent feature of the whole history of the educational system. The 1830s, like the 1960s was a moment of educational utopianism. Pursuing these ambitions, critical of existing efforts, wishing to transform the working class *and* their educators, experts naturally looked to the state. Their problem was how to install, at the centre of state power, the kind of directing force which their whole programme required.

V

We must now turn to the expert agitation and the reasons for its relative failure. It is useful to consider, very generally, the conditions that governed the chances of success. The most obvious difficulty was the massive institutional presence of the Established Church in the educational sphere. Educational politics were constructed around this dominating institution which, for many early Victorians, was the recognised ideological and moral agency of the state itself.

Historians have tended to define the legislative problem of nineteenth-century education mainly in terms of 'the religious difficulty' — the problem, that is, of finding some means by which children of different religious denominations could be educated in the same school, satisfying or overriding Anglican claims to monopoly yet defending the rights of Catholics and Dissenters. The expert initiative certainly posed this problem in a particularly acute form (though not for the first time). Personally most experts adopted some form of the Christian religion. They usually envisaged an education which would include fundamental Christian truths and a morality based on the Gospels. Yet their conception of education was basically unsectarian. They sought *cross-*

denominational, 'national', solutions. This relative distance from specific religious commitments was a further dimension of their statism. 'National education' must be education through the state because, in a religiously divided society, only the state could fully express national unities, and be the guarantor of secular progress. They thus posed dilemmas which were to frustrate the politicians for the best part of a century.

Yet the religious difficulty was only the most acute manifestation of a larger problem. As in the seventeenth century, so in the England of the religious revivals, many different kinds of conflict took on religious forms. The religious-educational differences between the Anglican Church, organised Dissent, and the various secularising tendencies represented by expertise, were regional expressions of bigger divisions within ruling ideologies. These divisions can in turn be traced, as we have traced expertise, to the heartlands of their genesis and reproduction: to particular social milieus, particular social groups and classes, particular sets of social relations, particular institutions. The Anglican Church, as an institution, had its own autonomies and history. It was legatee of a special relation to the state, and of the massive ideological inheritance of 'mother church'. But it was also closely associated with the rural order, allied to agrarian capital and the governing groups and dovetailed politically into the Tory Party. It was the bearer of a conservative and hierarchical conception of society that stressed stabilities and continuities rather than progress. This was necessarily reflected in its educational practices, making many Anglicans suspicious of educational utopias.[106] The vigorous persistence of an already capitalist agriculture, together with the evident utility in a threatening world of some historically sanctioned focus of loyalties, underpinned the church's survival right into the era of industrial capital. From the 1830s, indeed, it is accurate to speak of an 'Anglican Revival', part internal reformation, part adjustment to the urban industrial world.[107] The growing weight of Dissent, the threat of disestablishment, and secularising tendencies of just the kind represented by expertise, were the imminent spurs to revival. The educationalists' programme was already conditioned by this Anglican presence long before it was, in practice, weakened by Anglican opposition. Given the church's power within formal politics, some messy compromise on the lines of 1839 seems to have been inevitable.

It is worth considering, however, how this barrier might have been removed, or some compromise forced more favourable to the state educators. Such shifts did occur, after all; the story of Anglican conservatism was in the end a history of retreat. Conjuncturally, such shifts occurred over the first Reform Act, the protection of agriculture, and eventually, in 1870, over education. Each time, though in very different circumstances, anti-conservative alliances of a somewhat similar composition were forged: Whig or Liberal politicians, a middle-class mobilisation spearheaded by Dissent, a powerful popular push managed and contained by bourgeois leadership. One way of under-standing the expert campaign is to explain the *absence* of this classic liberal alliance. Why was it so difficult to muster from 1833 to the early 1840s?

It is easy to see, once the question is posed, that the elements in such a coalition were all awry. Until the 1860s, orthodox Dissent was lukewarm or hostile to state education. This was shown by the failure of the CSE to recruit outside the unitarian and Catholic heterodoxies. It was shown too by the wary attitude of the leaders of the British and Foreign School Society to all but the most modest expert schemes. The more thoroughgoing proposals were seen as as much of a threat to the Society's 'liberal principles' as the exclusiveness of the Anglicans.[108] Dissenters feared the erosion of 'scriptural instruction' by secularisers, *and* the adoption of Anglican teaching by the state. For these reasons they often opposed any state intervention on principle, a tendency to emerge more clearly, as 'voluntarism', after 1843. In the meantime, there was room for a more modest, defensive alliance between the British and Foreign School Society, the Whig leaders (several of whom were members), and the more pragmatic experts. Suspicion remained too deep, however, to permit a major agitation. The public association of state education with phrenology and secularism (in the person of James Simpson) and with Catholicism (in the person of Thomas Wyse) kept alive the possibility that Dissent might even campaign against a state measure, if 'ultra-Radicals' appeared in it at all.[109] It was only after 1860, with the 'voluntarist' change of mind, that the liberal-dissenting alliance for state education was on the agenda.

As important was the disposition of more popular forces. To understand this we have to return to the relations, over time, between 'progressive' educationalists and working-class radicals, and ultimately to the general history of the class struggle during the period. The starting point is the failure of an earlier populist strategy, the Broughamite strategy of the 1820s. Brougham's early schemes, especially the mechanics' institute movement, do represent an attempt to create an educational alliance with working-class adults. Workers were called upon to educate themselves, with middle-class aid to be sure, but without the stifling patronage of the past.[110]

But this alliance, while prefiguring the 1860s, did not really materialise. After 1832, and more surely after 1836, the lines between working-class counter-education and middle-class liberals were drawn more firmly. The poor law struggle and the rise of Chartism completed the process. For their part radicals rejected the enterprises of the educational transition (mechanics' institutes, SDUK and infant schools).[111] 'Brougham' like 'Whig' became a word of abuse, and a state system of education before the Charter was achieved was seen as a likely source of tyranny. The key radical strategy was substitutional; working people must educate themselves in their own way through their own efforts. Middle-class liberals, for their part, entered on the phase typified by expertise, in which parents were given up as a lost cause and attention was focused on the still uncorrupted child. Thus the trajectory of educational strategies conformed to the whole swing of bourgeois politics, away from the radicalism of the early 1830s, and towards the anti-Chartist alliance of order of 1838 to 1842. It was only after the defeat of Chartism that the populist alliance was once more feasible.

This context was reflected in the forms of the expert campaign. A quiet mode of agitation was favoured, aimed primarily at a middle-class public and at animation of the Whig politicians. The typical tactics were slow accretion of the 'facts' of educational 'destitution', and a mass of propaganda, much of it in the form of official reports spelling out the consequences. Where possible, Anglican opposition was bypassed by action on the educational peripheries of poor law and factory legislation, these 'exceptions' then being cited as evidence for the need for a general system. Sympathetic politicians, especially Brougham and Lord John Russell (the Home Secretary), were heavily canvassed.[112] With increasing urgency from the middle of the decade, Brougham and the MPs (not always working together) raised the issue in Parliament, securing and managing Select Committees (Roebuck's of 1834 and 1835; Slaney's of 1838) and sponsoring motions and Bills (Roebuck's of 1833; Brougham's of 1837 and 1838). They cited expert findings in their speeches and called experts as witnesses. Slaney played an increasingly important part towards the end of the campaign, drawing, with Kay's help, on the work of the Manchester men and the Poor Law Commission, and occupying the space held in common by Whigs, Dissenters and the more pragmatic experts.[113] In general, then, the campaign was esoteric rather than popular, influential not agitational. The main exception was the activity around the leading fraction of the CSE led by Wyse,

Simpson and Duppa.[114] In the two years before 1839, for instance,
Simpson stumped the country, speaking (separately) to middle-class and
working-class audiences.[115] He visited twenty-five towns and cities
urging his hearers to support a state system once a plan was matured.
Though he reported with glee on his large (and pacific) gatherings, his
campaign was largely ignored in the Chartist press and cautiously
evaluated by the Owenites.[116] He and Wyse seem to have failed to
secure even a middle-class mobilisation, though their campaign
undoubtedly alerted the church, infuriated the British and Foreign
School Society and wrecked Simpson's chances of becoming secretary
to the Education Department, a post he earnestly sought.[117]

The government, however, was gradually edging towards a confrontation it heartily wished to avoid.[118] Right up to August 1838, the
Cabinet wavered. Once they had decided to act, Russell toyed with all
kinds of eclectic and over-ambitious schemes before being taken in hand
by Lansdowne (the Lord President of the Council) and Spring Rice (the
Chancellor of the Exchequer).[119] When the government's decisions
were announced in February 1839, they were, indeed, a minimum
programme.[120] A new department was to be constituted by regularising
the meetings of four cabinet ministers as a Committee of the Privy
Council. Its province was to 'consider' all educational matters; its
effective powers were limited to administering the grant system started
in 1833 and hitherto handled by the Treasury. One state 'normal
school' was promised. This arrangement permitted the Cabinet to
continue its deliberations and to recruit 'expert' aid. It was given a kind
of propriety by the device of an Order in Council which possessed the
huge advantage of bypassing Parliament and resting the Committee's
authority (though not its money supply) on Royal Prerogative instead
of Statute. In the storm that followed, the normal school plan was
destroyed by Anglican opposition, the right of inspection was secured
only on the condition that most inspectors were clergymen of the
Church of England, but the Committee itself and its embryonic
department just survived.[121]

Analysis of the final decision to act suggests one last paradox.
Though the emphasis of the February plan (on inspection and the
normal school) owed much to expert recommendations, it was not the
educationalists who persuaded the Whigs to act but their Anglican
opponents. The threat of state education stimulated a group of young
Churchmen (including the young Gladstone) to press for immediate
anticipatory action by the National Society. The church was to set up
its own diocesan machinery, 'visitation' was to anticipate inspection

and 'seminaries' for teachers the state normal schools.[122] In August 1838, the Society's 'Committee of Inquiry and Correspondence' issued marching orders to the Church Militant on the lines of this plan.[123] The fear of a comprehensively Anglican system on this pattern in turn convinced the Whigs and their dissenting allies that government must act.[124] In this complicated pattern of rivalries, it is arguable that the emergence of the demand for state education was the decisive moment. It certainly set off the whole chain of events which boosted the founding of day schools in the years after 1839.

In this sense expertise cannot be said to have failed absolutely. The Committee of Council, moreover, did become the nucleus of educational administration. Dr Kay, who unlike Simpson, Duppa and Hickson avoided public identification with the CSE, did succeed in time in asserting some of that directing power. His policies as secretary were consistently those of the 1830s, pursued with stealth.[125]

Even so, 1839 was a disappointment. It is worth considering, however, the likely consequences of successs. A major expert victory would have necessarily involved a major blow against the Established Church and the whole conservative end of the ruling-class repertoire. At the same time working-class radicals may well have viewed it as a further act of tyranny, comparable to the new poor law, especially if it had involved compulsory attendance or an educational test as a condition of employment. It would have radically split ruling-class opinion while fuelling working-class hostility to the state. It would have heightened the crisis of 1839 to 1842, simplifying and rendering transparent the class nature of the education issue. As we have seen, none of this could have happened but we can see, as a result of this speculation, that there was a kind of counter-revolutionary logic in the expert failure. If their whole campaign can be analysed in terms of hegemony, so too, can its outcome. It represented a necessary compromise between fractions of the dominant class, in the ultimate interests of stability and order. Though they may aspire to stand outside society and history, 'experts' undergo their own 'education' too.

Notes

*This is an extensively revised version of a paper given before the History of Education Society in December 1974 and to the Centre for the Study of Social History at Warwick University in 1976. I am grateful to all who have commented on it, especially to Simon Frith, and to members of the State Group at the Centre for Contemporary Cultural Studies, for discussions of the theories.

1.   Landmarks in this debate have included the publication in English of *The Prison Notebooks* of Antonio Gramsci, ed. and trans. Quintin Hoare and Geoffrey Nowell Smith (London, 1971) and of the work of the French structuralist marxists, see esp. Louis Althusser, 'Ideology and State Apparatuses' in *Lenin and Philosophy and Other Essays* (London, 1971) and Nicos Poulantzas, *Political Power and Social Classes* (London, 1973).

2.   Though it is arguable that this lower level of generality is reached too seldom in the modern debate. Hence the importance of Perry Anderson, *Lineages of the Absolutist State* (London, 1975) and Barrington Moore, Jnr., *Social Origins of Dictatorship and Democracy* (London, 1967).

3.   E.P. Thompson, 'Peculiarities of the English', *Socialist Register* (1965). For Marx and Engels on Britain see *On Britain* (Moscow, 1962), or *Surveys from Exile* (London, 1973).

4.   'The Eighteenth Brumaire of Louis Bonaparte' in *Surveys from Exile,* pp.237-8.

5.   For the original use of 'revolution in government' as applied to Britain in the 1830s and 1840s see O.O.G.M. MacDonagh, 'The Nineteenth-Century Revolution in Government: A Reappraisal', *Historical Journal,* I (1958). Some later contributions have stressed localism, e.g. William C. Lubenow, *The Politics of Government Growth* (Newton Abbott, 1971).

6.   H.H. Gerth and C. Wright Mills, *From Max Weber: Essays in Sociology* (London, 1970), p.228.

7.   Ibid., pp.214, 217.

8.   Ibid., p.228.

9.   See especially 'Elections in England – Whigs and Tories'; 'The Chartists'; 'Corruption at Elections'; 'The Crisis in England and the British Constitution'; 'Lord John Russell' – all in *On Britain.*

10.   Richard Johnson, 'Administrators in Education before 1870' in Gillian Sutherland (ed.), *Studies in the Growth of Nineteenth-Century Government* (London, 1972), pp.110-38.

11.   Richard Johnson, 'Educational Policy and Social Control in Early Victorian England', *Past and Present,* 49 (Nov. 1970), pp.96-119 and 'Notes on the Schooling of the English Working Class' in Roger Dale, Esland and McDonald (eds.), *Schooling and Capitalism* (London, 1976).

12.   The general significance of this dichotomy is explored further in Richard Johnson, 'Barrington Moore, Perry Anderson and English Social Development', *Working Papers in Cultural Studies,* 9 (Spring 1976).

13.   The best account of Brougham's early career is Chester W. New, *The Life of Henry Brougham to 1830* (Oxford, 1961).

14.   Ibid., pp.209-25.

15.   See, for example, his letter to Victor Cousin, the French reformer, recalling this conversion. University College, London, Brougham Papers 696, Brougham to Cousin, 4 Sept. 1837.

16.   The Brougham Papers are therefore a key source, containing letters from Horner, Hickson, Simpson, Duppa, James Mill, Sarah Austin and Kay as well as the Whig ministers and the leaders of the British and Foreign School Society.

17.   There is no published biography of Slaney but see the valuable chapter in P.R. Richards, 'The State and the Working Class 1833-1841: MPs and the Making of Social Policy' (unpublished PhD thesis, University of Birmingham, Oct. 1975), ch.V.

18.   *Slaney Journals,* Shrewsbury Public Library, VI, 30 Oct. 1829.

19.   Ibid., VI, 5,16 and 22 Jan. 1830; Vol. VII, Jan, 1837 and

Sept. 1837.

20.   What follows is mainly based on J.J. Auchmuty, *Sir Thomas Wyse 1792-1862: The Life and Career of an Educator and Diplomat* (London, 1939). I have not consulted what Auchmuty calls 'the vast store of unedited manuscript material' constituting the Wyse Collection in Dublin. But James Murphy, *The Religious Problem in English Education* (Liverpool, 1959) is an excellent account of his Liverpool connections and his English campaign and must be read alongside this essay for a fuller reconstruction of the liberal educational politics of the late 1830s. For some criticisms of his conclusions see J.R.B. Johnson, 'The Education Department 1839-1864: A Study in Social Policy and the Growth of Government' (Unpublished PhD thesis, University of Cambridge, 1968). Cited hereafter as Johnson, 'Education Department'.

21.   Thomas Wyse, *Education Reform; Or the Necessity of a National System of Education*, (London, 1836), frontispiece.

22.   The standard biography is Robert Eadon Leader, *Life and Letters of John Arthur Roebuck* (London, 1897).

23.   For his relations with his Bath constituents see R.S. Neale, *Class and Ideology in the Nineteenth Century*, (London, 1972), ch. II.

24.   For the clearest expression of his educational views see 'J.A.R.', 'National Education', *Tait's Edinburgh Magazine*, II (March 1833), pp.755-65. And also his speech proposing the motion of 1833, *Hansard*, XX, cols. 139-66.

25.   For Brougham and Mill see New, *Brougham*, pp.151-6 and John Stuart Mill, *Autobiography*, 4th edn. (London, 1874), pp.90-1.

26.   S.E. Finer, 'The Transmission of Benthamite Ideas 1820-50' in Sutherland, *Nineteenth-Century Government*, pp.11-32.

27.   For Chalmers' position in an unusually concise form see 'The Supreme Importance of a Right Moral to a Right Economical State of the Community', *Works*, XX, pp.170-84. Also published as a pamphlet in 1832. For McCulloch, who did not accept Chalmers' position in full, see D.P.O'Brien, *J.R. McCulloch: A Study in Classical Economics* (London, 1970), esp. pp.280 and 346 ff.

28.   The most recent discussion of Mill's educational ideas is W.H. Burston, *James Mill on Philosophy and Education* (London 1973). But the account in Elie Halevy, *The Growth of Philosophic Radicalism*, trans. Mary Morris (London, 1928) is hard to beat. See esp. on utilitarianism and education generally, pp.241-4, 282-96 and 364 ff.

29.   The debate, of course goes back to A.V. Dicey's, *Lectures on the Relation between Law and Public Opinion*. The subsequent literature is too massive to list here.

30.   e.g. Black's *Morning Chronicle*, Bowring's *Westminster Review*, Fonblanque's *Examiner*, W.J. Fox's *Monthly Repository* and John Stuart Mill's *London and Westminster. The Quarterly Journal of Education* (1831-5) was edited by George Long, Professor of Greek at London University and an active member of the SDUK and the CSE. Among 'experts' who wrote for it were B.F. Duppa and McCulloch.

31.   Quoted in Joseph Hamburger, *Intellectuals in Politics:John Stuart Mill and the Philosophic Radicals* (Newhaven, 1965), p.184. I have followed Hamburger's argument about the political limitations of the utilitarian circle in the later 1830s.

32.   G.S.R. Kitson Clark, '"Statesmen in Disguise": Reflections on the History of the Neutrality of the Civil Service', *Historical Journal*, III (1959); Henry Parris, *Constitutional Bureacracy* (London, 1969), ch. V; O.R. McGregor, 'Social Research and Social Policy in the Nineteenth Century', *British*

Journal of Sociology, VIII (1957); Michael J. Cullen, *The Statistical Movement in Early Victorian Britain* (Hassocks, 1976); Lucy Brown, *The Board of Trade and the Free Trade Movement 1830-42* (Oxford, 1958).

33. Lucy Brown, *Board of Trade,* pp.76 ff; Cullen, *Statistical Movement,* ch. I and pp.139-44 (for the crime and education debate).

34. S.E. Finer, *The Life and Times of Sir Edwin Chadwick* (London, 1952) is the best source though it tends to exaggerate Chadwick's role – in everything.

35. The best source remains Katharine M. Lyell, *Memoir of Leonard Horner,* 2 vols.(privately printed, 1890). See also Bernice Martin, Leonard Horner: A Portrait of an Inspector of Factories', *International Review of Social History,* XIV (1969).

36. Quoted in S. Leon Levy, *Nassau William Senior 1790-1864* (reprinted, Newton Abbott, 1970), p. 106.

37. Ibid., p. 129.

38. Ibid., pp.73, 106-7.

39. For Horner's relationship with Lancashire businessmen, in which he retained a large measure of independence, see Michael Sanderson, 'Education and the Factory', *Economic History Review,* XX (1967), p.271.

40. For Scottish University education generally see G.E. Davie, *The Democratic Intellect:Scotland and Her Universities in the Nineteenth Century* (Edinburgh, 1961). Also useful is John Clive, *Scotch Reviewers: The Edinburgh Review 1802-15* (London, 1957).

41. Ibid., ch. VII.

42. Horner, for example, abhorred what he called 'all priestly domination' but did not identify closely with English Dissent. Lyell, *Horner,* II, pp.174-5.

43. New argues persuasively that Brougham's educational ideas were based on his Scottish experience. Popular enthusiasm for education in Scotland was often cited as an example to benighted neighbours by expatriate Scots.

44. The educational ideas of phrenologists deserve a closer study than is possible here. A good contemporary starting point is James Simspon, *The Philosophy of Education,* 2nd edn. (Edinburgh, 1836).

45. For Tremenheere see R.K. Webb, 'A Whig Inspector', *Journal of Modern History,* XXXVII (1955). The most revealing source for Duppa, who is otherwise very elusive, is his correspondence in the Brougham Papers. For Tufnell see Boase, *Modern English Biography;* for Symons see *DNB.*

46. *DNB.* See also his letter in Brougham Papers.

47. The main source is Frederick Hill, *An Autobiography of Fifty Years in Times of Reform* (London, 1894).

48. The standard life remains Frank Smith, *The Life and Work of Sir James Kay-Shuttleworth* (London, 1923). Useful but requiring careful use is B.C. Blomfield (ed.), 'The Autobiography of Sir James Kay-Shuttleworth', *Education Libraries Bulletin,* London University Institute of Education, Supplement 7. This is a transcript of the manuscript in the Kay-Shuttleworth Papers now at the John Rylands Library, Manchester.

49. Especially in the Manchester Statistical Society for which see Cullen, *Statistical Movement,* ch. VIII, and T.S. Ashton, *Economic and Social Investigation in Manchester* (London, 1934).

50. J.P. Kay, *The Moral and Physical Condition of the Working Classes Employed in the Cotton Manufacture in Manchester* (London, 1832). The first edition is cited throughout. For an assessment see Johnson, 'Educational Policy and Social Control'.

51. See the lists of subscribers and committee members printed in Central

Society for Education, *First Publication, Second Publication* and *Third Publication* (London, 1837-9), republished Woburn Press. Compare the party affiliations in Dodd, *The Parliamentary Pocket Companion for 1838.*

52.   For the statistical society groupings see Cullen, *Statistical Movement.*

53.   For examples of this general orientation see Wyse, *Education Reform*, p.2; *Quarterly Journal of Education*, I, no.2, p.213; Joseph Fletcher, Report to the Handloom Weavers Commission (Reports to the Commission, hereafter cited as Handloom Report) *PP* 1840, XXIV, p.107; Sarah Austin (trans.); *Report on the State of Public Instruction in Prussia . . . by Victor Cousin* (London, 1834), translator's preface, p.viii; Kay, *Manchester*, p.48.

54.   e.g. Porter's famous work of that title. For a typical celebration of machinery (to the neglect of its effects on human labour) see E.C. Tufnell, Report to the Factory Commission, *PP* 1834, XIX, p.208, the long footnote.

55.   For examples of these arguments see Hickson, Handloom Report, pp.688-9; Hill, *National Education*, pp.238-46; Fletcher, Handloom Report, pp. 99-110 (comparing Coventry and outlying districts).

56.   Actually it was a *defence* of Manchester. See Johnson, 'Educational Policy and Social Control'.

57.   e.g. J.R. Porter, *The Progress of the Nation*, 3rd edn. (London, 1851), p. 685, quoting from McCulloch's, *Principles of Political Economy.*

58.   On these 'vicissitudes' see Hickson, Handloom Report, pp.655-6.

59.   *Quarterly Journal of Education*, IX (Jan-Apr. 1835), pp.35-6.

60.   Hickson, Handloom Report, p.677. Even Simpson whose educational programme approached the egalitarian, saw equalisation as moral, distinctions of 'God's appointment' remaining. Simpson, *Philosophy of Education*, p.209.

61.   [J.P. Kay] 'Condition of the Working Classes and the Factory Bill', *Westminster Review*, XVII (Apr. 1833), esp. pp. 385-6. The attribution is clear from internal evidence but see also Kay-Shuttleworth Papers, T. Perronet Thompson to Kay, 5 Feb. 1833.

62.   e.g. Leonard Horner, *On the Employment of Children in Factories. . .* (London, 1840), esp. preface and p.5. For the phrenological standpoint on 'over-labour' see George Combe, *Lectures on Popular Education*, 3rd edn. (Edinburgh, 1846), pp.25-46 and Simpson, *Philosophy of Education*, pp.181-4.

63.   Roebuck, 'National Education', *Tait's Magazine*, II, p.755.

64.   e.g. Roebuck, Hickson, Hill, Brougham and Kay. For Kay's early politics see [J.P.Kay], *A Letter to the People of Lancashire, concerning the Future Representation of the Commercial Interest.* (London, 1831).

65.   For a short but typical discussion see Kay, *Manchester*, pp.36-8.

66.   The poor law story is too well known to require recapitulation here. For crime see Cullen, *Statistical Movement* and the typical expert treatments in *Quarterly Journal of Education*, I, p.215; Hickson, Handloom Report, pp.720-21; Fletcher, loc cit., p.212.

67.   e.g. Hill, *National Education*, pp.14-15.

68.   Chalmers, *Works*, XX, p.179.

69.   See Handloom Weavers Commission, Final Report, *PP* 1841, X, pp.860-1 (for a summary of recommendations). For the educational intentions of those involved in the report see Brougham Papers, 32, 194. Hickson to Brougham, 28 Nov.1837.

70.   For explicit discussions of the suffrage issue see Hickson, Handloom Report, pp.721-3 (which is also a revealing discussion of Chartism) and Symons' classic formulation: 'Admitting the general right of every

man to vote, I deny the right of every man to vote, whether he knows how
to vote or not', *Arts and Artisans at Home and Abroad* (Edinburgh, 1839),
ch. XIV.

71. For the general argument see Kay, *Manchester,* p.60. Tufnell, Hickson and
Fletcher took a similar position.

72. See note 62 above.

73. See, for example, the handling of cholera in Kay's *Manchester,* not merely
as an act of nature but as a providential event in a chain of 'moral
causation'. But also the interpenetration of questions of health, drink and
the inadequacies of working-class domestic economy.

74. Election speech at Sheffield 1868, quoted in Leader, *Roebuck,* p.325.

75. e.g. 'Domestic happiness is not promoted, but impaired, by all the members
of a family muddling together and jostling each other constantly in the
same room. The *usual* and *better* course, adopted by the middle and
higher classes, is that of separating for the day, and assembling only at
meal-times in the evening.' Handloom Report, p.694.

76. See for example the continuation of the Roebuck speech which focused
sentimentally on 'home'.

77. Chalmers, *The Christian and Civic Economy of Large Towns* (Glasgow,
1826), p.288.

78. e.g. B.F. Duppa, *The Causes and the Present Condition of the Labouring
Classes in the South of England* (London, 1831), p.3.

79. i.e. of labour power itself in the capitalist relation. Compare Marx's
formulation of 'reproduction' in *Capital,* I, Ben Fowkes trans. and Ernest
Mandel intro. (London, 1976), pp.711-24, 1060-65.

80. Wyse, *Education Reform,* pp.3-4.

81. The argument that follows is developed more fully in Johnson, 'Notes on
the Schooling of the English Working Class' in Dale *et al.,* op.cit.

82. For Hickson see note 70 above; for Roebuck, who actually spoke in favour
of the Charter on its first presentation to Parliament, see Leader, *Roebuck,*
esp. pp.126-7, 133-4.

83. Wyse, *Education Reform,* p.394.

84. *Prison Notebooks,* p.258.

85. Hickson, for example, was involved in advising Brougham about his Bills
but also urged action, without legislation on the basis of the grants of 1833.
See Brougham Papers, 17,065, 'Suggestions by Mr W.E. Hickson', 1 Dec.
1837 and c.p. [W.E. Hickson], 'Schools for the Industrious Classes. . .',
CSE, *Second Publication,* 1838, pp.398-9. The author has been identified
by internal references, especially the heavy use of 'juvenile witness' and
the actual places and schools cited in the article which also appear in
Hickson's other works.

86. e.g. Roebuck's plan of 1833; the extraordinarily elaborate proposals of
James Simpson (See Report of the Select Committee on Education in
England and Wales, *PP,* 1835,VII, Appendix 3); the evidence of Professor
Pillans (a Scottish educationalist) to the Select Committee of 1834 (*PP*
1834, IX, qqs. 405 ff.) and Sarah Austin's recommendations on the basis of
the Prussian system. *Foreign and Quarterly Review,* XII, no.24, pp.273 ff.

87. Kay, evidence to the Select Committee on the Education of the Poorer
Classes, *PP,* 1837-38, VII, esp. qu. 240 ff.; Fletcher, Handloom Report,
p.205.

88. e.g. Wyse, 'Education in the United Kingdom', CSE, *First Publication,*
p. 63; Hickson in CSE, *Second Publication* (cited note 85 above); and the original recommendations of Slaney's Select Committee which were defeated
by Churchmen on the Committee (See Select Committee on the Education

of the Poorer Classes, *PP* 1837-38, VII, pp. xii-xv).

89.   Wyse, 'Education in the UK', p.30.
90.   E.G. West, 'Private versus Public Education: A Classical Economic Dispute', ·
      Journal of Political Economy (Oct. 1964) and *Education and the State*
      (London, 1965).
91.   e.g. Sarah Austin, *Report on the State of Public Instruction in Prussia,*
      pp.ix-xix; Hill, *National Education,* pp.165-6; Horner, *On the State of*
      Education in Holland. . . by Victor Cousin (London, 1838), translator's
      preface, pp.xvi-xvii.
92.   *Education Reform,* pp.447-53.
93.   This, for example, is the main argument of those parts of *Education*
      Reform which deal with working-class culture, cf. Johnson 'Educational
      Policy and Social Control'.
94.   Cullen, *Statistical Movement,* esp. p.139.
95.   Ibid., pp.94-5.
96.   The reservations about private schools and Sunday schools are important
      if we are attempting to assess the overall provision of schools. But experts
      discounted the value of these.
97.   e.g. Wyse, *Education Reform*, pp. 446-8; Fletcher, Handloom Report,
      p.204; Hickson, CSE, *Second Publication, passim.*
98.   Wyse, *Education Reform,* pp. 15-21.
99.   e.g. [McCulloch], 'Reasons for Establishing a Public System of Instruction
      in England', *Quarterly Journal of Education,* I, no.2, pp 279-80; Roebuck,
      'National Education', *Tait's Edinburgh Magazine,* II, p.760.
100. e.g. Hickson' Schools for Industrious Classes', pp.356-61.
101. Hence the common argument that government should acquire some
      control over the nature and content of schoolbooks, e.g. Horner,
      State of Education in Holland, p.xlvii; Wyse, *Education Reform,* p.469.
      On 'everyday things' see Duppa, *The Education of the Peasantry in*
      England. . . (London, 1834), pp.23-5; Hickson, Handloom Report
      p.718, reprinting his letter to the Bishop of London; Pillans, evidence to
      Select Committee of 1834, *PP* 1834, IX, qu. 556-71, citing French practice
      with approval.
102. Simpson, *Philosophy of Education,* p.120. In general Simpson's conception
      of the necessary content of elementary education was very wide. See ch.V.
103. Especially Duppa and Hickson, Hickson writing extensively on this theme
      in the 1840s.
104. Hickson, CSE, *Second Publication,* 364-7.
105. e.g. 'The working classes have awakened first; they render it impossible for
      any others to sleep, unless they wish to be trode [sic] over.' Thomas Wyse,
      Speech Delivered at the Opening of the New Mechanics Institution, Mount
      Street, Liverpool.. . . September 1838 (Liverpool, n.d.), p.30.
106. It is not possible, here, to examine Anglican educational attitudes in detail.
      See, however, G.M. Goldstrom, *The Social Content of Education 1808-1870*
      (Irish University Press, Shannon, 1972).
107. For the fortunes of the church generally in the period see G. Kitson Clark,
      Churchmen and the Condition of England 1832-1885 (London, 1973).
108. What follows is largely based on letters in the Brougham Papers between
      Brougham, William Allen and Henry Dunn (the secretary of the British
      and Foreign School Society).
109. Henry Dunn to William Allen, 6 Sept. 1837, Brougham Papers, 9572.
110. The classic text from this period is Henry Brougham, *Practical Observations*
      upon the Education of the People, Addressed to the Working Classes and
      their Employers (London, 1825). This pamphlet which helped to launch

the mechanics' institute movement went through many editions.

111. The history of this relation can be traced in the unstamped press. See also Patricia Hollis, *The Pauper Press* (Oxford, 1970), esp. pp.143-5.

112. The Russell Papers (Public Record Office) are less revealing on this than the Brougham Papers perhaps because they are less.complete. But Kay was certainly in contact with Russell well before his appointment to the Education Department. As Home Secretary Russell was also in regular receipt of reports from the inspectorates. For Kay's contacts with Russell see Johnson, 'Education Department', pp.55 and 62.

113. For a fuller account of Slaney's role and the evidence on which this is based see Johnson, 'Education Department', pp.45-51.

114. For a fuller account of the campaign see Murphy, *The Religious Problem.*

115. Brougham Papers, nineteen letters between March 1836 and August 1839, 15,909-19; 15,369-74; 36,541.

116. For Owenite reactions see *New Moral World,* 16 Nov. 1838.

117. For his 'application' see Brougham Papers, 15,371 (14 Feb.1839) and 15,372 (16 Feb.1839)

118. This account is based on Johnson, 'Education Department', pp.53-61.

119. e.g., a system based on the poor law administration, on the Irish model or on the British and Foreign Society's plan of Bible Reading. See Russell Papers, 3B, Lord Cottenham to Russell, 25 Oct. 1837; John Lefevre to Russell, 25 Oct. 1838; Spring Rice to Russell, 29 Oct 1838, and Murphy, *Religious Problem,* pp.160-2.

120. For the scheme in full see *PP* 1839, XLI, pp.255-7.

1*21. For the origins of the clerical inspectorate see Nancy Ball, *Her Majesty's Inspectorate 1839-1849* (University of Birmingham, Institute of Education, Educational Monographs VI, 1963) and Johnson, 'Education Department', pp. 62-85.

122. H.J. Burgess, *Enterprise in Education* (London, 1958), pp.63-8; Johnson, 'Education Department', pp.43-4, 46-8, 52-4.

123 National Society, 'Address from the Committee of Inquiry and Correspondence', 1 Aug. 1838. There is a copy in the Russell Papers with passages heavily scored in ink!

124. Russell Papers, 3B, Russell to Allen, 13 Aug. 1838; Henry Dunn to Russell, 5 Oct. 1838.

125. For this familiar story see Johnson, 'Education Department', chs. II to V and c.p. Smith, *Kay-Shuttleworth.*

4 RELIGION AND SOCIAL CONTROL IN THE MID-NINETEENTH CENTURY

Jenifer Hart

Much religious teaching of the nineteenth century contained no social or political message. Indeed this is probably true of most of it. But some of it embodies social and political doctrines, either specifically or by implication. What were these doctrines? Do they reveal a hard core of agreement? In particular how did clergymen try to use religion as an instrument of social control, that is to control the 'lower' classes? This essay will be confined to the half century from about 1830 to 1880 and to the Church of England, for it is not possible here to discuss the interesting question of how far Nonconformists and Catholics held social philosophies similar to those of the Established Church. The picture of the latter which follows is based on an examination of a cross-section of the vast mass of surviving sermons and pamphlets. The method adopted was partly to look through collections of miscellaneous sermons selected at random, and partly to identify and study those whose titles suggested that they would throw some light on the social and political attitudes of the clergy. The main works on which this chapter is based are listed at the end.[1]

Stations in Life and Inequality

The notion that the existing social structure was the creation of Divine Providence — so common in eighteenth-century England — continued largely unabated down into the 1870s if not beyond. Most exponents of this doctrine do not explain how they know it to be true, though when they are dealing with one aspect of it, namely poverty, they submit various texts or facts in support of their statements. Ranks and grades in general however are simply declared to be the dispensation of Divine Providence. The language used may vary, but the message is identical. Thus: God has providentially assigned everyone to a station in life. He has been pleased to call us to a particular state of life. Distinctions of rank may be traced to divine arrangements. The social system derives from God, who willed different grades and orders of society and an inequality of ranks, wealth and power. Men do not come to their several stations by their own choice, or by chance, but by the appointment of God who disposeth of these things according to the good pleasure of his will. It has pleased God that in this world various social distinctions should exist. Christianity instructs us to look at differences of condition as resulting from the will of God; this takes off the harshness which cannot fail of attaching to them if they are viewed as merely human institutions. God has appointed some to labour with their bodies, and the inequality of our outward condition is inevitable. Differences and stations are ordinances of God and therefore sacred and just and wise. Our Lord had opportunities to lay down some new law as to the future condition of society and to show how the reception of his faith was intended to level all ranks, but he did not do this — indeed he did the opposite. At special meetings for working men held in conjunction with Church Congresses in the 1860s and 1870s, a number of speakers, mostly members of the higher clergy, propounded the same doctrine. For example: we must work together in the several stations in which God has placed us; the Church recognises orders and degrees under God's providence; God has placed people high or low in the social scale or has led them to their different places in this world; he has made distinctions which are to the end of time.

Some preachers do not stress the divine origins of ranks and classes, but rely on nature or history to support their inevitability. Distinctions are pronounced to be the order of nature; or, if we examine the records of history, we find that inequality of rank and conditions has prevailed universally. Distinctions of rich and poor are insuperable peculiarities of the human race. The sweat of the brow is the peculiar destiny of the working classes.

Given the divine origins of the social structure, it must of course not be criticised or altered. One should not find fault with distinctions of rank, because they are dispensations of God's providence. Each class must move in its own sphere. Again and again people are told that they must do their duty in that state of life in which it hath pleased God to place them, labouring faithfully with contentment. Children should be taught to be satisfied with any, even the humblest lot, and to discharge their duties with contented acquiescence. Any attempt to banish social distinctions would be a rebellion against the appointment of God, for it was God and not the higher orders of society who placed people in the rank they hold. The healthy gradations and distinctions of society should not be confounded or destroyed, nor should the capital of the social column be laid on a level with its base. In any case all can be happy in the social system although the distinctions may look harsh. Indeed the due subordination of one class beneath another lies at the very basis of all social happiness; and the highest happiness of man consists in a humble contentment with the lot which God has assigned to each person, whatever that may be. Many of the clergy, as others, were not unmindful of the practical, wordly advantages of their doctrines — in particular of the need to get manual work done and of the danger of educating children above their stations in life. Mandeville was criticised for having wished by education to disqualify the poor for their proper duties, raising their ideas above their social station. This line was constantly taken especially when support for the National Society for Educating the Children of the Poor was being solicited. National schools would keep to the golden mean: they would not unfit the poor for the discharge of those subordinate and necessary offices which Providence has laid upon them, but at the same time they would fit them for that state of future bliss which is expressly promised the poor in spirit. So no one need fear that in subscribing to the Society he would be lifting from their due condition those whom scripture acknowledges as destined to be hewers of wood and drawers of water.

Sometimes in the 1870s preachers seem to begin thinking that some degree of social mobility may be permissible. Thus Bishop Magee admitted in 1870 to an audience of working men that one can move up the social scale, but he added that they could not all rise to the top and that only those should who were led by God. He did not however specify how anyone was to know whether God was leading him or not. Similarly another speaker[2] at the same gathering said that there was no need to crave for a higher place unless God called one to it, and urged workmen to be humble and not to thrust themselves into prominence. Others warned against the danger of degradation when seeking to better oneself. Some improvement in the condition of the working man could be tolerated: he ought to be able at the close of the day to sit down with his family in a cheerful and comfortable home with practically all the refinements and appliances of a gentleman, though they would not be on the same scale. But unless these working men also had religious feeling and saw to it that their children had religious training, they would be but a superior kind of animal, almost like the brutes that perish. The speaker[3] did not desire to limit their advancement, but it should be 'true and real'. Others when talking about the 'elevation' of working men were not thinking of economic or social elevation. Thus Bishop Durnford in 1874 said that many of the higher classes (with whom he obviously identified) desired to elevate working men by encouraging them to love high and noble things, to be good fathers and good husbands, good neighbours and good to their employers, and above all true to themselves. And he added the standard exhortation

that they should do their duty in the place which Providence had
assigned them. That few of these speakers had economic elevation in
mind is indicated by the emphasis they all put on the dogma that wages
are fixed by a law of nature.

Although God had created ranks and social classes and required men
to maintain them, he himself paid them no attention: the lower classes
should respect the higher classes, but God did not. This message is
reiterated in various forms. The most usual is that in the sight of God
all are equal. He made us all: our souls are equally precious. There are
no ranks when sinners approach God. The immortal spirit of man is the
same in the sight of God: all earthly distinctions are cast into shade by
the soul which makes the peasant and philosopher, the monarch and
meanest man alike, and brings them all to one level. Social distinctions
are petty; earthly distinctions of position have no existence in the
presence of God; they have no permanence or reality. James Fraser,
later Bishop of Manchester, told servants at an Oxford college in 1853
that whilst to the worldly eye their condition involved temporal
disadvantages as compared with that of their masters, all distinctions
cease in Jesus Christ. One preacher[4] referred to the 'lower classes' when
speaking of the alleged increase of drunkenness among them, but then
added that he spoke after the manner of men when he used the terms
'upper' and 'lower', for in the sight of God we are all equal as regards
moral action. Another,[5] of a more macabre temperament, pointed out
that at death the man of 100,000 acres and the man who never owned
a rood were equal because each only needed six feet of earth. A.W.
Thorold, later Bishop of Rochester, and Winchester, said in the late
1860s that the doctrine of Divine Providence placed the beggar and the
king, the lonely widow and the powerful statesman, the decrepit
pauper and the conqueror in a hundred battles on the same level of
entire equality before him with whom there is no respect of persons. A
speaker[6] at the working-men's meeting of the Church Congress of 1870
said there is equality in the sense that we all share one master, 'Your
Lord and my Lord.' Sometimes indeed the working man was told that
he might stand higher in the estimation of God and in the kingdom of
heaven than the man of the highest station and dignity, if the latter
lived only for the pursuit of wealth; but this was not said very often,
perhaps through fear of stimulating arrogance in the wrong quarters.

Considerable emphasis was laid on the fact that the doctrines of the
church were equally within the reach of all minds and all stations. A
man can acquire knowledge of the truth however humble he is. One
does not have to pay with money for atonement from sin, or for

conversion or sanctification. Working men have as much right to the church as anyone else in the country; the church's ministrations and religion are as free to all as air and sunshine. In fact the church was often declared to be 'the greatest leveller in the whole country',[7] because the baptism, marriage and burial services were the same for everyone. All who are baptised can take part in the church's prayers and praises, and are entitled to the ministrations of the clergy, in particular to the burial service. Or as another preacher put it truth and liberty were offered freely and equally to all of every station and every country; they shine with the same lustre on the tenant of the cottage and the mansion. With God all can achieve equality of rights and interests, of advantages and situations, which the world has vainly struggled to establish; that is (as Bishop Fraser declared in 1878) it is only in the Christian Church that true equality, liberty and fraternity are realised.

Another theme is that men are alike in that they are all equally capable of happiness and misery, though Archbishop Tait when he was propounding this in 1875 admitted that it was remarkable, considering the vast differences in men's worldly circumstances. The fact that men all fell into the same sorts of sin was also emphasised.

The value of the doctrine of spiritual equality was clearly apparent to many preachers: as Augustus Hare put it in 1831 in a sermon called *Religion the Humaniser of Man, and Supporter of Society,* it softened the differences of condition in this life and made them seem comparatively unimportant. If the right kind of equality were respected, another preacher[8] declared, namely spiritual equality which is true and practicable, we should not even think of that pretended equality which is false and impossible, for a poor man has not a right to equal property, or rank, or power, or any perishable thing. This was an easier position to maintain than the one increasingly adopted later on, namely that there are not really substantial differences between the classes, but that all men are brothers and that 'we are all working men'.

Poverty

The subject of poverty was referred to in a great many sermons, but nevertheless there was a large measure of agreement about it. The position taken up was as follows.

The Almighty had arranged that there shall be poor people. Poverty is the direct consequence of the curse: those who toil prolongedly every day and earn but a scanty meal exemplify to the very letter the penalty to be paid by our fallen race. The providence of God has appointed some to be poor. For some wise and almost sacramental purpose, Christ has declared that the poor shall never be removed from the land. This is his will even though disease falls crushingly on the poor. The existence of the poor reveals the manifold wisdom of God. Poverty is hallowed by Christian teaching. The state of poverty has been sanctified or consecrated by the fact Christ was poor; he redeemed it from its curse. Poverty is a necessary element in the social life of a nation. It is not against the will of God that there shall be rich and poor. God has drawn the demarcation line between rich and poor which we cannot blot out. God cautions us against riches and often condemns them, but there is not one word against the state of poverty in the Bible. Indeed many things are said in its favour, and our Lord gave grace and dignity to that condition of life. Great stress is always laid on the fact that Jesus chose voluntarily to be poor, though the question whether he would have chosen the condition of the nineteenth-century poor was not discussed.

Sometimes the existence of poverty was justified not with reference to God's will, but because it is 'the order of nature', or simply by saying it is inevitable. There will always be distress. There are no human means by which the multitudes can extricate themselves from penury. At the beginning of the Christian era, the distinctions of society seemed to be done away with for ever, but soon it was clear that the distinction between rich and poor was not be abolished, and could not be. Even in 1879, poverty was considered to be natural, inevitable.[9]

Poverty was also constantly justified on other grounds, of an empirical or utilitarian nature. Thus the poor man is often happier than the rich man. It is hardly possible to make a more erroneous estimate of individual happiness than to judge of it by external appearances alone. Even if the rich man exhibits all the outward signs of unmixed prosperity, he may in fact be of all men the most miserable. And just as wealth does not bring happiness, so there is no necessary connection between unhappiness and a low estate. However the notion that the poor man was happier than the rich man was not held by everyone, at least not by the Exeter Hall preacher[10] who argued in 1857 that the poor man needed religion more than the rich man because if you take the hope of heaven from the rich man he still has something to live for (e.g. he can pamper every appetite); but what is left to the poor man if you take from him the bright hope that irradiates his trouble and sustains his toil? The poor man often leads a more godly life than his wealthier neighbour who has been led astray by the deceitfulness of riches and who is so preoccupied with pleasures and cares due to riches that he cannot spare time to think about God. As competitors for eternity the poor are not so badly off: for it is easier to draw off the affections of the poor from things visible to invisible than those of the rich. Poverty keeps the soul humble, dead to the world, sober (though this of course did not imply that the poor did not get drunk). Loss of wealth involves a gain in religiousness. Sometimes it is admitted that excessive poverty distracts the mind and hinders devotions, but even so it is not condemned by the preacher because he considers it in the end often most beneficial to the soul. So the poor have many spiritual advantages over the rich, even if they do not realise it: in mean dwelling places and houses of humble poverty have been formed from age to age those great but hidden saints of old who have been made perfect through suffering.

The poor also have an advantage over the rich in that it is easier for them to be charitable, to make sacrifices, to perform acts of self-denial. Poverty inclines one to seek the Kingdom of Heaven, while prosperity turns one back from it. The poor have less to answer for at the final day of retribution because less is committed to their charge. Indeed there are many more dangers in riches than in poverty. Another advantage the poor man has over the rich is revealed when they are faced with death: the rich man is then in a bad way, but poverty loosens ties to life and the poor man does not mind dying so much because he sees he is only leaving an inhospitable shore for a haven of eternal rest.

Poverty was also justified on the ground that the rich need the poor: if there was universal affluence, it was argued, there would be no opportunity for morality, or for spiritual improvement, or progress in genuine piety. We have a tendency to selfishness; we therefore need objects appealing to our compassion. It is difficult enough not to be selfish now. How much more difficult it would be if there were no destitution! The poor are therefore the blessings and benefactors of a community. They, like the halt, the maimed, the blind, the widow and the orphan keep us from hardening into a heartless mass, and preserve in healthful play our sympathies and sensitivities. Christianity has laid a debt of gratitude upon the poor, because it established a law of sympathy as a rule of social life. The poor should not be removed out of the land because they enable others by being nice to them to minister to Christ. The weary pilgrimage of the poor has two objects: to perfect them, and to draw forth into active exercise the forces of charity and compassion in what the world would call their more fortunate brethren. God's great object in creating poverty and wealth is to bring many brethren into glory. He sends us the poor to try our faithfulness.

Many other things were said to try to make these doctrines palatable to the poor. Some of them were directed at making them feel they were very special people. For instance, they are the jewels of the church, the brightest gems of the coronal of grace and sanctity. The working classes at a Westminster Abbey sermon in 1858 were told that the poor, even the beggar, were raised from the dust and the dunghill and set among princes where they inherited the throne of glory; so they are Kings, infinitely above comparison with any earthly potentate; the King of Kings sends an embassy to treat with us, with the very poorest and most miserable of us all as Kings, though we be as dust and ashes. Christ raised the whole position of the poor by choosing his earthly place amòng them. One of the privileges of the poor which is constantly referred to is that the gospel was and is preached to them. Moreover the poor should feel comforted by the fact that Christ's life was spent for their sake.

A common device was to use words in a different sense than the usual one, and thereby to attempt to bring comfort to the poor. For instance, Christianity can make the poor man *rich* by furnishing him with the golden treasure of contentment. How *rich* is the poorest peasant, W.W. Champneys declared in 1857, as he walks through the rich man's park, and enjoys those beauties with a greater and keener zest than the owner, as he lifts to heaven the unpresumptuous eye and smiling says 'My Father made them all.' Similarly the richest man in the world is *poor* if he cannot get all he wants. And the man who has to exchange a mansion for a humble cottage can say that affliction with the Saviour's presence and love is the best *prosperity*. The poor man is *enriched* through the gospel; it is a pearl of great price, like affluence to a beggar. If he receives the gospel, he is raised amongst his fellows, and the adventitious distinctions of property, rank and education are comparatively forgotten. He can no longer count himself poor, for all things are his. The poor beggar with nothing who loves God and Christ will really be *richer* than the wealthy man with every-thing who does not love God and Christ. God has given more to the beggar than to the rich man. Money does not make one rich: only love can do this. In sermons for *inter alia* Union workhouses, the inmates are assured that God intends to make them *rich,* not merely hereafter but now, by offering them pardon of sin and much else.

Another consolation offered to the poor was that though they may feel everything is against them, yet God has demonstrated this to be a fiction of their own desponding hearts, or a mischievous delusion of the devil, so that in reality all things are working for their own good.

Though they be 'as having nothing', they are possessing all things.

Allied to this is the exhortation to trust the Lord. Sometimes the assurance that the Lord will provide is given with no qualification: cast your care upon God; if he has given you life and bodies, he will not deny you the lesser blessings of food and clothing. Observe God's power and goodness in the provision he has made for the support and nurture of the least and weakest of his creatures. Take no thought for the morrow. Reliance was placed on Psalm 37.3: 'Put thou thy trust in the Lord, and be doing good: dwell in the land, and verily thou shalt be fed.' If you have true faith, you are brought under the care of the heavenly father to be clothed by him, and fed bounteously by him. Trust him to help your ignorance and poverty, to provide for your sickness, to save you from want. No good thing will be withheld from them that live a godly life. If we are following Christ, we may not doubt his protection; we shall find that means are at hand which will suffice for our wants. Take no thought for your life; for if God has given life, the nobler gift, will he withhold what is necessary to sustain and defend it? God provides enlarged possessions to some to provide for poverty. The experience of God's people in every age confirms the truth of expressions like 'it shall be given you'. Indeed the Lord is often providing now. What honest man is there without a home? What honest head without a pillow? one preacher[11] asked. Another[12] pointed out that God gives us our daily bread, and also much else besides, namely comforts and conveniences such as tea and wheaten bread, as well as necessaries, whereas Christ himself only ate rye bread. If you are poor, the Lord will feed you, for you are better than the fowls of the air. He will never forsake you. He has given his royal word you shall never want. By Christ's poverty, we become rich. Even the farmer who has lost all through bad weather should feel really safe, and as far removed from starvation after as before his losses. The message is the same even in the late 1870s: trust in the Lord and he will provide bread, etc. . . .

Sometimes the preacher is a little more guarded and includes a let-out clause. For instance, after reiterating the usual message that if the labouring classes make religion and the care of their immortal souls their first concern, all other needful things will follow, the speaker[13] admits there may be exceptions here and there for God's wise purposes, but that the promise would generally be made good. Others include other caveats. For instance: if we are trying to love God, no evil can befall us, and we shall want no manner of thing that is good; but it is God who judges what is good for us. In some sort all things are ours, but we may have nothing as the world judges. The man of faith has all the consolations that he requires. We shall want for nothing which it is good for us to receive. Orphans were told that the Almighty parent who had already given them a lot (i.e. life, and his own son) will freely give them all things that are essential to their real felicity if they believe in him. Our temporal wants may not be satisfied because we have not earnestly sought the aid of God and forsaken sin, or because God judges certain temporal gifts to be bad for us. Others were more sceptical about the Lord providing for the living, and stressed rather that if tribulations were borne properly, rewards would come hereafter, or that we should not worry about property because this is not our home: ours is in the heavens.

Another frequently expounded doctrine was that wealth and honours in this world are mere trifles of the hour, though (as usual) the possessor of earthly distinctions should be respected. What is the famine of the body when compared with the famine of the soul? The Rev. J.C. Ryle said in 1857 he knew many of his working-class audience did not know how to make both ends meet because they were poor, but he tried to reassure them by adding that all that happens to the body is comparatively nil. The body is merely a lodging for an immortal tenant. The Holy Spirit is the best thing which God has to give. There are worse things than poverty, e.g. temptation. Your spiritual birthright is a better possession than diamonds or gold, better than all the prizes of this world, because it endures, working men were told by Bishop Wilberforce in 1870. Riches and honours are perishable vanities which we cannot carry away with us when we die. In time of death, what is the use of money? Wealth is as nothing: a moment may snatch the golden bauble from our grasp. Riches cannot prolong life. It was felt that efforts to improve the housing of the working classes were not as important as seeing that they had a Bible in the home and the gospel in their hearts. A congregation was urged to contribute to church building because acts for feeding the soul are more pleasing to God than acts of charity to the body. The latter only affected the perishable, whereas providing churches affected the immortal part of men: their benefits are eternal, those of worldly charities only transient. Good deeds to advance religion promote the best interest of our fellow beings: whatever view we take of men, the instructions and comforts of Christianity are the best benefits that we can provide for them. The poor man's greatest need of all is of a better life hereafter.

The responses to his condition which are inculcated on the poor man follow logically from these views on poverty and riches. He should not try to change his lot: people should be educated to bear their poverty

like Christians, living and dying as Christ's poor ones. Nor should he
grumble at his lot: he should go through even biting poverty without
murmur. Neither should he envy rich or more prosperous persons.
Indeed he should not be angry even if men less in need than him are the
recipients of bounty, for a man's property is his to dispose of as he
likes. One preacher[14] admitted it was hard not be discontented under
poverty and distress, but advised the poor to direct their anger rather at
their own lack of godliness in not loving their neighbours. They should
not even be angry that some ungodly people do better than them, for
this would show distrust of God. The poor have much to be thankful
for. They should think of all the things God has given them, and not of
what they lack. Hugh Stowell, Canon of Chester, recounted in 1857 in
a sermon for the working classes how he saw a poor stone breaker
doing long and heavy work, and how at first he thought what a dreary
life he had. But then he realised that if the man broke stones in the
faith of Christ and peace of God, if he did it as doing his duty in the
state of life in which it had pleased God to call him, if he did it heartily
as to the Lord and not to men, then he had none to envy. Not only
should the poor man not envy the rich: he should sympathise with them,
for they have more anxieties than the poor, and indeed the poor man
will forget his own burdens in sympathising with the rich man.
Moreover if they fret at their lot, they will lose the benefit of its
discipline. If the poor have inward, spiritual peace, balm has been shed
over their souls which will preserve them from being galled and fretted
by the petty rubs of life. Even if God takes things away from us, we
must not complain, as they are not ours but his. Those who have lost
money and will sink to poverty should remember that Christ tasted a
far more bitter draught: this should be an antidote which can impose
sweetness in a bitter cup. In the 1870s there is more emphasis on the
notion that it is permissible for working men to want to have some
comforts, like a reasonable house and some leisure, but nevertheless
they are often urged not to be interested in material things. In any case
a man earning fifty shillings a week had in his command all that goes
to make the happiness and dignity and worth of human life, Bishop
Fraser told working men at Sheffield in 1878: no man ever made his
life really richer or brighter or happier by surrounding himself with
artificial wants and superfluous luxury.

Private Afflictions

Other afflictions besides poverty, such as sorrows, pain, madness, were
also sent by God. This was the standard doctrine. Even in the 1870s

trials are declared to be under the direct and immediate control of God and not arbitrarily dispensed; strictly speaking there is no such thing as an accident. God knows to whom he sends chastisement, why and what he sends, and exactly how far to go in sending us sorrows. Even if, as is sometimes suggested, we bring some troubles on ourselves, they may be used by God as instruments of Divine Providence.

Why does God send these afflictions? Sometimes they are said to be punishments for sin or at least in some general way the result of sin — even lunacy may be a visitation of anger; but this doctrine is much commoner in relation to public than to private disasters. The most frequently advanced theory to explain private afflictions is that they are good for people and that God has sent them to make men more holy. Thus he permits men to suffer in order to try both them and us. All our sufferings are sent to us by God with a merciful design, to wean our hearts from earthly goods; if poverty, sickness, sorrow or bereavement make us lovers of God, then God sends us these afflictions which are really blessings. He is doing this for the good of our souls. Conversely, seeming blessings are real curses if we love not God. Orphans were told that it was the merciful intention of God that their hearts should be made better by the loss of their parents and home. By reverses and trials on earth, God purifies our souls for heaven. The Christian who has been tried will admit that the cares and sorrows of life are productive of good, making him humble. Every sorrow can be made the means of sanctification. One learns about Christ through illness, a sick parishioner was told. We need afflictions as much as the child needs the rod; they are for our profit that we may be made partakers of God's holiness. Sometimes the idea that afflictions improve people is qualified: thus Bishop Hamilton declared in 1859 that it is only the good man who is made better by afflictions; bad men are made worse by them; they become more fretful, more selfish, more careful about their bodily wants and less able to apprehend the love of God. He also admitted that it was more difficult to connect any blessing with lunacy, and his doubts are understandable since he was preaching in a lunatic asylum. But the more usual view is that all forms of trial lead to blessed results, and that affliction is 'the best prosperity'.

Whether afflictions are punishments or sent to make us holier, they are signs of God's love for us. Thus even if you lose child after child or your wife, even if your affairs are in ruin, or your body is a burden and you are a loathsome spectacle like Job, nevertheless take these scourgings as a seal and pledge of God's love. It is gracious and conde-scending of God to take the trouble to afflict us with pain. Divine chastisements, e.g. poverty, bodily sickness, bereavements, are proofs of God's love for his children; they show that we are objects of his paternal regard. We may not understand God's dealings with us, indeed how should we? But even if we have suffered blow after blow we must not think God has forgotten to be gracious. Indeed afflictions are often sent in the greatest number to those whom God loves most; they are special marks of his favour. To die early is not a mark of divine displeasure, but perhaps rather of divine favour. Every sorrow is sent in mercy. The Christian knows that all God's dealings with him are kind and right.

It follows of course from these views on the origin and purpose of afflictions that the sufferer should either be thankful and rejoice at his suffering, or that he should at least be resigned to it and not complain. Afflictions are to be borne by Christians as occasions for rejoicing, particularly if they will see troubles as warnings to set their house in order, or as intimations that this world is not their home. They should be thankful for trials because Christ was made perfect through suffering. Even orphans should rejoice for they are partakers in Christ's sufferings. Afflictions, though painful, demand our warmest thanks, for they produce conformity to the divine image. As God uses worldly trials and disappointments to lead us to Christ, we have a very good reason to be thankful for these dealings with him, painful as they may be at the time. Trials sent by God are more advantageous than prosperity and ease. We should be grateful that God makes even afflictions and trials ministers of his mercy by preparing us for heaven and teaching us to love Jesus. Since sorrows to the religious mind are channels of blessing, we should thank God for them. In any case we all enjoy much more and suffer much less than we deserve.

Some preachers, perhaps sensing that gratititude would not come easily to the sufferer, put more stress on the Christian doctrine of resignation. For instance, as he does not know whether it is best for him to be delivered from his troubles or to remain as he is, he should submit to God's choice. Indeed everything that happens, happens well. Another reason for submission is that pain is deserved to the full, or that it does not equal Christ's. We should not look on suffering as an unkind and unaccountable interference with our happiness. On the contrary we should humbly bow to the rod which deals its strifes in this life in the hope that thereby we may be spared in the next. One reason for being resigned and submissive is that this may bring us a proportionate reward. But very often the exhortation is simply the general one to be content in whatever state we are. In any case sufferers are often told that they shall be delivered out of whatever troubles they may have. Thus the inmates of an infirmary were informed that the heavenly physician is never sought in vain. Similarly the congregation at Westminster Abbey in a special sermon for the working classes was told in 1858 by the preacher[15] that he had in trust to dispense to all a medicine which could heal all sickness, a specific for any case of threatening death; and that God's remedy could meet and satisfy any necessity. Preaching at a special evening service at St Paul's in 1864, Christopher Wordsworth, a Canon of Westminster, assured his audience that if we love the word of the Bible nothing can harm us. At another such service in 1865, Bishop Tait in a sermon on *The assurance of divine succour* exhorted his congregation to wait on the Lord in all anxieties, public and private: the conviction of his presence and of his readiness to succour will be our greatest security; God's merciful dealings in the past are the assurance of his trustful care for the future. A sick and apparently dying parishioner was told by her clergyman[16] that God would take better care of her children than she could, and that there was nothing to stay for on earth except disappointment, sickness, poverty, danger and sin. The recipient of this advice must incidentally have been disappointed to survive, as she did, for nearly fifty years more.

Public Disasters

A similar line was taken in relation to general, public disasters as to ones affecting particular individuals, though there is much more emphasis on their being judgements on sin, and punishments, rather than blessings. Because these disasters usually hit the poorer classes more severely than the middle and upper classes, it was possible for the clergy to see them as potential instruments of social control, and to use them as opportunities to lecture the lower ranks of the nation on the need both to put up with their fate resignedly and to lead a more godly life.

The standard doctrine was that disasters such as the cholera, famines, wars, the Indian mutiny, trade depressions, the cotton famine, the cattle plague and any other pestilence were sent by God because of sin — that is as punishments for sins, or as warnings to people to behave better. The precise sins committed are not always specified, but sometimes they are. Thus economic distress in 1830 was attributed to national ungodliness and the non-observance of the Sabbath, and distress among the agricultural classes was said to be an affliction from heaven because they refused to pay tithes. In 1832 economic troubles were attributed to the sacrifice of religion at the shrine of liberalism. The cholera in 1831-2 was said to be due to the existence of sedition, disorders, demonstrations, violence, infidelity, heresy, schism, the encouragement of Maynooth College, profanation of the Sabbath, licentiousness, drunkenness and swearing. The year 1848 was the occasion of a similar outbreak of pronouncements: the main sin mentioned was the division of the nation into two parties, rich and poor. This would not only bring civil strife, which was of course a reasonable view, but also war, famines, earthquakes, etc. At the time of the Irish famine, many said that the toleration of Romanism in England was the sin for which the nation was being punished, though others threw in the usual ones of blasphemy, disregard of the Sabbath, covetousness, idleness and the setting aside of parental authority. At some of the services for the working classes in Westminster Abbey in 1859, their sins are only alluded to in a general way, e.g. lack of spirituality and revolting against God, though the punishments likely to follow are detailed: drought, famine, earthquakes, volcanoes, tornadoes and hurricanes. The cattle plague of 1865-6 was constantly declared to be a judgement on sin, a punishment sent by God because we have sinned as a nation and individually. Indeed we merit more punishment than we get. Calamities are God's way of disciplining us. Thus they are useful: the cholera for example convinces us of sin and stirs up compassion towards the sick. It is sent for our good, out of love for our precious souls. Pestilence too is sent by divine mercy for our good. It were better for us to live always amid the ravages of famine than in a luxuriant land where there were none to ask pity. Moreover fear of famine makes people work. Although the mid-century cholera epidemic killed both the holy and the wicked, we must nevertheless be thankful for it, the preacher[17] declared in St James' Church, Westminster, in 1854, because many have been moved to think of holy words when dying. The fact that sanitation had been improved and that it availed nothing showed that the pestilence was the will of God.

War

There was not much occasion to make pronouncements about the attitude Christians should take to wars until the 1850s, though remarks in passing were sometimes made about the Napoleonic Wars, usually to the effect that the Lord had caused right to triumph over wrong. The Crimean War for obvious reasons caused much heart-searching, but few, if any, of the Church of England clergy denounced it, or war in general. Many of them felt bound to tackle the question whether wars in general and in particular this war were lawful, but they all seem to have come down firmly against what one of them[18] called 'pretenders to a treacherous peace theory'. It was wrong to think that war of every kind was forbidden by the gospel. Indeed war in general was declared to be lawful, which is not astonishing as wars were usually also declared to be due to God's providence for the working out of his wise and gracious purposes, and therefore to lead ultimately to good. Some preachers admitted that war was nasty leading as it did to a lot of suffering, but it is much more usual to find them emphasising the benefits of wars, such as an increased sense of responsibility and a more active knowledge and love of God, rather than dwelling on the horrors which wars entail. The Crimean War specifically was justified on various grounds: e.g. that it was being waged to defend the weak against oppression, that it was a war in defence of the British Empire, and that our victory would, or at least might, result in the conversion of Moslems to Christianity.

The justification of wars which would help to spread the gospel was much in evidence in relation to India in the late 1850s. We should hold India for God; if we neglect our charge, we shall draw down his judgement on us. God delivered India to the English in order that she could be converted, but this arrangement does not conflict with our national interests: indeed our position as a nation depends for the most part on our colonial possessions, and of these our Indian Empire is the most important. The Indian war was also justified on the ground that war is beneficial to everyone, for it recalls a truth often forgotten, namely that the course of the world is not ruled by chance, but by the governance of a living and almighty God. It also makes us think about our national sins, in this case in particular how we have neglected to bestow on India the choicest blessing which we ourselves enjoy, namely our religious faith.

Political Doctrines

Many clergymen were willing to make pronouncements on the fundamental classic problems connected with political obligation. Thus they expressed views on such questions as the source of authority, what makes government legitimate, the duties of subjects and (less frequently) the duties of rulers, and good and bad forms of government.

The usual message was as follows. Government is an ordinance of the Almighty. It is not of human origin, not a device of man, but of God. It would be wrong to think that the organised society in which one finds oneself was the creation of man, framed to meet the exigencies of his circumstances; on the contrary the world of mankind as it is, society in its conventional forms and in all its civil and domestic institutions was created by God and is part of his divine purpose. The machinery of society is approved by him. One preacher[19] in 1842 castigated the sects for not believing in the divine right of kings, or in the divine appointment of governments. The authority of civil sovereigns is direct from God himself. As civil government in general proceeds from God, any *de facto* civil government does so too. Rulers therefore are ministers of God; they have had powers delegated to them to administer the affairs of man. Indeed all people in any form of authority have had power providentially confided to them. They are accountable to God, not to their subjects. The judge for instance recognises God as the author and source of his authority, for there is no power but of God.

It follows from this analysis of the source of authority that subjects owe their governments unquestioning reverence. As the constituted authorities are ministers of heaven, they must be honoured. We owe our government and the magistrates an unfeigned respect and an affectionate regard. Indeed we should respect everyone in power however wicked they are, for God may permit the wicked to be in authority to mark more conspicuously the Christian's duty.

Even more emphasis is put on the need to obey the 'powers that be', namely those whom one finds in positions of authority. Nor should they be expected to give reasons for their decisions. Some preachers go so far as to see value in obedience in itself, and not in its object; but it is more usual for some goal such as the maintenance of order or of the *status quo* or of religion to be at least implied. In either case the message is clear: in resisting the administrators of civil government, one is resisting an ordinance of Christ; and *per contra* one manifests obedience to God by obedience to the authorities that are ordained by him. In any case all submission to authority is beyond dispute a Christian duty.

Occasionally the question whether there are any exceptions to these precepts is asked. One preacher[20] said that if a bad man fills an office, our respect is due to the office rather than to the man; he also admitted that the commands of rulers are sometimes opposed to the commands of God, in which case God is to be obeyed rather than man. But it is much more usual to find expressed the view that there is a duty to submit to even the worst of governments, sometimes because this is a chastisement or punishment of the Lord, but more often because any other doctrine would endanger the social order, or simply because the Bible offers no support for the contrary view.

One marked feature of all these pronouncements is that the religious principle is the only solid foundation of civil obedience. This was of course a dangerous doctrine in that the state might well be weakened if people lost their religious beliefs; it might have been wiser to base political obligation on secular considerations. But the expounders of this view were convinced that the word of God,i.e. religion, was the surest support and preservative of a state; and they felt that they were strengthening the social and political system by teaching that obedience to the law was a duty not merely to any human authorities but to God himself, or, as some put it, that one should submit to every ordinance of man for the Lord's sake.

But it is not only obedience to the government and the law which is enjoined. Echoing Hobbes — though surely without knowing it — they taught that one should not speak evil of those in authority. One should not resist by word or deed. Whatever be the form of government under which we live, the obligation of Christians is not to criticise or disturb it. The man who is a noisy,forward denouncer of society's manifest wrongs will not go to heaven whereas the quiet waiting sufferer will. Even murmuring is constantly rebuked. Working men were told by Bishop Wilberforce at the Church Congress of 1870 that they should not prate about their grievances. People who criticise the authorities are goaded by ambition, self-interest and self-love and are anxious merely to enrich themselves.

This leads into a general denunciation of the spirit of innovation and of anyone who advocates change: whatever is new must necessarily be false. Religion can strengthen the hands of a government by denouncing desires for change and by urging men to be contented with their lot. Complacency is specifically praised. The best Christian is the best patriot, and patriotism appears to mean supporting and preserving the *status quo.* Christianity is against restless desires for change. In any case, why should people desire to change things, since our laws are excellent in their origin, and the spotless purity of their administration is equally admirable? For the law of England extends its protection to all: it protects a man from any severer punishment than his sentence inflicts; it visits him in prison to look after his health and treatment, and takes not the conveniences of life utterly from him: thus it would protect the criminal on his way to execution from being torn to pieces by the mob. Another preacher[21] declared in 1836 that our kings are gracious, our governments lenient and our institutions free. And even allowing for the principle of *de mortuis nihil nisi bonum*, it was going rather far to describe George

IV as 'one of the greatest monarchs that ever sat on England's throne'.[22] In the 1830s much was made of the fact that slavery was unknown in England: the labourer could change his master whenever he pleased, unless bound to him for a term, and a slave who came here would be set free. Other privileges mentioned were freedom of worship and the fact that the government supported religion. There is no real grievance in England, the speaker[23] declared at an assize sermon in Liverpool in March 1848; for here the powers that be exist for the protection and well-being of the people.

When it comes to discussing particular forms of government, the range of views expressed is predictably narrow. Monarchy is of course generally praised; indeed one writer[24] went so far as to declare that monarchy alone in strict truth is government and that theoretically at least it is most perfect when most absolute. Some believed in the divine right of kings. American republicanism in particular is deplored. But the greatest effort is put into denouncing democracy. The case against democracy is seldom argued, though at times it is linked with dissent, for democracy would it was feared lead to the disestablishment of the church. More often the poor are simply told that they cannot play a part in the making or administration of the laws; or the idea that the people ought to be consulted is ridiculed. The labouring classes should not busy themselves in the concerns of the state: God does not require them to attend to these; they should do their own business not the nation's. A Christian is a subject of him whose kingdom is not of this world. He is a stranger and a pilgrim on earth, a citizen of a heavenly country. He can therefore have but little concern with the management of states and empires. The less he attempts to interfere in matters which are too high for him the better. By the 1870s, the emphasis is rather different: it is obviously felt necessary to move with the times. So whilst nothing is usually said in support of an extension of the franchise, stress is laid on the fact that the Church of England is the most democratic body in the land, not in 'the miserable sense' of democracy which is prevalent, but in the true sense of that word, namely that it believes in the brotherhood of man. The church is also said to be democratic because one can rise in it. Others go further and claim that Christianity is the only truly democratic religion the world has ever known, because it offers religion freely to all; moreover it gives all needful power, namely the love of God, to the working man.

Some of these political attitudes stem from distrust of independent thought and the unrestricted use of man's reason. Hostility to free thought was very common. Lust for independence of thought and action is declared to be a part of our fallen nature. If people judge things by their own reason, the result will be a reckless course in social and civil life. Submission of the intellect to dogmatic truth is recommended: it is wrong to consider the opinions of man as of more authority than the decrees of God. In the 1830s many preachers reveal anxiety about contemporary trends in the education of artisans: Satan is leading them to entertain questions which bear neither upon their station in this life nor upon their destinies in a better; the increased appetite for worldly knowledge brings vanity and self-delusion to the possessor. In the 1870s it is more usual to find reassurances such as that the gospel does not wish the working man to be undertaught, and that God is no favourer of ignorance; but even so it is clear that it is spiritual not secular knowledge which is regarded as the best for him. Liberal and enlarged views are denounced; the minds of men are afloat upon a wide sea of opinion without a pilot. Hence the church is the best educator, because she gives no licence to each teacher to disseminate his own notions. A preacher[25] before the University of Oxford in 1848 pronounced controversy to be bad, dangerous for the old, and even worse for the young, 'for God has formed their minds to believe and to obey'; they should be reared in an atmosphere of peace, sitting in docility at the feet of Truth and Law; if they presume to become arbiters of truth, what form of social or moral life can survive such a reversal of its primary laws?

Churchmen often talked about liberty and said things like 'the gospel will bring liberty to the people', but it was not liberty in the ordinary sense which they had in mind. For instance the standard liberties, such as liberty of the press and of movement, and trial by jury, were denounced at a Westminster Abbey sermon for the working classes in 1858;[26] and the line was taken that even political slavery was only 'outward' and temporary, involving as it did subjection only of the body; the most exalted freedom of the soul was compatible with it. The slave after all becomes free for ever at death, whereas the slavery of sin is a far worse fate, for it allows no hope. This was understandably a common theme in sermons against drunkenness: men should not harp on freedom from public evils which exist only in their imagination; they should realise that the severest and most tyrannical of all slavery is the tyranny of vice.

Work and Recreations

As one might expect, much emphasis was put on the importance of work, especially of hard work. In order presumably to sweeten the pill, work was elevated in various ways. For instance it was declared to be worship. We should not toil and slave only in order to eat and drink, but because it is God's will that we should do so. Work and labour are instances of the gracious action of Divine Providence in arranging this world. Daily work was a display of God's goodness and power. The fact that Christ was born into the lot of a working man had elevated manly labour and hard work in this our preparatory condition even if nothing else had. So work is glorious. God has ordained that anything which is great and useful in this world shall be attained by hard work. No other book dignifies labour as does the Bible. The work done by even the poorest classes is as great and dignified if they are working honestly as if they were ruling an empire.

However one could not toil absolutely all the time, and indeed it was admitted that a holiday was needed in order to come back to work cheerfully; so views were expressed on how much leisure the working classes should be allowed, and on what recreations were and were not approved. In the 1830s one day a year free from toil was regarded as adequate by a preacher[27] talking to certain Friendly Societies, and even then he cautioned them to be moderate in their festivities. Later on, in the 1860s, some people recommended rather more holidays because if the poor only had one once or twice a year, they got too excited and committed all manner of excesses. But in 1872 Samuel Wilberforce was still playing safe: it was important, he considered, to get more leisure hours for the working man from a physical point of view and also for his family and for his intellectual and spiritual well-being. But it was no use having extra leisure if this was spent in dissipation: better by far that the working man should not have hours of leisure than that he should have them to lower his moral and intellectual condition. Another cleric[28] at the Church Congress of 1869 was prepared to admit that amusement was necessary to man, though he was sure sorrow was better than laughter.

Some recreations came in for constant criticism, particularly country fairs which were considered to propagate vice, namely drunkenness and immorality, and to be seasons of imminent peril to the moral and spiritual interests of the young of both sexes. Even special fast days ordered by authority in times of national distress were allegedly turned into days of mere pleasure hunting if not of actual revelry. Others decried racing and excursion trains, particularly because they generated too much excitement and feverish unrest. Indeed criticism was levelled at all places where people congregated in crowds and got excited and possibly drunk, e.g. the theatre, music halls, dancing halls and even lecture halls, concerts and free libraries. Some of the clergy were worried about all indoor recreations except those which took place in the home. They complained that even penny readings and musical entertainments held in many parishes often became coarse and embarrassing for the chairman. Important though it was that the aristocracy should be pure and full of high aspirations, it was ten thousand times more important that the working classes should be so, for they were the marrow of the nation, Bishop Fraser declared in 1874.

In the place of these dangerous and degrading activities, the clergy recommended healthful invigorating manly amusements, especially ones which could take place out of doors. Cricket was considered the best, for as one speaker[29] put it at the Church Congress of 1869, 'the salt of good manners, good morals, and every manly virtue is to be found in the cricket field, and gives a tone to every good cricketer'. It was often stressed that the upper classes and even the clergy should join in the sports and pastimes of the people, partly to keep their minds under the control of the fear and love of God and to prevent coarseness and corruption, and partly because it would promote respect on the part of the working classes towards their natural leaders. But some felt doubtful about participation by the clergy. For as the Dean Close declared in 1866, the parish clergyman should appear dignified and grave; 'When his people meet him on the following Sunday in the House of God, it cannot promote their respect or reverence for his office or his work, to remember that he was bowled out at cricket by the parish clerk, or suffered at football from the hobnailed shoes of one of his humbler parishioners.' There was general agreement that dancing in particular should be supervised: English country dances were mostly considered safe because they did not involve pushing, kissing or squeezing, and Scotch reels were commended because they gave 'the maximum of disciplined exercise with the minimum of familiarity'.[30]

Advice to Other Classes

Very much less advice was given to the middle and upper classes than to the lower, and few sermons were addressed specifically to the rich.

However certain themes recur. Riches are sometimes considered dangerous because they arouse envy, hatred and revenge amongst poorer people or increase the worldliness of the poor, or because they encourage pride in the owner and cut God out of his thoughts. But others clearly found it difficult to condemn money making and prosperity in the mid-nineteenth century. So they said that wealth came in answer to prayer and as a gift of God's rich providence if people behaved well; that commerce and money making are of divine appointment, as they existed before the fall, and that they may be perfectly holy; and that one could be rich and good. And obviously if one believed, as most of them did, in stations in life and the value of inequality, one could not suggest that religion forbade what the Professor of Divinity at Dublin referred to in 1845 as 'that moderated and well directed attention to our worldly interests which the duties of our different stations require'.[31]

Most effort was therefore devoted not to discussing whether it was all right or not to accumulate wealth, but to what one should or should not do with what wealth one possessed. Here the main exhortation was to use it to minister to the spiritual needs of the poor; even if one gave to relieve temporal distress one should so give as to keep one's fellowmen from going astray. In practical terms this meant chiefly contributions to church building and education. At a Westminster Abbey sermon for the working classes in 1858, the richer members of the audience were told that they should be charitable: this meant getting their poorer brethren to fill the churches.[32]

The purposes of giving were often discussed. It was frequently said to be some benefit to the giver, if he did it from the right motives, that is out of love of God. This might be a benefit of a moral or spiritual nature, or of a material kind: the Christian giver is blessed in body and substance, preserved in health and in life and delivered from the will of his enemies. Do not charitable families always prosper? one preacher asked.[33] His answer was that they gained more than they gave away. Moreover gifts by the rich to buildings such as hospitals and almshouses would foster kindly dispositions towards the wealthier ranks. And even the more prosperous might suffer some misfortune at a later date and need for instance an asylum for the aged. One did not have to be a Scot to point out that God asks us not to give but to lend: and the loan will be repaid.

It is not difficult to understand why the authorities were anxious that the working classes should go to church, nor why many of them did not.

Notes

1. The language and phrases of the authors have been reproduced as closely as possible in order to give the flavour of contemporary thought; but it was not considered that any useful purpose would be served by attributing every statement to a particular person, partly because the views expressed often represent the conflation of many sources. For further particulars of the works mentioned in footnotes, reference should be made to the bibliography.
2. W.R. Clark.
3. H. Birley.
4. R. Armitage.
5. Sermon VII in Anon., *Seven Plain Sermons.*
6. W.R. Clark.
7. S. Best.
8. J. Miller, 1831.
9. Ellell.
10. H. Stowell.
11. H. Goodwin.
12. A.Hare.
13. J. Miller, 1831.
14. A. Hare.
15. C.J.P. Eyre.
16. A.W. Thorold, 1850.
17. J.H. Thomas.
18. R.W. Plumptre.
19. Anon., *Sermons for the Times.*
20. W.M. Dudley.
21. S. Best.
22. W.B. James.
23. S.B. Sellers.
24. Sermon III in Anon., *Parochial Sermons . . .*
25. W. Sewell.
26. G. Moberley.
27. R. Pearson.
28. J.C. Chambers.
29. W. Glaister.
30. J.E. Clarke.
31. Prof. C.R. Elrington, rector of Armagh. Sermon published 1845.
32. C.B. Scott.
33. Anon., *Expository outlines. . .*

Bibliography

Beneath are listed the sources on which this chapter is based. The items are all sermons, and their authors are all in Holy Orders, unless otherwise indicated.

The places mentioned show where the sermon was delivered when this is known.

Ackland, T.G. Bishopsgate, London. 14 April 1833.

Alcester Clerical Meetings: Minutes of the Alcester Clerical Association, 1842-60. ed. R. Seymour and J.F. MacKarness. 1862.

Allen, John. 'The way to comfort under Trial' in *Practical Sermons by Dignitaries and other Clergymen of the United Church of England and Ireland,* vol. III. 1846.

Alsop, James. Westhoughton, Lancs. 1858.

Anon. Christian Politics. 1826-1830. Printed in Colchester, (Pusey House, Oxford).

Anon. 'Daniel and his three friends'. *Seven Plain Sermons,* by the author of 'Plain preaching to poor people'. 1872. sp. Sermons nos. II, VI and VII.

Anon. 'Duties inseparable from privileges' in *Practical sermons adapted to the course of the Christian Year,* Part I. 1844.

Anon. *Expository Outlines: sketches and skeletons of sermons upon the most important paragraphs of the New Testament.* 1857. sp. sermons on Christian Diligence, Divine Chastisements, Trust in Providence, and Unsanctified Riches.

Anon. 'The Girls of the Period', *Union Review,* 1869.

Anon. *Parochial sermons bearing on the subjects of the day.* 1855. sp. Sermons nos. II and III.

Anon. A plain sermon on the presence of God's judgements in the land. 1831.

Anon. Plain Sermons, vol. I. 1849. 'Christ's Presence in Ordinances' by C.C.S.

Anon. Plain Sermons, vol. I. 1849. 'Love one another' by W.B.F.

Anon. Plain Sermons, vol. I. 1849. 'Meekness' by J.M.C.

Anon. Plain Sermons, vol. I. 1849. 'Our daily bread' by J.A.C.

Anon. Plain Sermons, vol. I. 1849. 'True Trust'.

Anon. 'The pollution of the Temple' in *Sermons for the times, by clergymen of the Church of England.* Second Series. 1842.

Anon. Sermon for the propagation of the gospel. Norwich, 1831.

Anon. Sermon at Spitalfields. 1856. 'The labourer: his toils, sufferings, and hope'.

Anon. *Sermons for the Christian Seasons,* 1853. (a) vol. II, no. 52. (b) vol. III, no. 72.

Anon. *Sermons for the people.* 1848. Nos. 8 and 9.

Anon. *Sermons selected from various sources and arranged for domestic use.* 1851. sp. Sermons Nos. II, IV, V, XIII and XXVI.

Anon. *Sermons for Sunday evenings.* 1872. sp. Sermons on 'The Sanctified uses of Adversity' and on 'An old Disciple'.

Anon. *Sermons for the times, by clergymen of the Church of England.* Second series 1842. 'The pollution of the temple'.

Anon. 'Social Evils and Christian Remedies', *Church of England Monthly Review,* vol. I, July – December 1856. p. 237.

Anon. Three sermons on social duties. 1863.

Armitage, Robert. (Curate of Sellack, Herefordshire.) Common Evils of Drunkenness, 1834.

Baber, Harry. Grosvenor Square, London. 1862.

Bardsley, James. Manchester, 1862.

Baring, Charles (b. of Gloucester). 'The Motives and Rewards of Obedience' in *Sermons for Sundays and some other holydays of the Christain Year,* vol. 2. 1859.

Barry, Dr A. (Princ. Cheltenham College). Ch. Congress, Wolverhampton. 1867.

Barter, William B. (Rector Highclere and Burghclere, Hants.) Winchester Cathedral. 8 July 1844.

Bartholomew, J. St David's, Exeter. August 1848.

Bennett, W.J.E. Knightsbridge, London. 1846.

Berens, Edward. Sermon preached before Special Commissioners at Aylesbury, Bucks., 10 January 1831, and in Salisbury Cathedral. 'The Christian's duty in turbulent times'.

Best, Samuel. Abbotts Ann. Hants. 1836.

Bickersteth, R. (b. of Ripon). Church Congress, Leeds. 1872.

Birley, Hugh (MP) Church Congress, Leeds. 1872.

Blomfield, C.J. (b. of London). St Martin's in the Fields, London. 18 February 1838.

Blunt, Henry. Sloane Street, Chelsea. 4 July 1830.

Borton, W.L. (Rector of Wickham St Paul, Essex). Sermon preached at St Giles, Cripplegate. 25 June 1837.

Bowdler, Thomas. Sydenham, Kent. 7 September 1834.

Boyd, A.K.H.Counsel and comfort spoken from a City Pulpit, Nos. II and XIII. 1863.

Brandreth,H.R.T., *Dr Lee of Lambeth.* London 1951.

Bridge, Stephen (Rector, Droxford, Winchester). In *Twelve Parochial Sermons*. ed. by J.S. Utterton, Archdeacon of Surrey, 1868.

Browne R.G.S., Vicar of Atwick (Yorks). Sermon on a Shipwreck. 3 November 1844.

Burgon, John William. Oxford. 15 October 1865.

Burrows, H.W. *Sermons for Sundays and some other holydays of the Christian Year.* Vol. I, no. 22. 1858.

Butler, William John. *Twenty-five Sermons for working men.* pub. 1847. Delivered at Ware Herts. 1844-6. Nos. 23 and 24.

Cadman, William. Marylebone, London. 1861.

Calvert, Frederick. Whatfield, Suffolk. 1835.

Carpenter, Henry. Liverpool. October 1862.

Carpenter, William. Manchester, 10 April 1862.

Cator, Charles. Carshalton, Surrey. July 1832.

Cator, Charles. Beckenham, Kent. 12 August 1832.

Cattermole, Richard. Brixton. January 1831.

Chambers, John Charles. Church Congress, Liverpool, 1869.

Champnes, Charles. Langley, Bucks. 5 December 1830.

Champneys, W.W. Exeter Hall. Sermon for the working classes. 1857.

Champneys, W.W. St Paul's special evening Services. 1865.

Chenevix-Trench, R. Itchen Stoke, Hants. 1845.

Clark, W.R. (Rector of Taunton) Ch. Congress, Southampton, 1870.

Clarke, J. Erskine. (Priest, Derby.) *Plain papers on the Social Economy of the People.* 1853.

Clarke, J. Erskine, Church Congress, Liverpool. 1869.

Clarke, W.B. Blandford, Dorset. 9 December 1832.

Clarke, W.B. Poole, Dorset. May 1834. Published with alterations 1838.

Close, F. (dean of Carlisle). Church Congress, York, 1866.

Conybeare, W.D. Cardiff Assizes. 28 February 1834.

Conybeare, W.D. Sully, Glam. 1837.

Coxe, R.C. St James, Piccadilly, London. 1838.

Cresswell, Daniel. Enfield, Middlesex. 5 December 1830.

Cunningham, J.W. *Sermons for Sundays and some other holydays of the Christian Year.* Vol. I, no. 17. 1858.

Dale, Thomas. St Paul's Cathedral Special Services. 1859.

Daniel, John. Sennen, Cornwall. June 1837.

Davies, C.M. London Sermons. 1875. One on 'Gulfs', one on 'Dress'.

Dudley, W.M. Poole, Dorset. 10 January 1836.

Durnford, Richard (b. of Chichester.) Ch. Congress, Brighton 1874.

Edge, William John. Nayland, Suffolk. 1838.

Ellell. *The Life Militant: Plain sermons for cottage meetings* 1879. sp. Sermons Nos. I, VI and XV.

Elliott, Edward B. Brighton. 14 February 1830.

Ely, Archdeacon of Ch. Congress, Bristol 1864.

Eyre, C.J.P. Westminster Abbey Sermons for the Working Classes. 31 January 1858.

Faber, George Stanley. Durham. 29 July 1832.

Feilden, Randle Henry. Walton-le-Dale, Lancs. 9 January 1831.

Fowle, Fulwar W. Assize sermon, Salisbury. 22 July 1832.

Fowle, Fulwar. Amesbury, Wilts. 1836.

Fraser, James. Oxford. 27 March 1853.

Fraser, James (b. of Manchester). Church Congress, Leeds. 1872.

Fraser, James (b. of Manchester). Church Congress, Brighton, 1874.

Fraser, James (b. of Manchester). Church Congress, Sheffield, 1878.

Garbett, Thomas. Deptford, Kent. 20 May 1832.

Garnett, Edward. Gray's Inn Road, London. 10 May 1853.

George, Aubrey. Female Orphan Asylum. 10 May 1846. In *Practical Sermons by dignitaries and other clergymen of the United Church of England and Ireland.* 3 vols. 1844-6., Vol. 3, 1846.

Gifford, J.G. Ripley, Derbyshire. 8 April 1838.

Girdlestone, Charles. Sedgley, Staffs. 14 November 1830.

Girdlestone, Charles, Sedgley, Staffs. 1832.

Glaister, William. (Curate of Southwell, Notts.) Church Congress, Liverpool, 1869.

Goodwin, Harvey. St Paul's Cathedral Special Services, 1859.

Gorst, J.E. (Mr).Church Congress, Brighton. 1874.

Gutch, Charles. All Saints, St Margaret's Street, London. 1863.

Hale, Mathew B. Wootton-under-Edge, Glos. 18 August 1839.

Hamilton, Walter K. (b. of Salisbury). Fisherton Lunatic Asylum. 26 May 1859.

Hannah, J. (Vicar, Brighton). St Paul's Cathedral. 1874.

Hare, Augustus William. *Sermons to a Country Congregation,* 1836. (a) vol. I. A visitation sermon. 12 July 1831. (b) vol. II, nos. I, II and XV.

Hare, Augustus William. *Miscellaneous Sermons to a Country Congregation.* 4th ed. 1839. Sermons given c.1829-34. sp. Sermons Nos. I, II, XVIII and XXIV in vol. I.

Harris, S. Bache. Ewell, Surrey. 7 October 1857.

Harwood, George (Mr).Church Congress, Bath, 1873.

Hedgeland, Philip. Penzance, Cornwall. 1860.

Henderson, J.T. Sermon No. 10 in *Plain sermons on various subjects by Clergymen of the Church of England.* Vol. II,1858.

Harvey, Ld. C.A. (b. of Bath and Wells). Taunton 1872.

Hessey, F. 'The imperfect sympathy of man with man' in *Sermons for Sundays and some other holydays of the Christian Year.* Vol. 2. 1859.

Hicks, J. Piddletrenthide, Dorset. 1843.

Holland, E.W. Church Congress, Southampton, 1870.

Holland, Francis J. Westminster Abbey. 1 May 1859.

How, W.W. St James, Piccadilly, London. 1874.

Hutton, Francis. 28 August 1831.

Hyslop, William (ed.), *Sermons No. I, II, VII and XXIII in Cheerful Words, Sermons specially adapted for delivery before inmates of lunatic asylums, unions, workhouses, hospitals, gaols, penitentiaries and other public institutions.* 1874.

Jacobson, William (b. of Chester). Church Congress, Liverpool, 1869.

James, John. Oundle, Northants. 11 July 1831.
James, W.B. Woolwich. 1830.
James, W.B. Privett, Hants. 9 January 1831.
Jones, John. St Asaph, Flints. 1846.
Jones, Joshua (Isle of Man). Oxford, 1876.
Kebbell, K. Wistow, Leicestershire. 1830.
Kidd, W.J. Sermon addressed to the Working Classes. Manchester, 1839.
Kidd W.J. St Mathew's Church, Campfield, Manchester. 12 July 1840.
Knox-Little, W.J. Manchester Cathedral. Special Service for the Working Classes.
    2 October 1877.
Lake, W.C. (Dean of Durham). Church Congress, Leeds. 1872.
A lay Churchman. Pamphlet on *Church and Party* 1865 (Denison Collection,
    Pusey House, Oxford).
A lay member of the Church of England. *Three Sermons.* 1873. Sermon no. 1.
Lay Sermons by a member of the legislature. 1865. Sermon on Sorrow.
Lear, Francis, Salisbury. September 1831.
Lee, Alfred T. Finchley, London. 1876.
Lee, Frederick George. *The Church of England and Political Parties.* 1868.
    Letter to Gathorne Hardy.
Liddon, H.P. Knightsbridge, London. 1870.
A London Curate. 1 May 1859.
A London Incumbent. *Simple Sermons after the fashion of the reformers.*
    1853. No. XXI.
Lockwood, E.I. Bedford. 1845.
Lyttelton, W.H. (Rector,Hagley, Worcs.) Church Congress, York, 1866.
Lyttleton, W.H. Church Congress, Stoke-on-Trent, 1875.
MacKarness, J.F. (b. of Oxford).Church Congress, Leeds, 1872.
MacKarness, J.F. (b. of Oxford).Church Congress, Bath, 1873.
McNeile, Hugh M. Liverpool. 28 February 1847.
McNeile, Hugh M. Exeter Hall sermon for the working classes. 1857.
Magee, W.C. (b. of Peterborough).Church Congress, Southampton, 1870.
Maguire, R. Clerkenwell, London. 1863.
Maitland, S.R. Assize Sermon. *In Practical Sermons by dignitaries and other
    clergymen of the United Church of England and Ireland.* 3 vols. 1844-6.
    Vol. 2, 1845.
Marriott, Charles. St Mary's, Oxford. 1853.
Massingberd F.C. South Ormsby, Lincs. 1846.
Melvill, Henry. Camberwell, London. 23 October 1836.
Melvill, Henry. Camberwell, London. 28 January 1838.
Melvill, Henry. Trinity House. 1840.
Melvill, Henry. Trinity House. 1842.
Melvill, Henry. St Martin's in the Fields, London. c. 1844.
Melvill, Henry. Trinity House. 1844.
Melvill, Henry. Liverpool. 1845 or 1846.
Melvill, Henry. Lothbury. 9 April 1853.
Melvill, Henry. 'The reproductive power of human actions' in *Pulpit Eloquence
    of the Nineteenth Century,* 1857.
Miller, John. Thoughts for the labouring classes among Christians, to help them
    towards comfort in both worlds. 1831. (Pamphlet).
Miller, John C. Birmingham. 1854.
Miller, J.C. Exeter Hall Sermon for the working classes. 1857.
Miller, J.C. St Paul's Cathedral Special Services. 1859.
Miller, J.C. Church Congress, Brighton, 1874.
Moberley, George. Westminster Abbey Sermons for the Working Classes. 1858.

Molyneux, J.W.H. Letter to his parishioners in Sudbury, Suffolk. 1855.
Moore, Daniel. Camberwell, London. c. 1865.
Myers, Thomas. St James, Birmingham. 30 July 1837.
Neat, J.W. Clandown, Somerset. 1848.
Nevill, Christopher. E. Grinstead, Sussex. 2 December 1832.
Nolan, Thomas. St George's, Bloomsbury, London. 1858. In Twelve Lent
    Lectures on 'The Signs of the Times'.
A North Wilts. rector. *Sermons*. 1869. Sermons nos. VII and X.
Nugee, George. Letter to Bishop of London. 4 March 1857.
Owen, Edward. Beaumarris, Angelsey Assizes. 29 July 1854.
Oxenden, Montagu. Wingham, Kent. 2 September 1832.
Pearson, Richard. Tunbridge and other Friendly Societies. 1830.
Pennefather, W. St George's, Bloomsbury. London.1858.
Plumptre, R.W. Ferryside, Carmarthenshire. 30 October 1853.
Pusey, E.B. Churches in London. 1837.
Ramsbotham, T. Manchester. 27 March 1862.
Randolph, E.J. (Rector, Dunnington, Yorks.) Church Congress, York, 1866.
Richardson, John. Church Congress, Bath. 1873.
Roberts, George. Holborn, London. 1853.
Roberts, J.L. St George's, Hanover Square, London. 26 November 1854.
Robins, Sanderson. Dover. 26 April 1854.
Robinson, J. Travers. Holborn, London. 1848.
Roe, Henry Farwell. Callington, Cornwall. 26 April 1854.
Rule, W.H. *Religion in its relation to commerce and the ordinary avocations of
    life.* Lectures in City of London. 1852. Preface, pp. V-VI.
Rumsey, J.R. Carlton, Camb. 26 April 1854.
Ryle, J.C. Exeter Hall sermon for the working classes. 1857.
Sadler, M.F. Bedford, 9 March 1866.
Scott, C.B. 'The Scorners of Ephraim'. Westminster Abbey Sermons. 1858.
Scott, John. Hull. 26 April 1854.
Sellers, Samuel Bamford. Liverpool. Assize Sermon. 26 March 1848.
Selwyn, C.A. (b. of Lichfield). Church Congress, Wolverhampton, 1867.
Sewell, William. Chiswick Alms Houses. 1848.
Sewell, William. Oxford. 1848.
Seymour, Richard. Stratford-on-Avon. Whit. Monday 1838.
Sharpe, William. Wells Cathedral. Assize Sermon. 15 August 1830.
Skinner, J. Facts and Opinions concerning Statute Hirings. Pamphlet. 1861.
    (Pusey House, Oxford).
Smith, B.F. Rusthall, Kent. October 1865.
Smith, B.F. Rusthall, Kent. 7 March 1866.
Smith, Percy. Sermon no. 5 in *Plain Sermons on various subjects by Clergymen of
    the Church of England.* Vol. II. 1858.
Somerville, Dudley. Leicestershire Assizes. 13 March 1853.
Soper, John. Crawley, Sussex. 17 May 1868.
Stanley, A.P. Westminster Abbey Sermons for the Working Classes. 2 January
    1859.
Stanley, A.P. Westminster Abbey Sermons for Working People. 24 February 1867.
Stanley, A.P. Sermon to Westminster Volunteers. 22 June 1873.
Stocks, T.F. Highgate, London. June 1857.
Stowell, Hugh. Exeter Hall Sermon for the Working Classes. 1857.
Stowell, Hugh. Westminster Abbey Sermons for the Working Classes. 2nd series.
    1859. No. 10.
Street, B. Grantham, Lincs. June 1854.
Swayne, G. Salisbury, 1866.
Sworde, Th. Thetford, Norfolk. 1845.

Tait, A.C. (b. of London). St.Paul's Special Evening Services. 1865.
Tait, A.C. (Archbishop of Canterbury). City of London.1875.
Thomas, J.H. St James', Westminster. 1854.
Thompson, Henry. Wrington, Somerset. 1831.
Thompson, Henry. Wrington, Somerset. 1832.
Thomson, William. (Archbishop of York). Special evening services at St Paul's,
    London. 1866.
Thomson, William (Archbishop of York). Sheffield, 1878. From Ethel H.
    Thomson, *Life and Letters of William Thomson,* 1919.
Thorold, Anthony W. Letter to a sick parishioner. 1850. In C.H. Simpkinson,
    The Life and Work of Bishop Thorold, London, 1896, pp.20-22.
Thorold, A.W. Sermons preached 1865-1869 in *Selections from the works of
    Bishop Thorold* with preface by the Bishop of Winchester. London, 1897.
Tristram, H.B. Church Congress, Wolverhampton. 1867.
Tuttiett, L. (Curate, Lea-Marston, Coleshill, Warwicks). Church Congress,
    Bristol. 1864.
Tyrwhitt, R. St. J. St Mary Magdalene, Oxford. 1859.
Vaughan, C.J. St Paul's Cathedral Special Services. 1859.
Villiers, H.M. (b. of Carlisle). Westminster Abbey Sermons for the Working
    Classes. 25 April 1858.
Villiers, H.M. (b. of Carlisle).St Paul's Cathedral Special Services. 1859.
Waldegrave, Samuel (b. of Carlisle.) Carlisle. 12 January 1866.
Walker, S.A. Bristol. 1860.
Watson, A. Sermon no. 36 in *Plain Sermons on various subjects by Clergymen
    of the Church of England.* Vol. II 1858.
Wilberforce, S. (b. of Oxford). Church Congress, Wolverhampton, 1867.
Wilberforce, S. (b. of Winchester). Church Congress, Southampton, 1870.
Wilberforce, S. (b. of Winchester). Church Congress, Leeds, 1872.
Wilding, James. Assize Sermon. Carmarthen. 1830.
Wilson, Richard. Mariners' Church, Liverpool. 13 November 1831.
Woodford, J.R. (Vicar of Kempsford, Glos.) Westminster Abbey Sermons
    for the Working Classes. 27 June 1858.
Woodford, James R. (Vicar of Leeds). Church Congress, Leeds, 1872.
Woodhouse, F.C. Manchester. 21 May 1863.
Wordsworth, Charles. (b. of St Andrew's). Westminster Abbey Sermons for the
    Working Classes. 7 March 1858.
Wordsworth, Christopher. Westminster Abbey Sermons for the Working Classes,
    14 March 1858.
Wordsworth, Christopher. St Paul's Special Evening services. 10 January 1864.
Wrench J. George (Vicar, Salehurst, Sussex). 1 May 1859.
Wright, J.H.C. Stockport, Cheshire. 2 April 1854.
Wright, William. Kensington, London. 1 May 1859.

5 THE PROBLEM OF WORKING-CLASS LEISURE. SOME ROOTS OF MIDDLE-CLASS MORAL REFORM IN THE INDUSTRIAL NORTH: 1825-50.

Robert D. Storch

In early Victorian industrial cities, the reform of working-class leisure and the transformation of popular culture opened a promising and indeed inexhaustible field for the operation of middle-class benevolence and for a wide range of organisations and movements devoted to that purpose. The impulse both to moral and social reform in this period was in turn pervaded and conditioned by another related and deeply disturbing problem: the vital question of the preservation — in the first instance — of a stable pattern of civil and moral order congenial to local elites in a fluid and turbulent urban context. This essay is not primarily concerned with changes in the nature and patterns of popular leisure and culture in this period, but rather with the examination of a corner of the collective mentality of the early Victorian middle classes as they confronted these issues. The rhetoric of fear and loathing which we will encounter in the course of these explorations can only be understood in conjunction with more general perceptions of the modern city and the potential for chaos and destruction which, it was felt, lay in the industrial masses once they left the comparatively structured and disciplined atmosphere of the factory or workshop and the direct or indirect supervision of their employers.

I

Everywhere one looks in the contemporary literature of description of the working classes at liberty or at play, and of their habits and customs, it is nearly impossible to take leave of a universe of discourse which reflected a profound sense of fear and disgust, coupled with muffled — and not so muffled — intimations of social catastrophe. Kay-Shuttleworth's well-known treatise, for example, was inspired by the fear that if attention were not paid to the misery, ignorance and vice of the workers, they might prove 'volcanic elements, by whose explosive violence the structure of society may be destroyed'.[1] Similar sentiments, in different imagery, were frequently expressed. A.W. Paulton, the anti-corn law lecturer feared 'a social earthquake from fermenting masses of misery'.[2] Joseph Livesey, the Preston cheese factor and temperance reformer was equally explicit: 'Unless the people are morally improved, being now brought into large masses, and possessing increased facilities for mischief, the result: . . . may sooner or later, be internal commotion if not a national wreck.'[3] W.R. Greg felt that unless the domestic habits and moral perceptions of the working classes were altered 'and that speedily, there are silent but mighty instruments at work. . . which, ere long, will undermine the system of social union and burst asunder the silken bonds of amity which unite men to their kind.'[4]

These apprehensions reflected a deep concern over the absence of a commonly affirmed array of values linking the different classes in society. One aspect of this was concern over indigenous working-class culture. As I have remarked elsewhere, by the 1830s the notion that the movements of the lower orders had comprehensible or legitimate objectives was replaced by the feeling that they aimed somehow at the utter unravelling of society.[5] Equally, the intense interest shown by the middle classes in what the working classes did after their release from the salubrious discipline of mill or workshop, reflected anxiety about the social implications of unsupervised working-class leisure. Thus it was not simply altruistic benevolence which led the middle classes to the subject. Contained within the various movements formed to structure working-class leisure one finds approaches to a number of important and interrelated middle-class objectives: the preservation of civil order, the imposition of new types of labour-discipline and the diffusion among the working classes of a new (and alien) system of moral authority.

All middle-class reform movements concerned with the altering of popular leisure and culture evoked two images of the working man: as he was and how he might become after 'treatment'. The goal was clear: the English working man was to be morally sanitised (and politically neutralised in the process) by an extensive reworking of his character structure. A large order of business! The threat of political and social revolution in the 1840s was successfully avoided. The other enterprise — the administration of a cultural lobotomy and the implanting of a new morally superior lobe — went on into the 1850s and beyond, with very mixed results. But how did this human 'ground to be tilled'[6] appear to middle-class writers and publicists in the 1830s and 1840s? An answer may be found in three interlinked themes which formed the core of middle-class jeremiads; the 'Great City' itself; the image of the urban crowd and its disposition; and the evocation of the working man as 'morally diseased', even half-savage.

The theme of the 'Great City'[7] has frequently been discussed by

historians, who have noted, even among its defenders, awareness of a
paradox about city life. On the one hand, the growth of cities meant
progress, knowledge and increase in wealth; on the other, encouragement to 'anarchical, Socialist and infidel forces',[8] to secret societies
that

> working in the gloom of night, may surprise us when surrounded
> by the best, the fairest of our land, when music floats through our
> halls – may even strike us in the house of God on that day devoted
> to prayer, may render our homes desolate, and involve country and
> city in one common ruin.[9]

But one aspect of urban life, to which modern man has become
accustomed, was new and alien to the early Victorians, almost uniformly
striking and potentially menacing to them. The vast crowds, which all
domestic and foreign visitors to Manchester remarked, were deemed to
possess a great potential for mischief and destruction, whatever the
purpose they assembled for: a fair or wake, a Chartist demonstration,
shopping or even going to or returning from work.[10] The mill
represented a social safety mechanism, since once there, the workers
'can hardly learn many bad habits, the severity of discipline and cease-
lessness of labour prevents that. . .The factory system while it develops
no moral germs within the soul does at least. . . preserve it from
contamination from without.'[11]

A sigh of relief could be breathed when the factory masses reached
their mills and donned the traces of their labour, but their sudden
appearance in the morning or evening could conjure up awful fears and
portents in middle-class minds. These apprehensions were far from
merely abstract; they were grounded in the concrete experience and
personal recollection of the materialisation of urban crowds for other
less benign purposes.[12] The tendency of middle-class early Victorians
to define working-class leisure as a problem was reinforced by the
unavoidable, but unnerving encounters they experienced with workers
away from their jobs on any occasion: St Monday, strike, unemployment or Sunday. Thus an outraged and shaken Leeds respectable
complained of the crowds of idle workers he had to pass through on
Sundays.

> Many. . . swear, most of them smoke; profuse expectoration is the
> consequence of the latter. . . habit; and as these would-be men are
> not particular as to the direction in which they eject their odorous

mouthfuls, you may find on reaching home that your own black coat, or your wife's. . . dress bears no slight souvenir of the gauntlet you have been compelled to run.[13]

Working people in the mass could appear then in various manifestations, some dangerous and overtly threatening, others more benign (at least on the surface); but could one always be sure which was which? Such contacts inevitably shaped bourgeois views of the moral state of the poor. Closer investigation confirmed their worst fears. We can, in fact, construct a composite image of the working classes as they appeared to some of the better known middle-class publicists of the time. They were portrayed as sunk in bestiality, improvidence[14] intemperance and lack of sexual restraint; their family lives appeared atomised and their 'homes' non-existent; they were viewed as exempt from the restraints of religion and apparently beyond the direct and indirect influences which could conceivably civilise them. In terms of their character-structure, they were perceived as the very negation of the bourgeois and his virtues.

> They live precisely like brutes, to gratify. . . the appetites of their uncultivated bodies, and then die, to go they have never thought, cared, or wondered whither. . .Brought up in the darkness of barbarism, they have no idea, that it is possible for them to attain any higher condition; they are not even sentient enough to desire. . . to change their situation. . . they have unclear, indefinite, and undefinable ideas of all around them; they eat, drink, breed, work and die; and. . . the richer and more intelligent classes are obliged to guard them with police.[15]

Joseph Kay's sentiment was echoed by many observers, who, like William Barry of the Leeds Rational Recreation Society, thought the worker was 'little higher than the beasts of the field'. He 'must ever be a thing of the earth. . . He seeks happiness in sensual gratification alone'.[16]

What else are these men describing in their images of the city, its masses and of the moral characteristics of the working man, but what Owen — the grandest moral reformer of them all — termed, in his highly idiosyncratic language, the 'Old Immoral World'? Most moral and recreational reformers did not construct panaceas as sweeping as Owen did, but all were agreed that something had to be done about the beastly state of the people. That Joseph Livesey could speak of the danger of a 'national wreck', or Owen of the collapse of the 'Old Immoral World', or that the language of others of their contemporaries could be so highly coloured, should not be so surprising. By the end of our period most had lived through or remembered the economic and domestic crises of the post-1815 period, Peterloo, a wave of agrarian disturbances in 1830, two Luddite terrors and Chartism. Our hindsight may be an obstacle to getting inside the minds of the early Victorian bourgeoisie. We know now that the social order was capable of withstanding those shocks; but to people who were alive between 1815 and 1850, the earth frequently heaved unpredictably. In this period, it was difficult not to conclude that commercial and industrial advance was outrunning 'moral' progress.[17]

II

One of the unpleasant paradoxes — or so it must have seemed to middle-class contemporaries — of early industrial society was the fact that the unparalleled discipline and restraint of the mill was accompanied by the appearance of as free and untrammelled a recreational life as had probably ever existed in England. The corollary of free labour was free leisure. Once freed from that discipline, the lower classes were by and large exempt from the supervision of their betters. This trend was made more apparent by the break-up of common recreations among the social classes.[18] Common leisure activities in the large urban areas often foundered on the precise rock of class conflict, with the result that each class was forced into its own distinctive leisure and recreational activities. This process of rupture between the whole manner of life and culture of the middle classes and that of the workers can from time to time be seen to appear almost in a twinkling, as in a polaroid snapshot. In Bradford, for example, the bitter and prolonged strike of weavers and woolcombers in 1825 marked an exact point of cultural rupture. Up to this time, the septennial celebration of 'Bishop Blaize' involved the whole community, and the famous procession through the town included the entire 'Trade': worsted manufacturers, woolsorters, combers (470 of them in 1825) and dyers. The celebration of 1825 was the last. Hard on its heels came the strike, the progressive impoverishment of the combers and the technological revolutionising of the industry. In June 1825, in the midst of the strike, the break was symbolically announced by a striking worker:

he had always entertained a high opinion of the town of Bradford, especially when he saw the humane speeches made by the manu-

facturers, with regard to the condition of their workmen, at the
Blase dinner; but that he now thought they were acting in a way
that cast a stain on their characters.[19]

In 1832 it was announced that Bishop Blaize had been given up in
compliance with the 'general sentiment of the town', with the usual
observation that the age was growing superior to such 'childish shows'
and that religion and intellect were 'getting the better of sensual
indulgences'.[20]

In the end Bishop Blaize was appropriated in different ways by the
different social classes. In 1839 the middle classes held a ball on the
eve of Bishop Blaize. The working classes, for their part, seem to have
turned out of the mills after breakfast, refusing to work and parading
the streets. In the evening, 'a great amount of drunkenness was
observed'.[21] Four months earlier a meeting of apprentices was held to
consider how to celebrate February 3. They had to conclude that 'there
will never be another full scale festival, as the masters seem disposed to
grasp and keep every farthing'.[22] A small vignette tells the rest of the
story. In February 1840 a 'formidable body' of combers at Ripon
staged their own version of a Bishop Blaize procession, parading through
the town and later making the rounds of the houses of the gentry to
collect money for drink. The local middle classes were thrown into
consternation, thinking it was a Chartist uprising! All took refuge, but
were reassured at the sight of 'Bishop Blaize' himself, carrying two
combs and mounted on a nag.[23] Times had indeed changed.

But although such common amusements might be abandoned as
primitive or 'childish', middle-class reformers were insistent on the
need for contact between the classes, contact on *their* terms, which
would control working-class leisure and recreation. For reasons already
outlined, the leisure activities of the working classes, both those that
were public (the popular fete) and those increasingly covert (pub life),[24]
were perceived as both a general nuisance and a vague threat to
civilisation at large, to a great degree symbolic of the chaos which
appeared to threaten the social fabric and of that 'process of
decomposition' which was thought to be active.

This is the week of the fair [a North of England correspondent wrote
to a temperance publication] and I have seen boys of 12 and 14. . .
quite drunk on the streets. . .My window looks to the street, and at
night . . . I have frequently covered my head with the clothes, that I
might not be shocked. . . by hearing the blessed name of Jesus. . .

taken in vain.[25]

Or Edward Baines' *Mercury:*

> Thus for a whole week. . . have the streets been crowded, the . . .
> public houses crammed, the pickpockets, sharpers, and showmen
> filled. . . On Saturday night, if a foreigner had chanced to pass near
> the cattle market, he would have seen a sight after which all stories
> of English virtue and morality would have fallen upon his ears in
> vain. Crowds of men and women . . . drunk, surging up and down
> the streets, gurgling round the entrance of the . . . beer-shops;
> pickpockets. . . unfortunate women. . . children struggling through
> the crowded booths. . . witnesses of all the disgusting immorality,
> the ribald jesting, the cursing and profanity. . . and other nameless
> things, in which these fairs and feasts abound.[26]

The spectacle of urban masses in full cry, or the nocturnal saturnalia
might very well have propelled sensitive spirits to take refuge beneath
the bedclothes. It was above all at play that the worker was evoked as a
kind of savage, an alien being with alien customs; a creature who would
have to be morally reformed if whatever bonds of social cohesion there
were were to hold fast.

But beyond this, three decades of experience had demonstrated the
intimate connection between popular fetes and the threat of disorder
or even insurrection.[27] Popular fetes were increasingly feared because
they could so easily explode into sudden and seemingly meaningless
violence, or into riot or protest. Fair days and other occasions of
popular revelry often doubled as opportunities for the settling of
accounts not only between rival neighbourhood groups or between the
men of different villages, but between social classes, as on Guy Fawkes
night.[28] Similarly during the great 1840 anti-police riots at Colne it
was declared 'that if a policeman appears on the ground at the approaching races at Burnley, they will destroy him'.[29]

Equally, the more private *foci* of working-class leisure were suspect.
Especially after the Beer Act of 1830 and the multiplication of a class
of drinking places which could be occupied by extremely humble men,
much began to be made of the alleged facts that they were located in
retired, out of the way spots in both town and country; that they did
not depend on the magistrates for their licences; formed a recreational
nexus which encouraged and sheltered the most abominable sports and
games; and were centres of actual or potential insurrectionary plotting.[30]

Yorkshire Luddism had its inevitable associations with certain public
houses; and so did Chartism.[31] Of course this was most natural. The
pub served as an all-purpose service institution in working-class life
(publicans provided much more than mere drink: house of call,
toilet facilities, a treasury for sick clubs, refuge from the wet and from
the wife, dominoes and cards, reading matter, food and music);[32] but
to the middle classes all this appeared quite frightening. It was no small
evil, reported an 1849 parliamentary committee 'to have a class of
houses thus established, frequented exclusively by the labouring population, who thus lose the benefit of some control from contact with
persons of superior stations.'[33]

Even ardent believers in the beneficent possibilities of the industrial
system could feel pangs of apprehension after the passage of the Ten
Hours Bill: 'Now. . . there is leisure enough for the working classes to
get wisdom and understanding. It is moreoever certain that they will
do this or something else not so creditable to them.'[34] The implication
was clear. For every increment of increased free time allowed to the
worker by his employer or the state, he must be persuaded to fill it
with activities of a sober, elevating or educational nature. The provision
and patronising of such activities could be made into excellent
insurance against national wrecks. Joseph Kay put it neatly:

> It cannot be in the interest of. . . wealthy proprietors that the
> labourers should continue the prey of low moral habits, to a large
> extent without religion, in gross ignorance, and consequently the
> prey of the . . . emissaries of disorganising doctrines. . . We. . .
> conceive that the same motives which induce merchants and
> manufacturers to devote a portion of their annual profits to the
> insurance of the capital they employ. . . ought to be sufficient to
> deter sagacious men from leaving their wealth exposed to the
> danger of popular tumults and secret violence, when a small annual
> expenditure, judiciously employed in introducing the elements of
> civilisation, would render society harmonious and secure.[35]

The improvement of popular amusements could be viewed as 'a point
of self-interest and self-protection. . . Our safety, the security of society,
of our homes and families, in the long run, are concerned with the form
in which they take their recreation.'[36]

There were other reasons for the attack on unsupervised working-
class leisure. In Bradford, it was linked with the wider bourgeois
struggle against the landed aristocracy and for free trade in corn.[37] It

was a commonplace of a certain type of middle-class discourse that the working classes shared with the aristocracy a regrettable taste for gambling, prizefighting and other brutal and demoralising amusements which could, if unregulated, lead to similar attitudes on political questions. More generally, the interest of employers in the recreational lives of working men was doubly keen in these areas which did not yet possess a fully developed factory system.

It is easy to overestimate the extent of the factory system in early Victorian England, even in the industrial north. In Sheffield, for example, well into the second half of the nineteenth century, older patterns of popular leisure (and the nature of work and production upon which they were grounded) survived in a remarkably healthy state. So one finds the old preference for leisure versus income (and the means to indulge it) and its consecration as 'St Monday'. The Sheffield artisan:

> is not tied to any stated hours of labour; he has a key of the wheel, and enters it at his own time, working when he likes, and playing when he likes. . . While. . . the factory-hand is necessarily in a condition of . . . dependence on the manufacturer. . . this authority on the one side and subjection on the other. . . scarcely exist in Sheffield. The relation of employer and employed there has very little in it of the relation between master and servant.[38]

Even large employers, like Joseph Rodgers who, by the mid-1840s, had established extensive control over all the processes of manufacture and even occupied their own 'wheel', could not get its grinders to work on Tuesdays: 'Tuesday is a "natty day" with grinders when nothing will persuade them to work — not even a barrel of ale, and yet [we] have more control over this class of workmen than any other manufacturers.'[39]

Older artisanal work patterns, and the leisure-culture (revolving around drink and pub life, betting, gambling and the general seizing of free time) attached to them, perpetuated themselves remarkably in such a milieu.

To respectable Sheffield, Leeds could appear as a kind of Utopia! The difference between Leeds and Sheffield, Dr G.C. Holland wrote, was that in Sheffield: '. . . men are masters of their own time and free from the ordinary restrictions of well regulated factories. They are not taught daily the value of time, or the effects of its misapplication.'[40] Holland thought the working classes of Sheffield to be 'morally debased' and almost beyond hope. A police superintendent complained that Sheffield apprentices were under no control, as they did not even lodge with the journeymen who employed them. As for the older men: 'The habits of the adults confirm the children in their vices. The great bulk of the men habitually spend their evenings in the beerhouses. . . [Morals in Leeds are better] because the factory system prevents their running wild in the same manner.'[41]

Just as, within the West Riding, Leeds and Sheffield constituted two very different zones of industry, we might posit the existence of two zones of working-class leisure. What characterised each was not so much different activities, but different temporal rhythms. Working-class recreational life was not primarily packed into the Saturday night and the Sunday. In Sheffield there could be a number of Sunday-like days. The streets and street life itself presented rather different aspects to Leeds or Manchester, and as we approach 1850 those differences tended to magnify. Whatever order and regularity could be found where the worker was tied to the discipline imposed by the factory was absent in Sheffield. A factory sub-inspector pointed out:

> Regular hours are best for the employer. . . and a little wholesome discipline and strictness in this respect. . . are most beneficial. Laxity. . . engenders a general want of obedience; and employers who . . . allow their hands to do as they like, find. . . that when some crisis arises they have not sufficient influence to carry out any measure that opposes itself to the prejudices and. . . habits of the workers.[42]

If the meaning of the 'problem of working-class leisure' in our period can be summed up, we may say that it symbolised a whole complex of other problems faced by the urban middle classes, all of which no doubt tended to run together in their minds whenever key terms such as 'improvidence', 'immorality' or 'crime' were raised. Specifically it tended to be symbolic of the related problems of civil order and the imposition or reinforcement of labour-discipline. It was from this frame of reference, and with the deepest forebodings, that middle-class missionaries, observers and theorists set about the moralisation of the working classes.

III

Since middle-class observers agreed on the dangerous undesirability of the insulation of the working class, moral reform schemes had at their centre the notion of somehow restoring a sense of wholesome *personal contact* between men of different social stations. Those who, like the

Leeds Unitarian Domestic Missionary Edward Hall, had been selected
to venture into darkest Holbeck and establish institutions designed to
alter, change or channel the uncongenial manifestations of popular
culture they discovered there, spoke a great deal of the evils of
residential segregation,[43] the unwholesome separation of classes in
industrial society, and of the need to bring the working classes within
the sphere of bourgeois values for everyone's good.

The consciousness that the English working class was now on its own,
as it were, that the wraps were off, accounts in part for the tremendous
interest (practically a nostalgia by mid-century) shown in the early
factory villages, or in later enterprises like Saltaire, which attempted
to reproduce some of their characteristics. In the numerous reports of
conditions at Turton, Egerton and Hyde we are as close to the presence
of middle-class quasi-utopian musings as it is possible to get:

> There the employer knows the employed and is known by them;
> an affectionate interest is created equally advantageous to both
> parties; the factory displays to a great extent the relations of a
> family, and the operatives regard themselves as members of one
> common household.[44]

In Samuel Greg's industrial community at Quarry Bank, it was possible
to implement a plethora of schemes for rational recreation and moral
reform. Greg was able totally to dominate the environment he created.
He provided his 'colony' with a full panoply of recreations: gardens,
schools, baths, Sunday school processions, a field for games and
gymnastics, drawing and singing classes and tea parties in the master's
garden for the especially docile and well-behaved. Every facet of life
at Quarry Bank was personally supervised by Greg or by trustworthy
superintendents. He wanted to encourage the development of 'sobriety,
modesty and good manners'; but he was not interested in eliciting the
mere forms and modes of bourgeois private behaviour. He wanted them
to really reflect changes in their 'feelings and character'. An ambitious
task! He felt that by minutely controlling the workers' environment, he
could not only recruit a stable and less migratory labour force (certainly
the main economic object of the exercise), but produce in his
employees the internalisation of a whole new set of values.[45]

But the facilities for duplicating such environments in large northern
cities did not exist, nor was the will to do so displayed by the majority
of employers. Moral reformers had to operate in a much less firmly
structured situation. There were some opportunities for control. Brutal

sports, mainly those which had to take place in the open, and some older forms of the popular fete could be suppressed with the assistance of the new police. The police could put great pressure on prizefighting in suburban fields, footracing on the roads or knur and spel, all of which were popular in the North, and which moreover involved a great deal of lower-class gambling;[46] and many old fetes were slowly pushed from the scene by mid-century. But a newer type of working-class recreational nexus, well attuned to the realities of an urban industrial context, was beginning to congeal and was certainly well in place by 1850. It centred on pubs and beerhouses,[47] but included, too, the newer 'singing saloons', the Northern form of the dancing 'casino'.[48] and ultimately the early music halls, all expressions of a notably urban and modern popular culture. That they were chiefly commercial ventures, and often proliferated in response to a large demand (and as a result of intense competition among drinksellers to claim portions of that demand) made them that much harder to compete with success-fully or attack.

Moral reformers, then, had to create instead, groups of workers psychologically as opposed to physically insulated from the contamina-tion of their fellows, by capitalising on a drive towards upward social mobility in the individual, or a religious or teetotal conversion. They had to form what may be called 'conventicles of respectability'. Such conventicles could serve as a transmission belt for the standard panoply of bourgeois values: thrift, self help, temperance, sexual continence and the cult of home. The organisational form conventicles might take varied: mutual improvement societies, temperance societies, societies for 'rational recreation' or even an Owenite Hall of Science.[49] But the ultimate aim was the same, the transformation of character and the encouragement or reinforcement of conversion experiences in working men.[50]

The ideal can be found in the middle-class sponsors of the Leeds Spitalfields Sewing School. Girls were gathered nightly and taught to sew and mend. The main objects were to reinforce the working class home by teaching domestic skills, but also to 'raise the moral . . . tone of the scholars, by reading to them, by advice, by encouraging easy intercourse with them; and. . . showing them what better educated people would do or say under [given] circumstances'.[51] Or in the effusions of a respectable in the Black Country who had converted a working man to thrift: 'That man's eyes are now open. . . *He sees and feels as we do,* and will influence others to follow his example.'[52] Had this man not begun depositing in the savings bank, 'the whole amount would have been spent in feasting, in clubs, or contributions to the trade unions'.

The key to success was always felt to be either direct or indirect middle-class supervision. One of the prototypes of the new rational recreation schemes of the late 1840s was the Rev. Sidney Godolphin Osborne's reformed beershop, very close to the germ of the later working-men's clubs.[53] He proposed that a room be taken where working men could enjoy a good fire, bread, cheese and coffee, but also a bit of beer and tobacco. A proper 'steward' would preside, and this place had to be filled by 'some respectable inhabitant'. Beer was to be fetched from the real beerhouse to a maximum of a quart an evening per man. The steward would monitor the quantity of beer consumed and the company itself, seeing that there was no credit allowed, no gambling, swearing or indecent conduct. It was the presence of the steward that constituted the bar between an 'ill-regulated beershop' and a 'well regulated place'.[54]

One of the original models of a 'conventicle of respectability' was probably the mechanics' institute, part of whose purpose it was to 'detach our youthful, or, if we can, our adult population from inordinate sensual gratifications by directing them to higher and purer sources of enjoyment'.[55] Brougham envisioned the institutes as an excellent means of diffusing political economy and the recognition of Malthusian necessities among the working classes. They could, he felt, be made 'not merely safe, but most wholesome for the community'.[56] The Rev. Thomas Allin of Sheffield believed that the type of education offered at a mechanics' institute would teach the workers 'the relations and duties of social life, inculcate a knowledge of property and government and damp down social passions'.[57]

The failure of the mechanics' institutes to achieve these objectives and to reach its target population is well known, and within the movement itself there was a great deal of self-criticism.[58] One response in the West Riding in the late 1840s was a debate as to the propriety of abandoning an exclusively pedagogical approach and introducing a measure of rational recreation and sociability as a means of attracting a clientele. Some concessions were made, like cheap trips, cricket matches and fortnightly concerts. But despite such attempts to combine instruction and amusement, the Yorkshire Mechanics' Institute movement never felt wholly comfortable with the dilution of its original objectives by even such bland recreational fare.[59]

The mechanics' institutes represented the first try (but not the last failure) to moralise the working classes by combining instruction with amusement. Some elements of recreation were introduced as a device to entice potential members to sample the real wares these institutions were founded to purvey and to retain a hold on current members. Ultimately they concluded that they had not succeeded very well in luring workers from the pub/beerhouse nexus, from the races, fairs, dancing casinos and new music halls. The message of diligence, continence and self-improvement was broadcast, but not enough ears were attuned:

> Voluntary teaching fails, paid teaching exhausts the exchequer, classes are ill attended, lectures do not pay. . .Our bill of fare appears to be good; there must be something in the way we present it which repels . . . May we not liken ourselves to unskilled anglers fishing in a well-stocked stream, with an ill-dressed bait?[60]

It is not my purpose here to detail the history and failure of most of the later schemes. They present a bewildering variety, ranging from the idea of creating non profit shareholding companies to set up museums, libraries and cheap concerts to compete with commercial recreational entrepreneurs, to the later working-men's clubs; the efforts made in Leeds and Lancashire by Mrs Hind Smith to buy up neighbourhood pubs and simply subtract the drink;[61] to the attempts to create temperance music halls.[62]

The first idea formed the original purpose of the Leeds Rational Recreation Society, founded in 1853. No museums or libraries were ever created, but it carried on a series of Saturday night cheap concerts for a number of years, became involved in a nationwide row with Edward Baines and militant Sabbatarianism over Sunday bands, and paid for a number of local Sunday band concerts.[63] As James Hole of Leeds recognised, Holbeck and Hunslet were never reached by its concerts. Shop-keepers and a smattering of self-improving working men became its clientele, and attendance at the Saturday night concerts became simply one more of the increasing number of badges or outward signs of respectability such people could display by the 1850s.

One might say as well that almost every subsequent effort to provide the masses with cheap and elevating entertainments outside the established channels of commercial enterprise ultimately took on the outlines of a conventicle of respectability, providing a threshold which people might cross out of the surrounding world of the brutal and 'rough'. By the 1870s reformers were openly admitting that this was what they were really about. The Rev. Henry Solly frankly stated that working-men's clubs were mainly meant for labour aristocrats;[64] others tried to gather conventicles among the poor of the East End. Both aristocrats and labourers, in theory, were considered to possess the potential for respectability, but schemes for reaching the masses at large became less frequent by the 1870s, and pained dismay at not being able to accomplish their moralisation became somewhat more rare.

Of course by this time the working-class political movement had been comparatively quiescent during two decades of relative prosperity, more powerful agencies of social discipline (the police and the compulsory school) had been well implanted, and the hysteria about national wreck and social anarchy (which provided so much of the impetus for the attitudes and movements we have been discussing) tended to fade a great deal.[65] If one follows the transactions of the National Association for the Promotion of Social Science into the late 1860s and early 1870s, the change in rhetoric and in the general ambiance of middle-class discourse is quite noticeable.

The 1850s were the heyday of an indiscriminate scramble among the Victorian middle classes to establish charities and cultural missions to the lower classes of all sorts;[66] an enthusiasm which petered out by the early 1860s to the accompaniment of cries such as the following:

> with all our boasted improvements, the mind, taste, and feelings of vast masses of the people are as yet scarcely touched, and remain pretty much what they were in days gone by. How to reach these masses with your manifold agencies is a problem, of which no one. . , has been able to give us a satisfactory solution. You establish schools – they are indifferent . . . You publish cheap books – they will neither purchase nor peruse them. . . Yet, in spite of everything, habits the most grovelling continue to flourish. In the midst of civilisation. . . there is. . . a kind of barbarism – not abject and poverty-struck, but vigorous and self-willed.[67]

How could one compete with the excitement of the St Leger? How to prevent 15,000 people congregating on Rombald's Moor in June 1850 to watch two men from Huddersfield and Halifax beat each other senseless; or the same number appearing at Bradford Moor Races in 1856? How to prevent thousands from being conveyed by the railway from Barnsley to Sheffield in January 1857 to gamble on a footrace? How to break into a popular culture which was capable of gathering huge crowds on Illingworth Moor near Halifax to watch Dan Moor of

Swill Hill and Joseph Hall of Haley Hill contest at the exercise of gathering one hundred stones placed one yard apart? (Bets were 'high and numerous'.) How to stop the prizefighting at the Punch Bowl, Hunslet (1840) or the Shepherds Inn, Pontefract Lane (1860); or dogfighting at the Turk's Head, Briggate (1839) or the Malt Shovel, Armley (1845), or other abominations at the British Tar, Hunslet (1845) or Black Bull, Woodhouse (1845)? How to compete with Bradford beerhouses which offered 'Dart Puffing', 'Winning Horse Boards', 'Railway Boards', 'Nigger dancing', and dancing for caps, ribbons and other articles? How to prevent Leeds beerhouses in the neighbourhood of the Rational Recreation Society's Saturday concerts from hanging out signs reading 'Free Concert Here'? How to entice Leeds workers from the 'Royal Alhambra', formerly 'The Casino', a wonderful new music hall (where one could view busts of famous criminals in an attached 'museum')?

It may have been true that in smaller towns and in the countryside the amusements of the working classes were dull and unvaried, but the more one looks at recreational life in the larger centres the more one is tempted to take issue with the reformers of the time who pleaded that there was little for working men to do in large towns.[68] It is true that there was little municipal or even private provision for parks, libraries or museums until after our period, just as it is true that working-class amusements were often brutish and low, even at times quite violent and explosive. It looks, though, as if, when middle-class contemporaries claimed that there was little to engage the workers, they meant very little that was elevating, rational, politically neutral, instructive, and that was moreover provided, planned and supervised by them. This was a problem, but for them rather than the working classes.

Middle-class attempts to moralise the poor were further vitiated by the frailty of the conventicle, which isolated and insulated its members from the values of the neighbourhood and barred them from the range of social relationships normal in working-class life. To venture beyond the conventicle and its deviant values meant courting the risk of falling away, being reabsorbed in the comrade-cluster of the pub, lapsing back into 'sensuality' and 'vice'.

That this frequently happened can be well documented. The Unitarians in Leeds, through their Domestic Mission, made a special appeal to adolescents, and tried to keep them together as a group: as sheltered from the temptations all around them as possible. The Domestic Missionaries in Leeds were active, intelligent and sympathetic; they knew and understood more about working-class life than anyone on the other side of the river. But of course they did not succeed.

Despite the provision of a full panoply of activities and amusements in connection with the mission, the reading room failed, and the Christmas singing and entertainments were attended only by a core group who clung to the mission.[69] Even they deserted at fair time, but worst of all they went off to the singing saloons and dancing rooms. 'Many instances have come to my notice of Sunday School teachers and scholars, as well as regular attendants at Christian worship, having been drawn into the vortex of sin. . .'[70] Even those most devoted to the conventicle would be lost after the age of sixteen; the pull of the world of work and the peer-group pressure of their mates would inevitably detach them from their former loyalties. 'Almost every week do I see the sad effects of the workshop in the insubordination and viciousness of Sunday scholars, who were, previous to their being sent out to work, orderly and well-intentioned.'[71]

It was the same with adult members of conventicles of respectability. A device such as the signing of the pledge was meant to reinforce the member's sense of separation from the ways of the surrounding community; the parading of ex-drunkards, with their lurid testimonies, was designed as a constant reminder of the dangers lurking outside; the boundaries of the conventicle were the boundaries of respectability. Middle-class sponsored and financed moral reform agencies such as the Domestic Mission or the later British Workman pubs were institutions of this type; so were many attempts at the moralisation of the workplace. Working men who attached themselves to such organisations knew that the price was often excommunication from the local community and sometimes persecution. There were anti-temperance riots on occasion; teetotallers could be burned in effigy at their doorsteps.[72] 'We have teetotallers here', a miner told a parliamentary committee in 1842, 'but very few; none of them miners; we could not follow 'the work up without beer. If one of that sort were to attempt to come amongst us, we would soon take him to the canal.'[73]

Many men, having signed the pledge, could not socialise with their mates any longer; some might be forced out of the shop. A Leeds teetotaller, having violated a shop rule, was asked to pay the usual fine, to be spent in drink. He proposed other ways of using the money and even offered to pay double the fine. He was persecuted and finally had to leave the shop.[74] That many fell away was no wonder. The gulf across which middle-class reformers spoke to working men was wide. They demanded detachment from the real, pulsating life of the community, its trade customs, patterns of conviviality and marriage markets: in short the very stuff of what we call culture. Strait was the gate into respectability; few were called and ultimately even fewer answered.

IV

Recently Brian Harrison has explored the profusion of Victorian moral reform groups and valuably drawn some of the complex links between them and the impulse to social reform.[75] When they are viewed on a local as well as a national level, one has the impression of an extremely vigorous kind of growth. Much has been made of the sense of disquiet and fear of disorder which pervaded middle-class discourse in the 1830s and 1840s, but the intention here is not to propound any oversimplified or reductionist explanation of the impetus of bourgeois moral reform. How for example does one account for the perseverance — even acceleration — of middle-class moral reform after 1850, when one can begin to speak of the existence of an increasingly self-assured mood among the upper classes generally in England? Why, after the collapse of Chartism and the threat of social anarchy which it — and other movements of the lower orders — was perceived to contain, did the mid-Victorian bourgeoisie not simply turn its back on the whole enterprise? Any analysis grounded upon the notion of a mere response to the challenge of disorder loses its power to explain as soon as such questions are posed. Why the perpetuation of the typically bourgeois impulse to remould the inner man, to transform him morally, after the immense social crisis which lasted from Waterloo to the last Chartist petition had been weathered?

What were the ultimate purposes of all this activity, and how can it be viewed under the rubric of 'social control'? Certainly a number of formal mechanisms of manipulation and coercion were created in our period: one need go no further than the implantation of the new poor law or new police. Many early Victorians consciously mused upon the possible good results such coercive or manipulative instruments might produce. On the other hand, there was a greater emphasis on the need for the diffusion of a standard set or array of norms which might (and *should*) be shared by individuals, across class lines and throughout society.

It might be thought that the early Victorian middle classes were pulled in two ways when they contemplated the great task of civilising and taming the masses. Some indeed did not view the road of moral reform and social reform as completely harmonious.[76] The nature of the peculiarly Anglo-Saxon variant of bourgeois ideology set up a certain tension between them which, to a certain extent, played itself out in the sphere of thought. On the actual plane of society itself it was perhaps otherwise, for were not moral reform, cultural missionising and the creation of conventicles of respectability not simply the other side of the coin of policing or sanitary inspection? There was nothing innately discordant about them in the final analysis. Chadwick himself certainly did not think so.[77] It is true however that there was an unmistakable chariness about the use of the state and a certain tendency to eschew its use. Many early Victorian reformers considered police coercion, the employment of the state and the use of administrative and bureacratic solutions to be less effective for some very practical reasons. In a world manifestly 'lacking in normative regulation and moral authority — a world deficient in. . . ideological community — only the reimposition of a system of common morality could restore [or ensure] social order'.[78]

The immuring of the working class within the factory, forcing it to dance to the tune played daily by that strict and uncompromising orchestra, the steam engine — that 'chorus' of 'wheels and shuttles' Herr Kohl noted[79] — seemed insufficient; even so gigantic and powerful an engine of compulsion was not quite equal to the task. 'I have arrived', said Mr Thornton, in *North and South*,

> at the conviction that no mere institutions, however wise, and however much thought may have been required to organise and arrange them, can attach class to class as they should be attached, unless the working out of such institutions bring the individuals of different classes into actual personal contact. Such intercourse is the very breath of life.[80]

This type of rhetoric informed many attempts at the moralisation of the workplace and the foundation of innumerable conventicles of respectability in our period and beyond.

Whatever the state, the police or Somerset House did, could greater orderliness and regularity among the working class be created, could the remoulding of the working class Home proceed without men of wealth and station personally lending their arms to the task apart from the state and outside the sphere of work? How could it be otherwise? Thrift, continence, the deferral of present gratifications could only be truly achieved if they proceeded from 'character', as an expression of the well-socialised 'inner man'. How could the state or the police *alone* change a man's character or transform the nature of a social class? What good protestant could assent to such a proposition?

To return once more to the nostalgia we noted for the early factory villages, we know what was supposed to transpire (and what to be communicated) during those elevating and civilising group-therapy sessions for workers held at Mr Samuel Greg's garden tea parties. But by mid-century such options were rapidly closing off, though dreams and schemes persisted beyond that point. The local and personal — the paternalist — basis of social control of Quarry Bank or New Lanark could not be reduplicated. The arena in which all the cultural forces of the middle classes had to be marshalled had become (now and forever) Manchester and Leeds, Glasgow and Bolton. The moralisation of the masses would have to proceed on that inhoispital ground. Domestic missions and conventicles of respectability were designed to fit these changing urban circumstances.

What other options existed in our period, especially since the mightiest modern engine for the purveying of new systems of moral authority, the compulsory school, was not yet in sight? In the end it was neither feasible nor possible to entice the masses into respectability the turf of the great industrial city proved too stony. The numerous conventicles set up for the purpose were usually highly artificial efforts, and often were unable to compete for the free time of the worker with the increasing number of attractions and activities offered by commercial recreational entrepreneurs. A great garden tea party was laid on, but on the whole the full complement of guests neglected to arrive. That prong of middle-class moral reform which attempted to deal directly with the worker ran head-on into an increasingly 'corporate' working-class culture,[81] more impenetrable and impervious to 'domestic missionaries' of all sorts than had originally been expected.

Some historians have observed that the nineteenth-century middle classes were considerably more anxious in the face of real differences of values within society than the components of previous ruling classes in European history.[82] Whether this was due to any striking peculiarities in the bourgeois world-view, or whether it was so at all, we might leave an open question. Nevertheless, it is the case that the task the figures and organisations we have dealt with thought they were involved in was precisely the 'reimposition of a system of common morality'. This they thought could be the only solid and durable platform of social order. In this respect these moral reformers and publicists were what we might term 'intuitive' or 'instinctive' Durkheimians. As they observed the urban working classes from their offices and counting-houses or from the suburban peripheries, and pondered their situation, they were dismayed to find that. 'they do not in the least comprehend that what is in the interest of society is their own also'.[83] This perhaps is another clue to the persistence of middle-class missionisings beyond 1850;

despite the fact that an immediate threat to the social order ceased to exist, the enterprise had to go on.

Notes

Research for this paper was made possible by an Edinburgh University Junior Research Fellowship, and it was presented there, in early draft, at a symposium on Class and Class Consciousness in nineteenth-century Britain. I am grateful to Professor G.F.A. Best who supervised my work at Edinburgh. Professor J.F.C. Harrison invited me to present a later version to his Modern Britain seminar at the University of Wisconsin. I benefited from his encouragement at that time and since.

1.   J.P. Kay, *The Moral and Physical Condition of the Working Classes Employed in the Cotton Manufacture in Manchester,* 2nd edn. (London, 1832), p.112.

2.   Quoted in *Northern Star,* 11 April 1840; 'Moral and Social Condition of Wales', *Blackwood's Edinburgh Magazine,* (Sept. 1849), p.327.

3.   *Livesey's Moral Reformer,* 6 Jan. 1838.

4.   W.R. Greg, *An Enquiry into the State of the Manufacturing Population, and the Causes and Cures of the Evils Therein Existing* (London, 1831), pp. 39-40.

5.   R.D. Storch, 'The Plague of the Blue Locusts. Police Reform and Popular Resistance in Northern England, 1840-1857', *Int'l Review of Social History,* XX,1 (1975), p.62.

6.   I paraphrase J.F.C. Harrison here, *Learning and Living* (London, 1961), chap. I.

7.   See e.g. A. Briggs, *Victorian Cities* (New York, 1970), pp. 59-65; R. Williams, *The Country and the City* (New York, 1973), chap. XIX; L. Faucher, *Manchester in 1844* (London and Manchester, 1844), p.92; *Moral Reformer,* 1 Jan. 1838; Joseph Kay, *The Social Condition and Education of the People in England and Europe* (London, 1850), I, p.374; R. Vaughan, *The Age of Great Cities,* 2nd edn. (London, 1843), p.222.

8.   H.S. Tremenheere quoted in M.J. Cullen, *The Statistical Movement in Early Victorian Britain* (New York, 1975), p.145.

9.   E.A. Antrobus, *London. Its Danger and its Safety* (London, 1848), p.22.

10.   See, e.g. W. Cooke Taylor, *Notes on a Tour in the Manufacturing Districts of Lancashire,* 2nd edn. (London, 1842), pp.6-7 and J.P. Kay, *The Moral and Physical Condition. . .,* pp.42-3.

11.   J.G. Kohl, *England and Wales* (London, Cass Reprint, 1968), p.137.

12.   Mrs Gaskell described these particularly well. See, e.g. the passages in *North and South,* Penguin edn. (London, 1970), pp. 226 ff., 232-3.

13.   *Leeds Mercury,* 10 Oct. 1863; G. Cruickshank, *Sunday in London. Illustrated in Fourteen Cuts,* (London 1833), pp.23-4; C. Babbage, *A Chapter on Street Nuisances,* (London, 1864), pp.16-18.

14.   See the factory inspector Robert Baker's pamphlet *It's Nobbut and Nivver Heed* (London & Leeds, 1860).

15.   Joseph Kay, *Social Condition and Education. . .,* I, pp.580-1.

16.   William Barry, *An Essay on the Most Desirable Plan for Supplying Innocent*

and Elevating Recreation for the Working Classes (London & Leeds, 1853), p.6.

17. See e.g. Joseph Fletcher, 'Moral and Educational Statistics of England and Wales', *Journal of Statistical Society of London,* X (Sept. 1847), p.213 and *passim.*

18. Anthony Delves, 'Popular Recreations and their Enemies', paper presented to Labour History Society Conference (1975); R. Malcolmson, *Popular Recreations in English Society 1700-1850* (Cambridge, 1973); and discussion in R.D. Storch, 'The Policeman as Domestic Missionary. Urban Discipline and Popular Culture in Northern England, 1850-1880', *Journal of Social History,* IX, 4 (Summer, 1976), pp.492-3.

19. *Leeds Mercury,* 18 June 1825. Descriptions of the celebration are in *Leeds Mercury,* 29 Jan. 1825 and 5 Feb. 1825, and Anon., *A Full and Particular Account of the Septennial Festival Held in Honour of Bishop Blase* (Bradford, n.d.). See also E.P. Thompson, *The Making of the English Working Class* (London, 1964), pp.425-6.

20. *Leeds Mercury,* 4 Feb. 1832. By this time a temperance society appeared, and Henry Forbes, one of its leading spirits, agitated against Bishop Blaize (letter to author from Dr Brian Harrison); J. Mayhall, *Annals of York, Leeds, etc.,* (Leeds, 1861), p.689.

21. *Leeds Mercury,* 9 Feb. 1839.

22. *Leeds Times,* 20 Oct. 1838.

23. *Leeds Times,* 8 Feb. 1840.

24. For the covert characteristics of pubs see R.D. Storch, 'Policeman as Domestic Missionary. . .', pp.487-9.

25. *Glasgow Temperance Record* (Nov. 1830); see discussion in B. Harrison and B. Trinder, 'Drink and Sobriety in an Early Victorian Country Town: Banbury 1830-1860, *English Historical Review,* Supplement 4 (London, 1969), p. 11; P.A. Whittle, *Blackburn As It Is* (Preston, 1852), p. 31.

26. *Leeds Mercury,* 16 July 1863.

27. Edward Baines, for example, referred to the Plug Riots as 'the late holiday insurrection'. *Leeds Mercury,* 24 Sept. 1842 and *Leeds Times,* 4 March 1843.

28. R.D. Storch, 'Policeman as Domestic Missionary', pp.490-1.

29. Sir Charles Napier to Home Office, 15 Aug. 1840 in Public Record Office, Home Office 40/58.

30. On the perceived connection between rural incendiarism and beershops, H.C. Select Committee on Sale of Beer, *Parliamentary Papers* (henceforth *PP*) (1833), XV, evidence W. Holmes, p.45; and on their alleged obscurity evidence W. Holmes, p.45; and on their alleged obscurity, evidence T. Tennant, p. 108; see E.J. Hobsbawm and G. Rude, *Captain Swing* (New York, 1968), pp. 60, 62.

31. See F. Peel, *The Risings of the Luddites, Chartists and Plugdrawers* (Heckmondwike, 1888), pp.43, 51, and Peel's *Spen Valley Past and Present* (Heckmondwike, 1893), pp. 314, 321-2; *Northern Star,* 11 May 1839; cf. E. Jenkins, *Chartism Unmasked* (Merthyr Tydvil, 1840).

32. G.J. Holyoake, *The Social Means of Promoting Temperance* (London, n.d.), p. 9; B. Harrison, *Drink and the Victorians* (Pittsburgh, 1971), pp. 46 ff., and 'Pubs', in H.J. Dyos and M. Wolff (eds.),*The Victorian City, Images and Reality* (London & Boston, 1973), I, pp.161-90. On the provision of music see Faucher, *Manchester in 1844,* p. 49 and B. Love, *Handbook of Manchester* (Manchester, 1842), p. 145. On their use as a house of call see 'The Tramping Artisan', in E.J. Hobsbawn, *Labouring Men* (London, 1964), pp.34-63.

33. H.L. SC on Sale of Beer, *PP* (1850), XVIII, Report, p.v and evidence H. Pownall, p.45.

34. January Searle, 'Huddersfield. Its Physical, Social, Manufacturing, Commercial and Religious Characteristics', *Tait's Edinburgh Magazine,* XVI (1849), p.239.

35. Quoted in Vaughan, *Age of Great Cities,* p.216

36. F. Fuller, 'How to Elevate the People. . . by Encouraging. . . the Masses to Pass their Leisure Hours Beneficially', *Transactions National Association for Promotion of Social Science* (1875), p.717.

37. *Bradford Observer,* 27 Dec. 1849 stated that as long as workers were concerned with brutal amusements 'the lords of the soil may count upon the recovery of their lost protection', cf. *Leeds Times,* 14 March 1840.

38. F. Hill, 'An Account of some Trade Combinations in Sheffield', National Association for Promotion of Social Science, *Trades' Societies and Strikes* (London, 1860), p. 530. In general see S. Pollard, *A History of Labour in Sheffield* (Liverpool, 1959).

39. Children's Employment Commission, *PP* (1843), XIV, evidence J. Rodgers, el 5, 30; see the stimulating article, D.A. Read, 'The Decline of Saint Monday 1766-1876', *Past and Present,* 71 (May, 1976), 76-101.

40. G.C. Holland, *An Enquiry into the Moral, Social and Intellectual Condition of the Industrious Classes of Sheffield* (London, 1839), p.12; Faucher thought that the mills were the *only* source of 'moral order' in Manchester. *Manchester in 1844,* pp.26-7.

41. Children's Employment Commission (1843), *op.cit.,* evidence Mr Raynor, e7, 11; cf. evidence J. Carr, el 3, 26.

42. Reports of Inspectors of Factories for the Half-Year Ending 31, October 1869, *PP* (1870), XV, Report Sub-inspector W. Johnston, p.217; cf. E.P. Thompson's remarks, 'Time, Work-Discipline and Industrial Capitalism', *Past and Present,* 38 (Dec. 1967), p.90.

43. Leeds Domestic Missionary Society, *Annual Reports* (1856 and 1857). Faucher, *Manchester in 1844,* pp.26-7; Cooke Taylor, *Notes of a Tour. . .,* p.14.

44. Cooke Taylor, *Notes of a Tour. . .,* p.147. See S. Pollard, 'The Factory Village in the Industrial Revolution', *English Historical Review,* LXXIX (1964), pp.513-31; *Morning Chronicle,* 29 Oct. 1849.

45. Samuel Greg, *Two Letters to Leonard Horner, Esq. on the Capabilities of the Factory System* (London, 1840), *passim.*

46. R.D. Storch, 'Plague of the Blue Locusts', pp.84-7.

47. See discussion in R.D. Storch, 'Policeman as Domestic Missionary. . .', p.488.

48. The marriage market *par excellence* of urban working-class youth.

49. For Halls of Science see Faucher, *Manchester in 1844,* p.51.

50. For some examples see S. Thomas, *From the Prize Ring to the Cross* (Huddersfield, 1900); T. Whittaker, *Life's Battles in Temperance Armour* (London, 1902), pp.66-7.

51. James Hole, *The Working Classes of Leeds. An Essay on the Present State of Education in Leeds and the Best Means of Improving It* (London & Leeds, 1863), p.48.

52. *Minutes of Committee of Council on Education,* I, (1846), Report of H. Moseley on the schools of the Midlands, p.179.

53. On the clubs see R. Price 'The Working-Men's Club Movement and Victorian Social Reform ideology', *Victorian Studies,* XV, 2 (Dec. 1971), pp. 117-47.

54. S.G. Osborne, 'The Beer-Shop Evil', in Viscount Ingestre (ed.), *Meliora. Or Better Times to Come* (1st series, Cass Reprint of 2nd edn. of 1852,

London, 1971), pp. i-ii

55. Rev. T. Allin, *Mechanics Institutions Defended on Christian Principles* (Sheffield, 1833), p.13. Brougham thought they would 'spread. . . the disrelish for sensual and vulgar gratifications', *Practical Observations Upon the Education of the People Addressed to the Working Classes and their Employers* (London, 1825), p.1.

56. Brougham, *Practical Observations*, p.5.

57. T. Allin, *Mechanics Institutions Defended*, p.15.

58. See *West Riding Union of Mechanics' Institutes Annual Report* (1840), p.7.

59. See Yorkshire Union of Mechanics' Institutes (henceforth YUMI), *Annual Report* (1847), p.74; (1850), p.14; (1855), pp.15, 97.

60. YUMI, *Annual Report* (1864), p.135.

61. This experiment can be tracked through its journal *The Leeds Monthly*, later *British Workman Review*.

62. For the most successful of them (ultimately!) see C. Hamilton and L. Baylis, *The Old Vic* (New York, n.d.), and J. Booth, *A Century of Theatrical History, 1816-1916. The 'Old Vic.'* (London, 1917).

63. Sabbatarians argued for early closing and provision of rational recreation on Saturday, but there were violent conflicts with other reformers who argued that workers were in most peril on Sundays. The literature is inexhaustible but see: 'The Sunday Screw', *Household Words*, I, 13 (1850), pp.289-92 and 'A Shoemaker' [J.D. Devlin], *The Sydenham Sunday* (London, n.d.); E. Baines, *On the Performance of Sunday Bands in the Parks of London* (London, 1856) and *On the Attempt to Change the Character of the Christian Sabbath* (Leeds, 1853); J. Donkersley, *The Yorkshire Comedy, Founded on Fact Entitled – Hydrofoggy or the Rehearsal of Sunday Closed. In Two Acts* (Huddersfield, n.d.).

64. Rev. H. Solly, *Working Men's Clubs and Alcoholic Drinks* (London, 1872), pp.4, 13.

65. See G. Stedman Jones, 'Working Class Culture and Working Class Politics in London, 1870-1900; Notes on the Remaking of a Working Class', *Journal of Social History*, VII, 4 (Summer, 1974), pp.460-508 and E.P. Hennock, 'Poverty and Social Theory in England: the Experience of the Eighteen-Eighties', *Social History*, I, 1 (Jan. 1976), pp.67-91.

66. M.B. Simey, *Charitable Effort in Liverpool in the Nineteenth Century* (Liverpool, 1951), pp.56-9.

67. William Chambers (ed.),*Chambers' Social Science Tracts Embracing Subjects Connected with Social, Political and Sanitary Economy* (London & Edinburgh, 1860-63), tract no. 4 'Misexpenditure', p.2.

68. For the profusion of working-class recreational activities in this period see Hugh Shimmin, *Liverpool Life* (Liverpool, 1856) and J. Lawson, *Letters to the Young on Progress in Pudsey* (Stanningley, 1887), pp.57-8 and *passim*.

69. Leeds Domestic Mission Society, *Annual Report* (1858), p. 27.

70. Ibid. (1863), p.13. This was a frequent complaint: see *Ipswich Series of Temperance Tracts* (London, n.d.), III, tract 102.

71. Leeds Domestic Mission Society, *Annual Report* (1866), p.13.

72. *Leeds Times*, 28 Nov. 1835; *Leeds Times*, 29 July 1843.

73. First Report Children's Employment Commission [Mines], *PP* (1842), XV, evidence C. Bleaden, p.67.

74. *Leeds Temperance Herald*, 29 May 1837; *Border Herald*, April 1841.

75. B. Harrison, 'State Intervention and Moral Reform', in P. Hollis (ed.), *Pressure from Without in Early Victorian England* (London, 1974),pp.289-322.

76.   Ibid., pp. 305-9, 316.
77.   See above, pp. 63-72.
78.   J. Karabel, 'The Marxism of Marxism', *Times Literary Supplement*, 15 Oct. 1976.
79.   J.G. Kohl, *England and Wales,* p.146.
80.   E. Gaskell, *North and South,* p.525.
81.   P. Anderson, 'Origins of the Present Crisis', in *Towards Socialism* (Ithaca, N.Y., 1966), p.34; J. Obelkevich, 'Notes Towards the Definition of Working Class Culture', unpublished Princeton University Davis Centre paper (1975), p.8.
82.   C. Lasch, *The World of Nations* (New York, 1974), p. 316.
83.   Joseph Kay, *Social Condition and Education,* I, p.581.

6 THE METROPOLITAN FAIRS: A CASE STUDY IN THE SOCIAL CONTROL OF LEISURE

Hugh Cunningham

In 1885 the Home Secretary, Sir William Harcourt, ordered the Metropolitan Police not to interfere with steam roundabouts, 'these innocent amusements of the poorer classes. . . even if such amusements are presumed to constitute unlawful fairs within the Police Acts'.[1] This deliberate refusal to use the power of the law against fairs contrasts strongly with official policy in the early part of the century when respectable minds saw in the metropolitan fairs a nursery of crime and a hotbed of vice. It was presumed at that time that economic and moral progress would lead to their natural demise, but no one saw any harm in hastening that event by bringing to bear the forces of law and public opinion. As a result many fairs were abolished. Others, however, particularly those on the outskirts of London, survived and grew. The railway and the application of steampower to fairground entertainment on the one hand, and continuing plebeian demand on the other, gave new impetus to a form of entertainment which was thought to be obsolete. And at the same time, as Harcourt's action shows, the government became more tolerant. Why was this so?

Partly it was because government had more power to its elbow. New legislation in 1822 and 1871 gave power to abolish unchartered fairs and to limit the hours of chartered ones. Government thus gained control of a direct kind. At the same time the formation and development of the Metropolitan Police after 1829 played its part in turning an unpoliced society obsessed with problems of law and order into one which accepted a considerable degree of bureaucratic intervention in daily life as the price of social stability.[2] The police, with the law behind them, could reduce if not abolish the threat posed by the fairs to social disorder. But this new-found power of two key agencies of social control, the law and the police, was insufficient in itself to account for the government's increasing tolerance. Equally important was a change in the values and norms of showmen, who from the middle of the century became respectable and wealthy entrepreneurs of leisure, patronised by Royalty. As a result the police, instead of acting instinctively to suppress fairs, began to cooperate with showmen in organising them. The visitors to the fairs, too, changed their habits. In the first half of the nineteenth century the fair could be seen as social control in the form of a necessary release from work for the people; thus Dickens described Greenwich fair as 'a periodical breaking out, we suppose, a sort of spring-rash: a three days' fever, which cools the blood for six months afterwards, and at the expiration of which London is restored to its old habits of plodding industry. . .'[3] By the end of the century, in contrast, fairgoing had become a relatively routine ingredient in an accepted world of leisure. Thus by a tightening up in the forces of law and order, and by a convergence of norms between showmen and fairgoers on the one hand and authority on the other, fairs became tolerated, safe, and in due course a subject for nostalgia and revival.

Fairs, throughout history, have necessarily attracted the attention of authority. As trading centres they called for special laws, and even special courts, the pie powder courts. And as their trading function declined, there remained in the pleasure fair a clear problem of public order. Eighteenth-century Quarter Sessions records are full of the attempts of magistrates to abolish, restrict and control fairs.[4] In London itself, Tottenham Court fair had been abolished in mid-century,[5] Southwark fair in 1762, May fair in 1764, and the restriction of Bartholomew fair to three days from its former fourteen was finally effectively enforced from about the middle of the eighteenth century. By the early nineteenth century such magisterial efforts were beginning to gain a groundswell of support from the public.[6] And as concern with the problems of public order became acute in the metropolis after the Napoleonic Wars, an increasing number of witnesses before Select Committees pointed to fairs as one among other causes of prostitution and crime. Fairs were thought to attract 'most of the worst characters in the Metropolis', and in the bid to eradicate the meeting places of criminals the eighty or more fair days in and around London each year were an obvious target.[7] In 1822 the Select Committee on the Police of the Metropolis recommended that legal, that is chartered, fairs should be forced to close from 11 p.m. to 6 a.m. in order to prevent 'scenes of vice and debauchery during the night'. More important, it suggested a new method for the suppression of illegal, that is un-chartered fairs, which as the law stood could only be dealt with by a writ of Quo Warranto in the Court of King's Bench, 'a tedious and expensive process'. The Committee proposed that any two magistrates who considered a fair either illegal or continuing beyond its legal duration should have power to summon the owner or occupier of the ground to appear at a petty sessions to show his title, and if this was not satisfactory, to declare the fair illegal. Since, however, the Committee was 'not prepared to leave to the petty sessions the power of determining absolutely in matters of property', the owner or occupier could, if he so wished, appeal to the Court of King's Bench.[8]

This proposal was immediately enacted as part of the Metropolitan Police Act of 1822 (3 Geo. IV. c.55), and it was quickly put into operation. Two fairs, Shoreditch[9] and the West End or Hampstead fair, had already been suppressed shortly before the Act was passed. In Hampstead the move for suppression stemmed from the magistrates after disturbances at the 1819 fair. With support from the Vestry and a committee of householders, and with encouragement from the Home Office, the local magistrates in 1820 assembled a force of some 150 men, including fifty special constables, to ensure that no fair was again held. Despite opposition from tradesmen and from householders who gained money from letting their yards and gardens during the fair, William Masters, Vestry Clerk and Clerk to the Magistrates, could justifiably spend 10s. 6d. of public money for the insertion of a news report in the *Morning Advertiser* in July 1820 headed 'West End Fair abolished'.[10] The Hampstead magistrates had assumed the fair to be unchartered, and had dared anyone to challenge their display of force; they had not actually secured a verdict in the courts against the fair. From 1822 legal action was the obvious first step for any local authority with an unchartered fair on its hands. In 1823 the Act was used successfully to suppress Bow, Brook Green, Tothill Fields, Edmonton and Stepney Michaelmas fairs.[11] At a stroke the number of fairs in London was severely reduced, and the showman and the pleasure seeker alike had to adjust to a new world. For these were no minor declining fairs that were thus abolished; Shoreditch had been attended by 30,000, Edmonton by 40,000.[12] As the 'Elegy on the Death of Bow Fair' put it:

No more the Fairing shall the fair allure,
For Fairs no more the fairing may expose:
In pleasure-lovers, work shall work a cure!
And Sundays only show the Sunday clothes!

Take warning then, ye fair! from this fair's fall!
One act (the Vagrant Act) hath been its ruin!
Listen, oh listen, to *Law's serious call,*
For fun and pleasure lead but to undoing![13]

But the elegist was too pessimistic. Other fairs, and important ones, survived. The magistrates tried to use the Act to rid themselves of

Camberwell and Peckham fairs in 1823, but the law officers did not consider the evidence produced sufficient to warrant abolition.[14] Peckham fair was eventually abolished in 1827, but Camberwell not until 1855.[15] Similarly the inhabitants of Pinner appealed to the Lord of the Manor, Lord Northwick, against the attempt of the Edgware magistrates to abolish both Harrow and Pinner fairs, determined, they said, 'to defend their public right in every legal way'. Both fairs survived.[16]

Most important of all, Greenwich, unchartered though it was, survived the attempts to abolish it in the 1820s. Although Francis Place reported in 1824 that 'the fair had been put *down* by the Justices and the Saints',[17] it was in 1825 and 1826 that the main moves against the fair were made. A petition of Easter Tuesday 4 April 1825 to the Justices of the Peace from the Vicar, Churchwardens, and the Overseers, Governors and Directors of the Poor represented that the fairs at Easter and Whitsun were without charter, and in recent years, and especially with the suppression of neighbouring fairs,

> that the numbers of the profligate part of the lower orders have been increased, that the money heretofore spent in the Town, or to the benefit of the Tradesmen generally, is now almost entirely squandered in the numerous Booths and Shows, to the detriment of the Parish and (what is the great foundation of this appeal) that a very great addition is made to this evil by the increased − the open and powerful − incentives to licentiousness among the middle and lower orders of the community.[18]

According to the *Weekly Dispatch* the petition had only twenty-seven signatures, and on the very same day, 4 April, the Clerks to the Magistrates, with the approval and knowledge of only two magistrates, issued a notice forbidding the fair. Some weeks later a regular meeting of the magistrates approved the action.[19] What is odd at this point is that the magistrates should have reverted to the methods of their Hampstead colleagues in 1820, rather than use the legal machinery set up under the 1822 Act. The showmen considered the notice to be a bluff, and this belief can only have been confirmed by a further magisterial notice issued on 17 May which expressed a determination to prevent booths or stalls being erected in roads, streets or highways, and to stop obstructions, but did not declare the fair illegal. Richardson and the other leading showmen started to erect their booths for the Whitmonday fair, but on Whitsunday officers of the parish, attended by forty special constables, ordered Richardson to 'clear off forthwith'. Richardson refused, but when the officers threatened to pull down his theatre, he and others moved off to Wandsworth fair. But the huge Crown and Anchor Dancing Booth, and other shows remained, and the parish officers left them in possession. The fair was reported to be numerously attended.[20]

Having failed to secure abolition in 1825, the magistrates in 1826 hoped for more success by making use of the 1822 Act. They issued summonses against the three owners of the ground upon which the fairs were held, calling upon them to show their right and title. Only one of the parties involved, a Mr Delaney, appeared at the Petty Sessions, and while the magistrates declared the fairs illegal, Delaney entered into the required recognizances to appear in the Court of King's Bench to meet any information filed against him. This prevented immediate abolition, and meant that the fairs were held as usual in 1826.[21] Moreover, no action seems to have been brought against Delaney in the Court of King's Bench. At the least whiff of opposition, it seems, the magistrates stepped down from their attempts to enforce abolition. In ensuing years they attempted to restrict rather than abolish the fair, mainly through trying to persuade Princess Sophia, Ranger of the Park, to shut the park gates against the public; but she refused to do so.[22]

So Greenwich fair survived, though at this distance of time it is impossible to discover the balance of forces within Greenwich which enabled it to do so. What is clear, though, is that having beaten off the attack of the mid-1820s Greenwich fair lived to enjoy an Indian summer in the 1830s and 1840s. Precisely at the time when they had become established in the middle-class consciousness as 'relics of a barbarous age',[23] fairs received a new lease of life from that symbol of progress, the railway. In February 1836 the railway between Deptford and Spa Road, Bermondsey was opened; in December 1838 it reached Greenwich. On Whitmonday 1839 the railway carried 35,000 passengers to Greenwich. As T.C. Barker has written, 'the railway's main function, so far as short distance passenger traffic was concerned, was to provide for the occasional pleasure trip rather than the regular journey to work'.[24]

Fairlop fair, held in July, booming as a fair in the 1830s and 1840s must have gained from the opening of the Eastern Counties Railway to Ilford in 1839, though in this case the journey by road had a peculiar significance. The fair had been established by Daniel Day, a block and pump maker of Wapping, who from about 1725 had established a custom of meeting with his friends and tenants at Fairlop Oak on the first Friday in July. They travelled from Wapping in a boat on wheels drawn by horses. So popular did the fair become that in 1828 'in consequence of the vast concourse of persons who have resorted to it from the Metropolis, whose numbers have annually increased, it is extended to three or four days; sometimes to more than a week'. It was a truly popular festival of the East End, the journey to and from Wapping as important as the fair itself. Vans, gigs, omnibuses and carts were gaily decorated, and the boats of the watermen and block-makers were drawn by six post horses with postillions superbly dressed. It was in 1840 that there was an attempt at Ilford Petty Sessions to abolish the fair (which of course was unchartered). When the Lord of the Manor, who had been summoned, said he would challenge the case in the Court of Queen's Bench, the magistrates quickly changed their tune and said their only wish was to restrict the fair to the original one day, and to prevent the desecration of the Sabbath. This was agreed. A further attempt to abolish the fair through a show of force in 1846 ended only in the discomfiture of the magistrates and the police; according to Admiral Harvey, 'They ordered the booths to be taken down, but the numbers assembled shewed the impossibility and danger in effecting such an object; the vulgar wit with which they were assailed, was such as exceeded everything of the kind he had ever before heard.'[25]

It was not the action of the magistrates, but an Act of Parliament which brought an end to Fairlop fair in its original venue. In 1853 Hainault Forest was disafforested, and the original site of the fair shut off from the public. But so deeply entrenched was the habit of celebrating the first Friday in July that an alternative site was found in a field opposite the Old Maypole Inn at Barkingside, then at the Bald Hind at Chigwell, and later back at the Old Maypole. Well into the second half of the century Fairlop fair day remained a day of celebration and festival in the East End.[26]

The other big fair of the 1840s was at Stepney, 'glorious old Stepney Fair, then the biggest gathering of the kind in England', as Sanger described it in 1848. Partially suppressed, it seems, in the 1820s and 1830s, this Easter and Whitsun fair was revived on a big scale in the 1840s, visited according to the *Illustrated London News* by not less than 200,000 people on Easter Monday 1844.[27]

The revival of Stepney fair seems to have been possible because of the reluctance of the police to interfere with it. By 1843, *The Times* was full of praise for a well-conducted fair, and reported that 'neither the Commissioners of Police nor magistrates are at all disposed to interfere with these harmless recreations of the people at the proper seasons. The excellent arrangements of the police of the K Division, their great forbearance, and their disposition to afford every facility to the visitors, are deserving of great praise.'[28]

This new police attitude is visible from the late 1830s, and reflects a considerable police confidence that popular festivals could be controlled. In a joint performance before the Select Committee on Metropolis Police Offices in 1838 Col. Rowan and Richard Mayne, the Commissioners of the Metropolitan Police, claimed that the conduct of the populace was much better since the establishment of the police, 'that there has been a great improvement' at fairs in particular and that 'there is a general disposition on the part of the people, on all occasions where the police are called upon to act, to assist them.'[29]

In that same year, 1838, the government gave permission for a fair to be held in Hyde Park to celebrate the coronation of the Queen. It was not only a remarkable financial success for the showmen, but also witnessed unprecedented cooperation between the police under Superintendent Mallalieu and the showmen, headed by Nelson Lee and John Johnson. At the end of the fair Mallalieu received a silver cup from the showmen at a dinner at the Champion Tavern, Paddington.[30] In 1850 Lee and Johnson suggested a repeat on the occasion of the Great Exhibition, arguing that if there was such a fair, 'persons least likely to benefit the Great Industrial Exhibition may be withdrawn from the immediate Neighbourhood of Hyde Park by a class of Entertainment found to be most attractive to them'. Far from being a threat to public order fairs were now being presented as an aid to it. Whether or not the government swallowed this argument, the fair was held, though on this occasion it was a financial disaster for the showmen.[31]

This was partly because heavy rain drenched the ground, but also, one may suspect, because the Great Exhibition proved a formidable rival. The apparent revival of fairs in the 1830s and 1840s, after the attack on them in the 1820s, was built on shaky ground. In the 1850s Bartholomew, Camberwell, Greenwich, Stepney, and, as we have seen, Fairlop in its original form, were all abolished. This was possible not only because of renewed attack by the authorities, but also because showmen themselves found fairs less and less profitable. Thomas Frost, the most percipient observer of the mid-century metropolitan fairs, noted that while the crowds increased, the showmen's receipts diminished and their expenses rose. The people flocked to the fairs at least in part because they were cheap, an increasing number of the shows costing no more than 1d. After mid-century improved transport, higher earnings and more leisure time encouraged the growth of permanent places of entertainment for the masses. It became less and less profitable for showmen to wander from fair to fair, staying at each place only three or four days.[32] For the big showmen the circus offered a better future than the fairs. At a low point in the third quarter of the nineteenth century, fairs were to revive on the basis of mechanisation whose origins were rural rather than urban. By the late nineteenth century fairs had been reconstituted. The chief attractions were mechanised swings and roundabouts, in place of the theatrical shows and dancing booths of the first half of the century.[33]

Of the fairs abolished in the 1850s, Camberwell succumbed in 1855 when a group of individuals purchased the rights of the lord of the manor, and turned the land where the fair was held into a public park.[34] Stepney's decline is less easy to trace, and may possibly have been caused by the land where it was held being built on. It seems to have been finally abolished in 1860, though little is heard of it throughout the 1850s.[35] The more significant disappearances were those of Bartholomew and Greenwich.

Few 'deaths' have been more protracted than that of Bartholomew fair. From the mid-eighteenth century, to go no further back, the City authorities had attempted to control or abolish it, often leading to serious rioting. In 1761, 1762, 1798, 1816, 1825-6, and almost continually from 1830 the Court of Common Council considered ways of ending the fair, eventually deciding to kill it off by restricting the type of show allowed and by raising the rents for the showmen.[36] This caution stemmed not only from the legal opinion that abolition would require an Act of Parliament, but also because until at least the 1830s the fair remained a popular occasion, which it would have been difficult to move against openly without provoking retaliation. The voice of the Licensed Victuallers, loud in support of the fair, was heard in the Court of Common Council, and outside Lady Holland's mob could prove too powerful for the forces of law and order. As Charles Pearson, the City Solicitor, put it in his important report of 1840, 'It is at all times difficult by law to put down the ancient customs and practices of the multitude. . .' With faith in the improving habits of the people, and in order to avoid 'exciting any of those feelings of discontent and disapprobation with which its compulsory abolition would probably be now attended', he suggested a limitation of the days of the fair, and a refusal to let standings for show booths.[37] Swings and roundabouts had been abolished since 1819. The fair was left to the vendors of gingerbread and toys, and in 1855 died the 'natural death' which Pearson had predicted. The showmen had resisted the strangulation of the fair, petitioning against the raising of the rents (for Johnson and Lee they were raised from £25 to £70), refusing to pay the 50 per cent increase demanded by the Court of Pie Powder, but were rewarded only with an alternative and unsuccessful site in Britannia Fields.[38]

Greenwich fair was already in decline at the time of the successful move to abolish it in 1857. A minor riot involving artillerymen in 1850 did the fair no good, and the star attraction, Johnson and Lee's Theatre, successors to the great Richardson, appeared for the last time in 1852; they were finding it more profitable to stay in one place for two or three weeks.[39] The time, then, was propitious for a public campaign against the fair.[40] The crucial steps seem to have been taken by Lord Haddo, son of Lord Aberdeen, the Ranger of the Park, who, resenting the intrusion of the people into the park, got up, without publicity, a petition of 136 householders living in the immediate vicinity of the fairground, calling for the suppression of the fair. This was supported by the Superintendent of Police and laid before Sir Richard Mayne, the Commissioner of Metropolitan Police, on 23 February. The latter directed that the Superintendent should apply to the magistrates for summonses against the owners of the land on which the fair was held, calling upon them to show by what authority the fairs were held. That is to say resort was made to the 1822 Act, available at any time since that date for the abolition of the notoriously unchartered fair, but only now, when the fair was in decline, successfully used. It was this small petition, rather than a second larger one, which led directly to the abolition. Opposition to abolition, manifest at a public meeting and in a petition, was of no avail. The Superintendent of Police dismissed the opponents of abolition as seeming to 'consist principally of Publicans, Beer and other small shopkeepers, living on the spot and deriving pecuniary advantage from them', and Sir George Grey, the Home Secretary, regretted that he was unable to meet a deputation in favour of the fairs. Two of the owners of the land on which the fairs were held indicated privately their intention not to contest the case, and the third, Mr Hockley, a publican, did so only, it was believed, so that he could delay the end of the fairs, and gain the profits on one last occasion. He, too, eventually gave way, and the fairs were thereby legally abolished. At Easter, the police reported, 'all passed off quietly at Greenwich. . . the discontinuance of the Fair having caused no excitement whatever. . . There was a very considerable attendance of

Holiday Visitors, and although of the lowest classes, they behaved in an orderly manner.'[41] But at least someone felt strongly about the abolition; a Seven Dials 'Lament for Poor Old Greenwich Fair' includes the lines:

> Oh cruel was the naughty rogues how could they ever dare
> To sign a long petition to kill old Greenwich fair
> May they never see a comfort may they never taste a nut
> May they die upon the river with a scratcher in their guts.[42]

The abolitions of the 1850s left inner London bereft of fairs. A Londoner in search of a fair now had to travel to find one, and the railway enabled and encouraged him to do so. Previously local and semi-rural fairs found themselves invaded by hordes from the metropolis. The first community to complain was Croydon, where the October fair had always been a major event, but which 'was never visited by so many thousands of persons as in the years of its decadence, which commence with the opening of the railway'.[43] In September 1854 two Quakers requested the Commissioners of the Metropolitan Police to interfere to prevent the fair being held for more than two days. The police could find no charter for the fair, and thereupon applied to the Croydon Bench for a summons to be served on the owner of the fair, Mr Thomas Brooker, a cattle dealer, 'but the Magistrates, after taking the whole day to consider the application, refused to grant the Summons', one magistrate declaring that the Quakers 'want to have it all their own way, but won't with us'. Faced with this magisterial intransigence, the police informed the two Quakers that they could take the case no further. In March 1855 a more impressive petition, signed by 1,148 of the 'Clergy, Gentry and Inhabitants' was received at the Home Office. Going further than the Quakers, the memorialists wanted the October fair restricted to one day only for the sale of animals. The difficulty in obtaining abolition at this point lay not with the Home Office, but with the Croydon Bench, as the police thought it unlikely that the new signatures would alter the magistrates' decision of 1854 not to grant a summons. In any case, the Superintendent reported, although at the 1854 fair twenty prisoners had been arrested, he 'did not observe any particular act of disorder and it was generally remarked, that the last Fair passed off more quiet, and with less disorder, than had been known for some years'. Faced with this evidence from the police, the first of a number of police reports which openly disagreed with the petitioners for the abolition of a fiar, the Home Secretary, Sir George Grey, decided that no action should be taken.[44]

The memorialists, however, persevered, and their investigations unearthed the fact that there *was* a charter for the fair — and for three days. This discovery made it much more difficult to abolish the fair, but it was tempered by the fact that the charter was granted to the Archbishop of Canterbury, who, the memorialists suggested, might be persuaded to resign his right. Since the opening of the railway, they claimed, the fair 'has been known to bring down in one day as many as 13,000 Persons into this District, a large number of whom are of the worst possible Character'. Would Grey communicate with the Archbishop, and would he in the meantime restrict the fair to three days? The Home Office response is interesting, an early indication of official support for fairs: 'This Quaker prejudice against fairs is not shared by others, and the Government are neither called upon to address the Archbishop nor to interfere in the limitation of days.' Grey gave his approval that a letter in this sense should be written to the memorialists. Between them, the Croydon magistrates, the police and the Home Office saved Croydon fair.[45]

Thus matters remained until the late 1860s when a new legislative onslaught on fairs commenced. The background to it is not entirely clear for none of the bills received even cursory debate in Parliament. The first move was a Home Office bill in 1868 to give extra powers for the prevention of recently-founded unchartered fairs, presumably aimed at the 'New Fairs' on vacant land described by Sanger.[46] Secondly, and more important, was a privately sponsored bill in 1871 'to facilitate the abolition' of fairs in England and Wales. Certain fairs, the preamble stated, 'are unnecessary, are the cause of grievous immorality, and are very injurious to the inhabitants of the towns in which such fairs are held'. The procedure for securing abolition was simple. The Home Secretary, on the representation of the magistrates or of the owner that the abolition of a fair 'would be for the convenience and advantage of the public' and with the consent of the owner, could order a fair to be abolished. The only proviso was that notice must be given of the day on which the Home Secretary would consider representations in favour of or in opposition to a fair. Short and effective, the Act was used to eliminate many fairs, particularly in the south-east of England.[47]

Although it seems probable that the Act was initiated with a rural rather than an urban problem in mind, it was soon applied to metropolitan and suburban fairs. Blackheath and Charlton were the first to be abolished, in March 1872, after the magistrates had called a special petty sessions to consider representations made to them about both fairs. Opposition to abolition came from thirty-five inhabitants and rate-payers, marshalled by John Turner, a publican, who rented land on which Charlton fair was held; their memorial, commented the Home Office, 'savours of the Publican and the signatures are of a very shaky character'. There was also opposition in the form of a letter from a Mr W. Hammond, who makes his meaning clear despite some shaky grammar and a total lack of punctuation: 'I send in an objection which is very short and simple that it is very plain there is one law for the *poor* and another for the rich.' It was ridiculous, he went on, to pretend that the disturbance to Charlton at fair time was in any way comparable to the disturbance to Epsom during the Derby, yet no one proposed to abolish the latter. 'All I can say is the more these places are done away with it takes the people freedom away and makes them very disloyal what they are doing on Blackheath now the people are all up at arms in their hearts.'

This defence of the poor was of no avail. The police were concerned at the 'great annoyance to the inhabitants of the neighbourhood who are of a highly respectable class', and the Blackheath Justices, in a report to the Home Office, made it clear that the weight of respectable opinion was in favour of abolition while 'it is evident on the face of the memorial in opposition that many of its signers are people of no position'. In the 1880s the Home Office might have paid some attention to the 'people of no position', but in 1872 the Home Secretary, despite the fact that some of the technicalities of the Act had not been adhered to, gave his assent to the abolition of what the Plúmstead Board of Works called 'the only so-called Pleasure Fair remaining within the Metropolitan District'.[48] In the same year, 1872, Harrow fair, which had survived attempts at abolition in 1829 and 1860 (the latter spearheaded by C.J. Vaughan, Headmaster of Harrow School), was abolished without a murmur of protest.[49]

Attention now turned to what had become the two major fairs for East Enders, Harlow Bush and Barnet. The former was abolished in 1879, the latter survived. Both were in origin cattle fairs, and in essence it was the greater importance of trade at Barnet which ensured its survival. Harlow Bush fair was held on 9 and 10 September on the Common. According to the memorial in favour of abolition from 116 'Owners of Property, Ratepayers and Inhabitants' the fair had 'of late years become the resort of the most dissolute and disorderly persons for the most part from the East end of London who congregate not for the purpose of any legitimate trade or business but with rare exceptions for dissipation, profligacy and immorality of the worst kind.' There was, however, a petition against abolition. It claimed that it was still an important cattle fair, and that the occasion 'as a Pleasure Fair and means of innocent recreation is eagerly looked forward to by the whole Countryside and as such is attended and supported in many instances by the Gentry and Clergy of the District.' The reference of the matter to the police produced a most interesting reply from Superintendent Simpson. During his eleven years of service in the area he had not known 'any Disorderly conduct or Immorality unusual to so large an assemblage of persons principally from the East-end of London'. The pleasure seekers, he continued, 15,000 to 20,000 in number, 'prepare for the day's outing by subscribing to a penny Weekly Fund to the Bus and Van proprietors, each Van being accompanied by one or more musicians'. They arrived at the fair about noon, and started to return about 4 p.m., so that by 7 p.m. only fifty or a hundred people remained, mainly local inhabitants. He admitted, however, 'that a much larger number of the rough class from the East End of London attended the fair of 1878, and were rather disorderly'. Nevertheless Simpson ended his report on a note almost of bravado. 'As a matter of course', he wrote, 'the enjoyment of the above class of people would be interfered with by its abolition.' Simpson's superior, Admiral and Chief Constable McHardy, in forwarding the report to the Home Office, could not fail to note Simpson's clear belief that there were no grounds for abolition; nevertheless, 'taking everything into consideration', he advocated the suppression of the fair. At the Home Office, the Under-Secretary of State, Sir Matthew White Ridley, favoured abolition, but it was thought wisest to seek further comments from the Chairmen of the Quarter Sessions, Sir H.S. Ibbetson and J.W. Perry Watlington, the latter hardly disinterested since he was one of the magistrates who had supported abolition in the first instance; not surprisingly he reiterated his views. Ibbetson also supported abolition, claiming that when he was a boy 'it used to be respectably conducted, and was really a people's holiday, but since the London roughs have taken possession of it' it was becoming annually a greater nuisance to the neighbourhood. Simpson, he wrote, was 'very unwilling to admit the possibility of its being supposed that he was not equal to deal with any amount of disorder'. With the chief witness in favour of the fair thus discredited, Richard Cross, the Home Secretary, decided to abolish.[50]

Although Barnet was first and foremost a cattle fair, the pleasure fair side of it grew, especially with the coming of the Great Northern Railway in 1850, and more conveniently the branch line to High

Barnet in 1872. Already in 1857 the *Barnet Gazette* was complaining of the 'torrent of lawless ruffianism from London' encouraged to come by the railway, and in 1859 it favoured abolition of 'the so-called Pleasure Fair'.[51] Opposition to the fair continued through the 1860s and 1870s, but it was not until 1888 that it showed signs of becoming effective.[52] In May 1888 Walter Justice, Solicitor to the owner of the fair, W.H. Richardson of Southampton, wrote to the Home Office, stating his client's wish to abolish the fair under the 1871 Act. The September fair, he said, was attended 'by the lowest class of buyers and sellers, and the scum of London who make holiday there'.[53] These 'scum' were primarily the costermongers. As a costermonger told James Greenwood,

> Bartlemy had its fair, but it was 'bolished. Camberwell had its fair, and quite a 'spectable class went to it, mecanicks and their families, but somehow it grew ugly, and it was 'bolished too. Then there was Greenwich. Gents went to Greenwich with tall hats and collars and cuffs, and females dressed in the wery height of fashion, but Greenwich was 'bolished. The townpeople complained of the orful goings on, and the perlice was down on it. But *our* fair, the fair wot's kep going by the London costermonger, is as flourishing and rosy as ever.

There was, as he said, 'nothing stuck up' about Barnet fair. Like Fairlop and Harlow Bush, the journey to the fair, preferably by road in a newly-painted vehicle, was as important as the fair itself, where the entertainments were traditional and small-scale — waxworks, monstrosities, a sparring booth, a Kaffir eating live rats, dancing. It was this well-supported traditionalism, the fair established as an annual festival in the calendar of working-class North and East London which was one factor making the survival of the fair possible.[54]

But there were other and more important ones. Opposition to abolition quickly showed itself, and from apparently respectable quarters. The Barnet Local Board, a Public Vestry of the Inhabitants of Chipping Barnet, the East Barnet Valley Local Board, the Barnet Rural Sanitary Authority, the MPs for the area and 2,459 signatories of a petition all opposed abolition. It would be a mistake to be led by this evidence to believe that the respectable authorities of Barnet favoured the pleasure fair — the truth was that the fair, particularly as a horse, cattle and sheep fair, was immensely profitable to the town and to neighbouring farmers who could rent out their land for grazing. It was

this which gave weight to the movement in favour of the continuation
of the fair.

As was the custom when there was dispute over the abolition of a
fair, the case was referred to the police. Enclosing his Superintendent's
report, Thomas Pearson could 'see no reason from a Police point of
view why this long established Fair should be abolished'. An average of
about 20,000 persons, reported the Superintendent, 'principally of
the tradesmen and labouring classes, attend daily, the Great Northern
Railway running special trains from London, whilst at the same time
it is largely attended by the Country Folk residing in the vicinity, and
for several miles around'. Of the offences committed during the previous
five years, almost half were for cruelty to animals, the cases being
brought by the officers of the RSPCA. There was very little disorder,
continued the Superintendent,

> and it is certainly not within the knowledge of Police either from
> their own observation, or from information given by other persons,
> that acts of immorality are committed. The fair is almost the only
> source of amusement brought within reach of the poorer country
> people during the year, and it is much enjoyed by them, and in
> addition it is a means of assisting small and struggling tradesmen of
> the town, as well as private persons who let lodgings.

Once again, as in the case of Harlow Bush fair, the police seem
sympathetic to the fair, and their evidence, added to the opinion of
established local interests, was sufficient to make the Home Secretary
decide against abolition. Barnet fair continued.[55]

The police also played an important part in securing the continuation
of Pinner fair, which the Magistrates, the Vicar and other inhabitants
wished to abolish in 1894. According to the police, during the last
twelve years there had been no summons or charge in connection with
the fair, no case of felony reported to the police, and no disorder or
case of immorality. On the positive side, 'it is reported that the Fair is
looked forward to by several hundreds of the poorer classes living at
and around Pinner, as their only holiday in the year; and, purely as a
matter of personal opinion, the Police consider that the abolition of this
Fair would, to some extent, interfere with the enjoyment of the poorer
classes of the community.' The Home Office referred this police
opinion to Mr R. Loveland Loveland, Deputy Chairman of the Middlesex
Quarter Sessions. He was strongly in favour of abolition, claiming that
there had been a considerable change in the character of the fair with

the opening of the Metropolitan Railway Extension through Pinner, and that the police were reluctant to prosecute for drunkenness. To Loveland's claims that the railway brought 'the rough element and disorderly and disreputable men and women', the police replied that those who came from a distance appeared 'to be mainly of the respectable though poor classes who come for a day's pleasure'. Faced with this conflicting evidence, the Home Office decided against abolition; as N.F. Reynard stated in a Minute,

> the persons petitioning for its abolition are apparently well to do people who find the Fair a nuisance whereas the people desiring its retention are mostly apparently the poor and illiterate. The record of the Fair is exceptionally good and if it be abolished many persons of the labouring class would I think be deprived of a day's harmless amusement with they are accustomed to look forward to with pleasure.[56]

The police and the Home Office, indeed, in the 1880s and 1890s seem to have been surprisingly favourable to the continuation of fairs and other types of public working-class entertainment. Harcourt, as Home Secretary from 1880, 'decided that a fair was not to be discontinued merely because it was no longer needed for business and gave trouble to the police, if it still provided once or twice a year a popular amusement for poor people'.[57] This attitude we have seen reflected in police reports on Barnet and Pinner. It is apparent too in police comments on Edgware and Feltham fairs. A move to abolish Edgware fair in 1883 was countered by a petition of local inhabitants, described by the inspector of police as those who 'although poor are respectable people most of whom I know personally'. His superintendent stressed that the fair was a small local one in a place 'absolutely devoid of amusement. . . in my opinion the abolition of the fair would interfere with the reasonable enjoyment of the shopkeeping and poorer classes'. Similarly in Feltham in 1887 where a petition in favour of abolition, signed by 102 people, and supported by the magistrates, was countered by one signed by 183 people, including thirty-three illiterates. 'The abolition of the Fair', wrote Commissioner Sir Charles Warren, 'is a class question on which as Commissioner of Police I can say little beyond the fact that it gives the Police trouble to keep order, and that while one class certainly enjoy it, its existence is the cause of annoyance to others.' In both cases the Home Office decided against abolition.[58]

In 1874 Thomas Frost concluded his study of the London fairs by

claiming that 'the nation has outgrown them, and fairs are as dead as
as the generations which they have delighted, and the last showman will
soon be as great a curiosity as the Dodo'.[59] Frost was wrong, and for a
number of reasons. First, he failed to anticipate the ability of the fairs
themselves to adapt to new conditions, and to make a positive virtue
of the mechanical skills of the industrial revolution. The fair itself
became mechanised, and as such had the power to excite and give
pleasure to the people.[60] Secondly, Frost overemphasised the 'mass'
quality of entertainment in the nineteenth century. Not only in
country areas but also as we have seen when looking at some of the
London fairs (Edgware and Pinner for example), many people, despite
the music halls and the trains, continued to look to their immediate
locality for their entertainment. Thirdly, he failed to recognise that
those fairs which no longer existed had not so much died as been
killed. None had simply faded away. Abolition always required a
positive and often resisted act by authority. A change, therefore, in the
attitude of authority towards fairs offered them considerable hope of
survival. This change was first evident in the confident police attitudes
in the 1830s, and it reached its height under Harcourt's leadership at the
Home Office in the 1880s. Harcourt wished to do all he could 'to
favour these cheap pleasures of the poor'.[61] Such an attitude brought
him into conflict with magistrates, ratepayers, clergymen and others
who continued to see fairs as dangerous orgies. But since it was the
Home Office which had to approve the abolition of any fair Harcourt
was in a position to resist the irate petitions of worthy local inhabitants
anxious to avoid an annual eruption from the East End into their quiet
neighbourhoods.

In Harcourt's case an aristocratic Whiggish attitude to 'the people'
may have been at the root of his desire not to meddle with the amusements of the poor. But there are other less idiosyncratic reasons. As
Britain became a mature industrial society, the early industrial revolution
emphasis on work to the exclusion of all else had less and less force.
From at least mid-century very few people wished to deny all amusements to the poor. What is new in the last quarter of the century is the
growing belief that the poor could be safely entrusted to organise their
own entertainment. The heavy hand of middle-class patronage could be
removed not only because it was unsuccessful, but also because it was
unnecessary. This was partly because observers at music halls and such
like found the audiences well behaved, and the fare harmless if hardly
uplifting,[62] but also because the entrepreneurs of entertainment had
ceased to be classed by magistrates as rogues and vagabonds and had

become the recipients of Royal patronage. In Sanger's autobiography
few passages are more striking than that in which he skips from a
description of the hostile attitude to showmen prevalent in the 1830s
to the quotation of his own letters from the Queen at the turn of the
century; and few features are more noticeable than Sanger's friendly
relations with the police from about mid-century: a police inspector,
'an intimate friend', gives him a hint about his penny gaff; a detective
in Liverpool, 'a friend of mine' finds him some 'savages'; finally and
most dramatically in 1871 when he wants to gain publicity for his new
venture at Astley's by cashing in on the thanksgiving for the Prince of
Wales's recovery, he persuades his 'very good friends' the police to
pretend to resist his show tagging on behind the official one, and then
to give in to it.[63] By the late nineteenth century showmen had become
respectable, they cooperated with authority.

The people, too, were perceived to be, and were, much less of a
threat. The police now knew the people as well as the showmen. They
controlled Barnet fair by returning known thieves to London.[64] They
were confident in allowing Edgware fair to continue because most of
those who wished it to do so were personally known to the inspector.
From the police point of view late nineteenth-century society was much
less anonymous and therefore less dangerous than early nineteenth-
century society. But it was not only changes within the police which
made fairtime a less threatening occasion; it was also the new perspective within which late nineteenth-century observers saw the fair as a
routine and legitimate occasion for leisure, rather than as one of those
'violent delights' of Londoners which Jerrold portrayed as typical as
late as 1872.[65] This new routinisation of leisure, combined with greater
police authority, led to a change in leisure behaviour. There was no
late nineteenth-century equivalent of Lady Holland's mob, breaking
windows and holding the authorities to ransom at Bartholomew fair.
There was no longer any fear, as at Camberwell in 1819,[66] that radicals
would use the opportunity of a fair to their own political advantage.
Rather, in the late nineteenth-century fair there was a balance between
order and freedom which all the participants — authority, the showmen,
the visitors — were keen to maintain. To attract the people, the showman had to provide an entertainment which gave an appearance of
freedom to the participants — a sense of colour, of speed, of escape —
and this he did in a skilful amalgam of tradition and innovation. But it
was an entertainment which was highly organised, which had to be
paid for, and in which the experience of freedom contained a large
measure of fantasy. There was nothing in any of this to frighten an

authority which accepted leisure as an integral and necessary part of urban life. Only puritans and ratepayers continued to object.

Notes

1. Police Order of 28 Apr. 1885, HO 45/9639/A33890; cf. Sir E. Troup, *The Home Office* (London, 1925), pp. 209-10.
2. To the older studies of police history such as C. Reith, *A Short History of the British Police* (London, 1948), *A New Study of Police History* (Edinburgh, 1956), and T.A. Critchley, *A History of Police in England and Wales 900-1966* (London, 1967), should now be added A. Silver, 'The Demand for Order in Civil Society' in D.J. Bordua (ed.), *The Police, Six Sociological Essays* (New York, 1967); W. Miller, 'Police Authority in London and New York City, 1830-1870', *Journal of Social History*, VIII (1975), pp.81-101, and two articles by R.D. Storch: 'The Plague of the Blue Locusts: Police Reform and Popular Resistance in Northern England, 1840-57', *International Review of Social History*, XX (1975), pp.61-90, and 'The Policeman as Domestic Missionary: Urban Discipline and Popular Culture in Northern England, 1850-1880', *Journal of Social History*, IX (1976), pp.481-509.
3. C. Dickens, *Sketches by Boz*, 'Greenwich Fair'.
4. S and B. Webb, *The Parish and the County* (London, 1906), pp. 495, 528-9, 533-8; E.G. Dowdell, *A Hundred Years of Quarter Sessions* (London, 1932), pp.29-31; S. Rosenfeld, *The Theatre of the London Fairs in the 18th Century* (London, 1960).
5. S. Rosenfeld, ibid., p.129 refers to the mid-eighteenth-century suppression order, but claims that the fair continued until 1827; the document she refers to, however, clearly dates from 1727. It is true that there were some remnants of a fair in 1808, but at that date it seems to have been finally stamped out (Heal, A XI, 73, Camden Local History Library).
6. L. Radzinowicz, *A History of English Criminal Law*, III, (London, 1956), p.191; *The Times*, 3 and 6 Sept. 1804; J. Strutt, *The Sports and Pastimes of the People of England,* 1st edn. 1801 (London, 1830), pp.368-9; press cuttings in 'A collection of cuttings, playbills, MSS notes, and other material relating to Bartholomew Fair and Pie Powder Court' (Guildhall Library, MS. 1514); Bartholomew Fair Papers, Camden Local History Library G.7; 'Collection of cuttings relating to Bartholomew Fair' (British Museum c. 70.h.6); Robert Howard to John Eliot, 6 Sept. 1802, Greater London Record Office, Acc. 1017/1371.
7. Select Committee on the State of the Police of the Metropolis, *PP* 1816 (510), V, pp.50, 170; Select Committee on the State of the Police of the Metropolis, *PP* 1817 (484), VII, pp. 387, 393-4, 402-4, 524; Select Committee on the Police of the Metropolis, *PP* 1822 (440), IV, pp.148, 153-4, 165, 167-8.
8. *PP* 1822 (440), IV, pp.101-2.
9. Ibid., p. 148.
10. HO 42/192; Papers on West End Fair, Camden Local History Library, H 394.6.
11. *Weekly Dispatch*, 6 Apr., 11 and 25 May, 6 July 1823; *The Times*, 4 and 12 Sept., 1823; HO 43/32, p.27.
12. *PP* 1822 (440), IV, p.148.

13.   Copy in Tower Hamlets Central Library.
14.   *Weekly Dispatch,* 6 July 1823; HO 43/32, HO 60/1.
15.   For the abolition of Peckham fair see HO 60/1; Select Committee on the
       Police of the Metropolis, *PP* 1828 (533), VI, pp.138-40; W.H. Blanch,
       Ye Parish of Camerwell (London, 1877), pp. 313-4. For Camberwell
       see below, p.170.
16.   Greater London Record Office, Acc 76/1804 (Northwick Coll.).
17.   B.M. Add. MS. 35144, f. 182 (Place Papers).
18.   Quoted in R. Longhurst, 'Greenwich Fair', *Transactions of the Greenwich
       and Lewisham Antiquarian Society,* VII (1970), pp.204-5.
19.   *Weekly Dispatch,* 5 June 1825.
20.   Ibid.,29 May 1825; R. Longhurst, loc. cit., pp.205-6; *Morning Chronicle,*
       24 May 1825.
21.   *Weekly Dispatch,* 9 Apr. 1826.
22.   Ibid., 21 May 1826; as *Bell's Life in London* put it (1 Jan. 1828), the
       Princess's conduct 'was worthy of a member of the illustrious House of
       Brunswick, whose ambition it is, not only to preserve the glory of this
       Empire, but to reign in the hearts of its people'.
23.   James Grant, *Sketches in London* (London, 1838), p.320; cf. J. Hogg,
       London as it is (London, 1837), pp.320-1.
24.   T.C. Barker and M. Robbins, *A History of London Transport,* I (London,
       1963) I, pp.45-6,, 56-7.
25.   *PP* 1828 (533), VI, p. 215; press cuttings in Tower Hamlets Central
       Library; Fillinham Collection (B.M.), vol. IV.
26.   Ibid. c.f., C.M. Davies, *Mystic London* (London, 1875), pp. 122-8.
27.   G. Sanger, *Seventy Years a Showman* (London, 1926), p. 157; W. Hone,
       Every-day Book (London, 1878 edn.), I, p.221; *The Times,* 23 Apr. 1840,
       3 June 1841; *Illustrated London News,* 29 Mar. 1844 (cutting in Tower
       Hamlets Central Library).
28.   *The Times,* 20 Apr. 1843, 3 June 1841.
29.   Select Committee on Metropolis Police Offices, *PP* 1837-8 (578), XV,
       qq. 2091-9.
30.   T. Frost, *The Old Showmen and the Old London Fairs* (London, new
       edn., 1881) pp.326-9; cf. Fillinham Collection (B.M.), vol. IV and 'A
       Collection of cuttings, memoranda and printed ephemera relating to fairs
       in and around London' (Guildhall Library).
31.   HO 45/OS 3291; T. Frost, ibid., pp.355-6.
32.   T. Frost, ibid., pp.320, 348-9.
33.   D. Braithwaite, *Fairground Architecture* (London, 1968), pp.19, 31-65;
       I. Starsmore, *English Fairs* (London, 1975), esp. ch. III; S. Alexander,
       St Giles's Fair, 1830-1914 (History Workshop Pamphlet, no. 2, 1970),
       pp.44-52.
34.   W.H. Blanch, op.cit., pp.313-14; Fillinham Collection (B.M.), vol. IV;
       cf. H.J. Dyos, *Victorian Suburb* (Leicester, 1961), p.153.
35.   Notice of abolition (1860) in Tower Hamlets Central Library.
36.   H. Morley, *Memoirs of Bartholomew Fair,* new edn. (London, 1880), pp.
       340-87; S. Rosenfeld, op.cit., pp.3-4, 63-4.
37.   For Pearson's report, Minutes of the Court of Common Council, 2 July
       1840; for the licensed victuallers, Journals of the City Lands Committee,
       vol. 115, pp. 114-16 (10 July 1823), vol. 117, pp.140-2 (5 Aug. 1825), vol.
       118, pp.90-2 (10 May 1826), Minutes of the Court of Common Council,
       21 June 1826 (all these in the Corporation of London Records Office); for
       Lady Holland's mob, Bartholomew Fair Papers, Camden Local History
       Library, G.7. T. Frost, op.cit., pp.191, 256; 'A collection of cuttings,
       memoranda and printed ephemera relating to fairs in and around London'

(Guildhall Library), referring to 1834. On Pearson, see T.C. Barker and M. Robbins, op.cit., p.100 n.

38. Journals of the City Lands Committee, vol. 111, p.129 (22 July 1819). The decline in the number of showmen can be traced in the 'Smithfield Court Book, containing proceedings in the Court of Pie Powder 1790-1854' (Guildhall Library), and the raising of rents and opposition thereto in Journal of the City Lands Committee, vol. 123, p.413 (27 July 1831), and annually thereafter, Journals of the City Markets Committee annually and esp. vol. II, pp.282-4, 308 (1840), and 'Smithfield Court Book. . .', 5 Sept. 1831, 4 and 5 Sept. 1838.

39. T. Frost, op.cit., pp.354-6.

40. See Rev. C.F.S. Money, *Greenwich Fair: A Nursery for Crime* (London, n.d.); 'An Address to the Inhabitants of Greenwich', printed for The British and Foreign Young Men's Society; *Borough of Greenwich Free Press*, 28 Feb. 1857 (all in Kent Collection, Local History Centre, Mycenae Rd, Greenwich.

41. *Kentish Mercury*, 7 Mar. 1857; HO 45/OS 6453.

42. Copy in Kent Collection, Local History Centre, Mycenae Rd, Greenwich.

43. T. Frost, op.cit., p.246.

44. HO 45/OS 6097.

45. Ibid. For similar police and Home Office reactions with reference to Barking fair in 1859, see HO 45/OS 6876.

46. 31 and 32 Vict. c. 106; G. Sanger, op. cit., pp.165-6; cf. G. Godwin, *Town Swamps and Social Bridges*, 1st edn. 1859 (Leicester, 1972), pp.98-9.

47. 34 and 35 Vict. c. 12; for the bill's sponsorship by Viscount Bury, R. Eykyn and C.S. Read, *PP* 1871 (60), II, pp.53-6. For the effects of the Act, see Subject Index and Box List to Home Office Papers, 1871-8, 1879-1900, 1900-9 (HO 45).

48. HO 45/9297/9886.

49. Greater London Record Office, Acc. 643 (Northwick Coll., 2nd deposit); HO 45/9310/13356.

50. HO 45/9571/77833. Ibbetson was Ridley's immediate predecessor in office, and in 1878, as Parliamentary Secretary to the Treasury, piloted through the House of Commons a bill to make Epping Forest a public recreation ground. (*D.N.B.*).

51. M. Jones, 'The social control of Barnet Fair in the nineteenth century' (Univ. of Kent BA dissertation, 1973), pp.7-9.

52. Ibid., pp.9-10.

53. HO 45/10436/B4198.

54. J. Greenwood, *Low-Life Deeps*, new edn. (London, 1881), pp.304-11; M. Jones, op.cit., p.16.

55. HO 45/10436/B4198.

56. HO 45/9878/B15620.

57. Sir E. Troup, op.cit., p.209; and for Harcourt's angry defence of the poor, HO 45/9639/A33890.

58. HO 45/9635/A28972; HO 45/9781/B2564.

59. T. Frost, op.cit., p.377.

60. D. Braithwaite, op.cit., I. Starsmore, op.cit.; and S. Alexander, op.cit.

61. HO 45/9639/A33890.

62. Select Committee on Theatrical Licenses and Regulations, *PP* 1866 (373), XVI, qq. 778-80, 969, 1297-9; P. Bailey, 'Rational Recreation and the Entertainment Industry; the case of the Victorian Music Halls', Paper to the Conference of the Society for the Study of Labour History (Nov. 1975), pp.17-18, 30-8.

63.   G. Sanger, op.cit., pp.100-8, 197, 233, 239-41.
64.   M. Jones, op.cit., p.19; cf. S. Alexander, op.cit., p.7.
65.   G. Doré and B. Jerrold, *London, a Pilgrimage,* 1st edn. 1872 (New York, 1970), pp.66-7, 161-2.
66.   HO 42/192.

7 ROCHDALE MAN AND THE STALYBRIDGE RIOT. THE RELIEF AND CONTROL OF THE UNEMPLOYED DURING THE LANCASHIRE COTTON FAMINE*

Michael E. Rose

First of all you see they catch the lion in their toils: then they cage him within bars of iron, clip his claws, draw his teeth, tame him with soup and gruel and having severely gagged him so that he cannot give either a roar of defiance or a howl of misery, they invite the world to look at him and admire him as the very pattern of all popular lions — the contented lion, the peaceable lion, the once fierce English lion turned into the harmless Lancashire lamb.[1]

Thus the Reverend Joseph Rayner Stephens, former Chartist sympathiser and bitter opponent of the New Poor Law of 1834, described the plight of the unemployed Lancashire operative to a public meeting in Stalybridge in February 1863. Few of Stephens' middle-class contemporaries would have shared his regret at the taming of the working-class lion. Indeed, as Gareth Stedman Jones has pointed out, the generally quiet and orderly conduct of the unemployed in Lancashire during the cotton famine provided 'indisputable evidence of moral and political maturity'.[2] 'Rochdale Man', the respectable self-helping, self-educating working man with his cooperative society, savings bank and chapel, had been severely tested by the experience of mass unemployment and had not been found wanting.[3] His reward for good conduct was to be the award of the franchise in 1867.

The Victorians looked back on the episode of the cotton famine with considerable satisfaction, especially when they compared the tranquil order of 1862 and 1863 with the riots and disturbances of 1819, 1826 and 1842.[4] Later historians have tended to re-echo, albeit less smugly, this tradition of long suffering patient behaviour on the part of the unemployed.[5] It is not the intention of this chapter to attempt to overturn the tradition, although there was undoubtedly more discontent at the relief policies pursued than some accounts have given credit for. Rather what follows constitutes an examination of the way in which unemployment relief, both official and voluntary, was controlled in order to prevent demoralisation and a possible breakdown of public order which many feared would be the result of long continued

185

distress in the cotton manufacturing districts.

Far from having immediate confidence in the capacity of 'Rochdale Man' to bear his privation nobly, there was growing alarm as the numbers of unemployed in the cotton districts mounted in 1861 and 1862, and the small savings of those thrown out of work became exhausted. In London, the Poor Law Board carefully monitored the situation.[6] In November 1861 it circulated all the twenty-eight boards of guardians in the distressed areas requesting a report from them on the present position and prospects of their district, and in May 1862 a special commissioner, H.B. Farnall, was despatched northwards to communicate with clergy, magistrates, boards of guardians, voluntary relief committees and all others involved in relieving the unemployed.[7] Farnall possessed two important qualifications for this task. In the first place, he had been a poor law inspector in Lancashire and the West Riding during the early 1850s and thus had some knowledge of the care required in handling local boards of guardians who were deeply suspicious of any interference by the Poor Law Board in their relief policies.[8] In the second place, and perhaps more significantly, Farnall was, at the time of his appointment in Lancashire, the poor law inspector responsible for poor law unions in the Metropolis. He was thus at the centre of the controversy surrounding the relief of distress in East London during the hard winter of 1860-61 when it was alleged that the poor law system had broken down and that indiscriminate private philanthropy had rushed in to fill the gap with disastrous results.[9]

The East London distress of 1860-61 led to the establishment of a Parliamentary Select Committee in February 1861 to enquire into the whole question of poor relief administration under the provisions of the Poor Law Amendment Act.[10] The select committee took nearly three years over its enquiries, and subjected the Poor Law Board and its policies to detailed scrutiny. The Board thus felt itself to be very much on trial in the early 1860s, especially as numerous calls for its abolition were made to the select committee.[11] Thus the Board's servants must have viewed the onset of distress in Lancashire with considerable alarm. Failure to control the administration of relief there would add strength to the arguments of those who were seeking to abolish centralised control of poor relief.

It was not merely a few civil servants fearing for their jobs who were alarmed at the mounting distress in Lancashire. Those who were concerned about the poor and their relief at both national and local levels, poor law inspectors, clergymen, magistrates, members of boards

of guardians, philanthropists, political economists and social thinkers,
feared a social catastrophe in Lancashire. The unemployed cotton
operatives, it was felt, would undoubtedly reject the none too tender
ministrations of the poor law system. Private charity would come to the
aid of those who refused to pick oakum or enter the workhouse.
Indiscriminate giving, however, could lead to relief being given in aid of
wages or other earnings. Cash doles might be spent in public houses.
The unemployed might soon come to find the bread of idleness sweeter
than that earned by the sweat of their brows. Unsupervised, and with
time on their hands, they would gather on street corners and provide
fuel for firebrand agitators like the Reverend Stephens. They would
become truculent and demand relief as their right. A once proud and
prosperous manufacturing district would become pauperised, its
condition resembling that of Sussex or Dorset in the bad old days of
the Speenhamland system. Pauperism, 'the social enemy of the modern
state', as C.S. Loch called it, had to be avoided at all costs in
Lancashire.[12] 'Many humane men with the best intentions caused an
amount of demoralisation in London last winter which it would take a
long time to overcome', wrote William Heys, the vice-chairman of
Stockport board of guardians to the Poor Law Board early in 1862.[13]
His letter requested a copy of the first report of the Select Committee
on Poor Relief, so that he and his fellow guardians could study it and
prevent the errors of East London being repeated in Stockport. If
pauperisation were to be prevented, control would have to be exercised
not merely over those in receipt of relief but also over those charged
with its distribution.

As far as the official agencies of poor relief were concerned, the central
authority, the Poor Law Board, could in theory control the actions of
the local boards of poor law guardians. Unions in manufacturing districts
were subject to the terms of the Outdoor Relief Regulation Order of
1852. Whilst less stringent than the Outdoor Relief Prohibitory Order,
which forbade all relief to able bodied persons except in the workhouse,
the Regulation Order laid down that no able bodied person should be
relieved if he was in work, that if relieved he should be set to work by
the guardians, and that half the relief given to him should be in kind
not cash. Any relief given which did not comply with these conditions
had to be reported to the central authority.[14] Failure to do this could
lead to the amounts paid being disallowed by the district auditor and
surcharged on the guardians. The Order had brought widespread protests
from boards of guardians in manufacturing districts when it was first
imposed in 1852, and remained a source of friction between boards of

guardians and the Poor Law Board.[15]

Boards of guardians complained that the Order interfered with their powers of discretion in giving relief. A period of short-time working in industry could, in their view, be got over more easily and cheaply in relief terms if they were allowed to pay a small dole to those working short-time who needed something to eke out their reduced earnings. Payment of relief in kind involved the trouble of purchasing provisions and distributing them amongst the scattered townships of the union. It was also unpopular with small shopkeepers since provisions would be distributed by the relieving officer and not purchased from them by those relieved. It was, however, the labour test which aroused most hostility from the guardians. Provision of organised labour, usually stone breaking or oakum picking at the workhouse, involved additional expenses such as the appointment of staff to supervise the work. Those sent to the labour test might have to walk long distances to and from the workhouse. Worse still, during a period of economic depression, respectable workmen who were unemployed through no fault of their own would have to perform the taskwork required in company with idle and dissolute persons to whom, in the guardians' view, the contemptuous term 'pauper' really applied. Mr Wimpenny, the chairman of Ashton board of guardians, complained to the Poor Law Board of the 'incongruous assemblages' which would result if the guardians were to enforce a labour test. These gatherings, he argued, would include the very worst as well as the respectable, and the latter would be demoralised by the presence of the former.[16]

Many boards of guardians in the cotton districts saw the onset of distress in 1861 as providing an ideal opportunity for them to press for repeal or suspension of the hated Order. 'The guardians have great reason to fear that the country has not for years experienced such a crisis as that which it is now entering and they trust that under existing circumstances they may be allowed absolute discretion in the cases of able bodied men until an improvement takes place in the staple trade of this district', the Ashton guardians told the Poor Law Board in November 1861.[17] A few months later, they were writing to other boards of guardians in the area inviting them to join in a deputation to the Poor Law Board to press for a suspension of the Order.[18]

At the same time, the poor law inspector in the area, J.L. Manwaring, strongly advised the Poor Law Board against any relaxation of the Order. He feared that any such action might allow the guardians to grant outdoor relief indiscriminately. 'Several of the guardians present were millowners', he reported after a visit to the Ashton board, 'and no doubt would like to give relief to some of their workmen in aid of wages.'[19]

This advice from their inspector placed the Poor Law Board in a severe dilemma. If they gave in to the demands of the guardians and suspended the Order, they ran the risk of a revival of the Speenhamland system which could demoralise the Lancashire operatives. On the other hand, too rigid an enforcement of the rules regulating outdoor relief could earn them the active hostility of the local boards of guardians, and serve to reawaken the anti-poor law feeling which had remained close to the surface in this area since the disturbed period of the late 1830s and early 1840s. Speakers at a Stalybridge meeting in 1862 attacked the Poor Law Board for attempting with 'cobweb rules' and 'paper precepts' to control 'the feelings welling up from the depths of society'.[20] 'The Oldham Guardians have openly defied the London Board', Dr J.H. Bridges wrote to Frederic Harrison early in 1863, 'and give relief without oakum. The office sends them several letters every week and they throw them under the table.'[21]

In fact, the central authority proved to be far less rigid than Bridges implied. Whilst they did not suspend the Relief Regulation Order, they allowed numerous cases to be relieved without complying with its demands. To save the guardians the onerous task of reporting the details of each individual case, a special form was provided on which only the weekly numbers of exceptional cases had to be entered.[22] In December 1862, over 5,000 adults were being relieved by Ashton guardians outside the terms of the Order at a time when just over 7,000 adult able bodied paupers were in receipt of poor relief.[23] Boards of guardians paid out small allowances of between 1s and 2s per head weekly to distressed operatives, and assumed that this meagre sum would be augmented from other sources, short-time earnings, income from other members of the family or charitable aid. 'Surely no one expected that what the guardians gave was enough of itself', remarked the chairman of the Ashton board in defence of its relief policy.[24] Despite continual protests from Inspector Manwaring that relief in aid of wages was taking place, the Poor Law Board persisted in their policy of maintaining the letter but not the spirit of the Relief Regulation Order, satisfied that the very low amounts of relief paid by the guardians would be unlikely to demoralise the recipient.[25] By keeping the guardians on a light rein, the Board hoped to maintain some control over relief policies, whilst at the same time preventing an open rebellion against their authority which could prove dangerous in areas where anti-poor law feeling was already running high. At the same time, by obtaining the passage of the Union Relief Aid Act of

1862, the Poor Law Board hoped to improve the financial position of the Lancashire Unions in a period when mills and shops were closing and parishes in distressed areas were experiencing considerable difficulty in meeting the growing demands of the boards of guardians.[26]

Of much greater importance than the Union Relief Aid Act in taking pressure off the rates in the distressed areas, however, was the rapid organisation of private charitable funds for the relief of the unemployed. It had always been traditional in periods of depression in industrial areas for leading local inhabitants to organise distress committees and solicit subscriptions for the relief of the unemployed. In the early years of the cotton famine, a whole rash of committees were formed in the cotton towns, so that, by April 1863, H.B. Farnall estimated that there were 158 of them spending £23,000 a week and saving an increase of 4s 3d in the poor rates.[27] Essential though such voluntary effort was to prevent a collapse of the hard pressed poor law system, it posed a greater problem of control than did the demands of boards of guardians for discretionary powers. Indiscriminate charitable giving had, it was felt, done much to pauperise East London in the winter of 1860, and a similar fate might befall Lancashire unless private as well as public aid could be distributed in a strictly regulated manner. An additional source of danger lay in the fact that, following the letters of 'A Lancashire Lad' in *The Times* in the spring of 1862, donations for the relief of distress began to pour into Lancashire from other parts of Britain and the world.[28] Whilst funds raised locally might on the whole be expected to be administered with economy, since those who had contributed most towards them were usually prominent in their distribution, no such barrier to imprudence existed in the case of national funds. Philanthropists whose hearts were larger than their heads might well be tempted to give relief without enquiry into the circumstances of the applicant or the requirement of some task in return for the aid given.[29]

An instrument for the control of charitable relief emerged however in the shape of the Central Executive Relief Committee. This body of twenty-six members under the chairmanship of Lord Derby resulted from the merger of two committees set up in the summer of 1862 to raise funds for the relief of Lancashire distress. The Central Relief Committee had been formed in June 1862 by leading businessmen of Manchester and other cotton towns, and it was followed in July by the Cotton Districts Relief Fund, set up after a meeting of Lancashire landowners at Lord Ellesmere's London residence, Bridgewater House.[30] Landed and industrial philanthropists thus came together in one committee to control the distribution of national funds for the relief of Lancashire distress. The only major exception to the new Committee's control of national relief funds was the fund raised by the Lancashire and Cheshire Operatives Relief Fund, launched by the Lord Mayor of London in May 1862.[31] This Mansion House Committee was to draw upon itself a good deal of adverse criticism for distributing relief funds outside the controls laid down by the Central Executive Committee.

Whilst Lord Derby was appointed as the figurehead chairman of the Central Committee, the main influence on its policies was probably that of its vice-chairman, Sir James Kay-Shuttleworth. Now an extensive land-owner in north Lancashire, Kay-Shuttleworth had served as an assistant poor law commissioner during the formative years of the New Poor Law in the 1830s.[32] Deeply impressed by his experiences as to the evils of pauperism and the value of the 'principles of 1834' in combating it, and imbued with a political philosophy which combined liberal individualism and professional elitist control, Kay was well suited to directing the policy of the Central Committee.[33]

Controlling as it did the main source of relief finance outside the poor law, the Central Committee was in a strong position to decide upon the mode in which relief was given to the unemployed by the 180 local relief committees in the area which became virtually its sub-committees.[34] Under Kay's direction, two main principles informed the Central Committee's relief policies. In the first place the amount of relief given to an unemployed man and his family was to be sufficient to keep them in good health, but must not make them better off than they would have been if at work. Relief should constitute about one third of normal wages.[35] A weekly allowance of between 2s and 2s 6d per head seems to have been that most commonly aimed at. This sum coincided closely with Dr Edward Smith's dietary survey of 1862 which estimated that an income of 4s 6d per week for a married couple with an additional 1s 6d or 2s for every child was about the minimum required for healthy existence.[36] Even at these meagre levels, the administration of relief must be strictly controlled. To prevent unwise spending of cash aid, some portion at least of the relief had to be in kind or in the form of tickets to be exchanged at certain shops. Relief committees were urged to organise a regular system of visiting those relieved to ascertain their needs, and those who attempted imposture were prosecuted.[37]

The second major principle underlying the distribution of charitable relief was that of requiring some return in the form of work for any relief granted. This the Central Committee argued, in a report published in September 1862, was essential 'not only for the preservation of public health and order but for the right moral guidance of all whose usual occupation is at an end'.[38] There existed however the problem of devising some form of relief work which would not carry with it the degrading overtones of the oakum picking and stone breaking associated with the poor law and which would be suited to unemployed factory workers accustomed to relatively light indoor work in high temperatures. The solution to this problem, at least in the winter of 1862-3, seemed to lie in the formation of educational classes for men and boys and sewing classes for women, to be held in suitable public buildings, or even in idle mills. Educational classes, the Central Committee felt, were 'eminently useful in maintaining order, in promoting cheerfulness and in preventing the contraction of evil habits during a period of unwanted leisure, as well as in communicating rudimentary knowledge', whilst the sewing classes were of value 'in keeping up the habit of continuous daily work and shutting out from each day the temptations incident to much unoccupied time'.[39] Any educational values the schemes might contain were secondary to their main purpose of keeping the unemployed under surveillance in a disciplined environment and preventing them from contracting habits of idleness.

By getting the local relief committees to observe these conditions when aiding the unemployed, the Central Committee hoped to diffuse amongst them 'the true principles of the Poor Law'.[40] Cooperation with the official poor law machinery was welcomed. At the central level, there were close contacts with the Poor Law Board, H.B. Farnall serving as an active member of the Committee. At the local level, the Central Committee invited boards of guardians 'to arrange with us a clear settlement of principles upon which we may hope adequately to relieve the misery that surrounds us', whilst at the same time warning them that the Committee 'will not feel justified in so apportioning their grants as to make them compensate for any deficiency occasioned by a low standard of parochial relief'.[41] In some unions, the desired cooperation was achieved, and some boards adopted the device of educational and sewing classes as alternatives to the labour test.[42] Such amicable cooperation was not however universal. In the Ashton Union a meeting between the guardians and the relief committee to decide upon common scales of relief 'terminated rather abruptly'[43]

Despite this setback, it seemed that, as the tide of unemployment and distress mounted in the later months of 1862, the Poor Law Board and the Central Committee had succeeded in controlling the conditions of relief and effecting cooperation between private charity and official poor relief at the local level. Indeed the success of this policy was later to be hailed as the inspiration for the policies developed by the Charity Organisation Society.[44] The unemployed themselves, however, were a good deal less enthusiastic at being subjected to the 'true principles of the Poor Law'. If anything, the relief committees with their strict enquiries, relief in kind or by ticket, and, in some cases, insistence on attendance at classes, proved more inflexible in their demands than did the despised boards of guardians. Operatives protested at the unrepresentative nature of the relief committees, some of which they alleged had had their origin in relief organisations launched by the operatives themselves. A meeting of the unemployed in Stalybridge in February 1863 complained that the local relief committee's mode of proceeding was becoming increasingly like that of the board of guardians 'in dealing with the class whom they denominate, truly or otherwise, hereditary paupers'. The meeting also complained of compulsory attendance at sewing or reading schools. Such attendance, they argued, would have been quite acceptable had it been voluntary, but compulsion altered the case and showed 'a distrust of their behaviour when at large, which is wholly at variance with the high praise and ample recognition of their submission and loyalty accorded to them on so many occasions by members of Her Majesty's Government.'[45] In Manchester, a deputation from the educational classes presented a petition to the guardians on behalf of their 1,600 unemployed members. The petition opposed the recent decision of the guardians to enforce school attendance on Saturday, and sought a further day off during the week to enable the reluctant scholars to look for work. The leader of the deputation, John Leonard, told the guardians that 'he and his companions had done all in their power to preserve order in the Bengal Street School'.[46] In Ashton, deputations from the male adult schools met in the Oddfellows Hall to protest against the policies of the relief committee and the board of guardians, and in Oldham a meeting of the unemployed appointed a deputation to wait upon the relief committee with a statement of their grievances.[47] The Lancashire unemployed were proving to be far from aquiescent in the relief policies imposed upon them.

It was at the height of these peaceable organised protests against relief methods that there occurred what the *Manchester Guardian* described as 'the single marked exception to the peaceful and orderly demeanour of the whole of our manufacturing population', in the shape of the Stalybridge Riots of 20 March 1863.[48] As has been seen, the Stalybridge Relief Committee had been singled out as a target of criticism by several meetings of unemployed operatives in the area, at which the Reverend J.R. Stephens had been a leading and extremely

vociferous speaker.[49] As if in defiance of this tide of protest, the
Stalybridge committee, which was finding like other local committees
that its funds were shrinking and that the Central Committee was
exercising rigid economy in its grants from the central fund, decided
to reduce the grant paid to the unemployed at the schools from 3s 4d
to 3s a week, to hold back one day's pay as a condition of good
behaviour, and to pay in tickets rather than cash because of allegations
that cash doles were being spent in beer houses.[50] This sudden decision
seemed to confirm the allegations of the unemployed about the failure
of the relief committee to consult them and its contemptuous treatment
of them as paupers unable to spend their relief wisely. When members
of the relief committee began a tour of the schools to announce their
decision, their cab was stoned and the windows of the school were
broken. A crowd then went around Stalybridge smashing windows
including those of the police office, a grocer's shop belonging to one
member of the relief committee and the house of the committee's
secretary. The relief committee's store was broken into and £800
worth of goods stolen, after which a rather half-hearted attempt was
made to set the place on fire. After about two hours, a troop of hussars
arrived to reinforce the borough's hard pressed fifteen man police
force, and the Riot Act was read. The crowds dispersed, but there was
further trouble on the following day, and over the next few days
attempts were made, in imitation of the Plug Riots of 1842, to march
to the neighbouring towns of Ashton, Hyde and Dukinfield and 'turn
out' the schools there. There were disturbances in all these places, and,
at Ashton, Hugh Mason, a prominent local mill-owner and magistrate,
read the Riot Act seated on the shoulders of two policemen. The
summoning of troops and the swearing in of large numbers of special
constables followed, but the disturbances rapidly subsided, and, apart
from some unrest in Stockport later in the week, the trouble did not
spread more widely.[51] About sixty arrests were made in Stalybridge,
and twenty-nine rioters were later brought to trial at Chester Assizes
where they received relatively light sentences of between one and six
months imprisonment. Others were dealt with summarily in the
borough magistrates court.[52]

   Although it was by far the most serious disturbance of the peace
during the Lancashire cotton famine, the Stalybridge riot does not rank
high in the scale of historical revolt. Indeed, in dramatic terms, it would
provide better material for an Ealing comedy than for a 'Battleship
Potemkin'. Explanations for violence occurring in this area come easily
to hand. The Ashton Union was the most heavily hit of all the cotton

manufacturing unions by the distress. Twenty-five per cent of its population was on relief in December 1862 and 32,000 of its 56,000 cotton workers were unemployed. Relief expenditure in the union rose from £10,000 in 1861 to £93,000 in 1863, and the guardians were hard pressed financially.[53] Its public men were not noted for their sophistication. The local paper described Stalybridge town council as one in which 'cock fighting and dog fighting were discussed as elegancies of civilisation and in which the excitement of tongue fighting beat cock fighting and everything else'.[54] Not only was there a total lack of cooperation between the relief committees and the Ashton board of guardians, but there were two rival relief committees in Ashton. The 'official' borough relief committee, chaired by Hugh Mason, followed closely the dictates of the Central Committee of which Mason was a member. By contrast, the 'rogue' General and Municipal Relief Committee, chaired by the Reverend F.H. Williams, an Anglican clergyman, was not recognised by the Central Committee and relied on the Mansion House Committee for any finance other than that raised locally. The two committees indulged in lengthy slanging matches in the local press with Williams accusing the Borough Committee in general, and Mason in particular, of anti-clericalism.[55]

This serious division in the machinery of relief control occurred in an area with a tradition of unrest stretching back to the Chartist disturbances of the early 1840s and beyond.[56] The renewed activity of the Reverend J.R. Stephens, one of the most virulent popular agitators of the 1830s and 1840s, also had an inflammatory effect on popular feeling towards the dispensers of relief.[57] Indeed, some hostile commentators were ready to apportion a major part of the blame for the disturbances on the 'old practised demagogue.'[58]

There existed however an even more obvious scapegoat than the Reverend Stephens on which to place the blame for the disturbances in Stalybridge. Of the twenty-nine rioters sent for trial at Chester, twenty-eight were Irish, and the majority were in their late teens and early twenties, the youngest being a lad of fourteen. 'The lasses in their blue Garibaldi jackets cheered on the wild Irish lads', commented one reporter on the riot, whilst the chief constable of Cheshire reported to the Home Office that the actual number of rioters did not exceed a few hundred, the majority being 'youths of the lowest class of Irish'.[59] The riot could thus be seen more as the result of youthful high spirits and Celtic temperament than of any sinister design on the part of 'Rochdale Man' to disturb the public peace.

Given that the Stalybridge riots were so exceptional and so easily explicable in terms of the peculiarities of the area, what is remarkable is less the riots themselves than the reaction to them. Both of the contemporary historians of the cotton famine devoted a considerable amount of space in their books to description and discussion of the events in the Stalybridge area.[60] Newspapers, both local and national, carried lengthy descriptions of the disturbances and leading articles commenting on their significance.[61] Far from there being a feeling of confidence in the good sense and respect for constitutional propriety of the respectable operatives of Lancashire, there was a very real fear that the Stalybridge disturbances heralded the beginnings of widespread social and political unrest in the area on the scale of that of the early 1840s. In response to an appeal by a group of Stalybridge clergymen, the Mansion House Committee made an immediate grant of £500 to the funds of the local relief committee in the hope of keeping relief payments at their former level and thus preventing further violence.[62] This action was roundly condemned by the Central Executive Committee who saw it as weakly giving way in the face of threats. The Committee nevertheless sent Kay-Shuttleworth, Farnall and the secretary, J.W. Maclure, hurrying down to Stalybridge to restore order. The trio severely lectured the unemployed, threatened to cut off all funds from the Central Committee and leave the operatives wholly dependent upon the board of guardians. Despite this high-handed tone, they met a deputation from the unemployed men in the schools and worked out a compromise whereby half of the 3s relief was to be paid in cash instead of the whole being given in tickets.[63] In Parliament, the Home Secretary was asked whether he was not 'seriously alarmed' by reports from the cotton districts and whether the area was 'not likely to be seriously disturbed during the recess'. Sir George Grey's reply was not entirely reassuring and he felt that there might be 'renewed attempts at disturbance'.[64] 'The Mayor had all your fears and had arranged for a meeting of the magistrates in Burnley this morning', Kay-Shuttleworth's son, Ughtred, wrote from Gawthorpe Hall to his father in Stalybridge. He continued:

> They would increase, probably treble the police force, have the Lancers in readiness, and be ready to swear in special constables. They would also probably send out scouts. The Mayor expects that the Bacup valley would be the first to rise in this neighbourhood. Todmorden is looked on as pretty safe. He thinks that Padiham would. . . be before Burnley. His policy would be on the first signs of disturbance to seize if possible all the leaders. . .[65]

Whilst this might be seen as the somewhat overwrought imaginings of a young man, his father was very far from scorning his notion of a general rising in the Burnley area. 'Tell Mr. Thompson *not* to lower or reduce the Padiham scale of relief. Let him *keep it as high as it* is now.'[66] When it came to his home ground, Sir James was not going to make the same mistake as the Stalybridge relief committee had done.

Whilst the fears of further major disturbances were proved to be unfounded, the Stalybridge riots did mark something of a watershed in the history of relief policy during the cotton famine. It seemed that in spite of, or perhaps because of, the controls which had been devised, the Lancashire unemployed were sinking into pauperism. 'The people are becoming demoralised by the attempt to shut them up in one vast moral workhouse to await the revival of the cotton trade', commented *The Times,* whilst the *Economist* argued that the longer a quarter of a million people were supported by alms not wages the more certain they were to be demoralised.[67] With this demoralisation came truculence, the demand for relief as of right. 'The Stalybridge people have got up a disturbance and gone and helped themselves at the relief stores. There was no reason why they should not do so. The things were sent for them, they were not given them, and they had a right to them, so they have taken them', one speaker was reported as having told a meeting at Padiham.[68] 'They have in a great many instances demanded as a right what they formerly received as a favour', wrote a sub-inspector of factories from Dukinfield.[69] 'If the Government abdicates its function Lancashire is left to riot or to rot. Of pauperism or rebellion, which is the greater evil?' Dr Bridges enquired of Frederic Harrison in April 1863.[70]

In this dilemma over future relief policy in Lancashire, there was growing pressure for the large-scale adoption of one of the favourite nineteenth-century remedies for pauperism. Emigration agents had been active in Lancashire since the onset of the cotton famine, but they had received little or no encouragement from boards of guardians or relief committees.[71] The Central Committee agreed to disseminate information about emigration schemes but were opposed to committing any finance to aid them.[72] H.B. Farnall had pointed out as early as December 1862 that 'in the event of a great number of operatives being without work, their emigration may become necessary'.[73] After Stalybridge the pressures to step up the emigration of a population threatened with pauperism mounted.[74] 'Let the people go free', demanded *The Times.* 'Spend money to disperse them. Otherwise they will be converted into a mob of sturdy beggars and truculent paupers.'[75]

This advice was strongly supported by its correspondents like the Reverend Charles Kingsley and Sidney Godolphin Osborne who were intensely critical of the role of the Lancashire mill-owners in the relief of their unemployed.[76] There was some substance in their argument that the manufacturers who dominated the relief agencies in Lancashire were behaving like the southern farmers whom the 1834 Poor Law Commission's Report had accused of keeping labourers in the parish, 'like potatoes in a pit', until they were needed for the harvest field.[77] 'To emigrate the hands would be a fatal step for these districts', the factory inspector, Robert Baker, told the Home Secretary, pointing to the shortage of labour which would occur when the cotton trade revived. 'The people will then be the masters', he added, 'for already they are thinking of the time when things will be different.'[78]

In the spring of 1863, therefore, those responsible for the relief of distress in Lancashire were faced with the urgent necessity of taking some new relief initiative if the working population were not to become further demoralised or be dispersed to the far corners of the earth. The only possibility, short of a revival of the cotton trade which was slow to develop, appeared to be the provision of work for wages in place of the degrading labour tests and irksome educational classes. 'Questions arising out of the consideration of measures for the employment of able bodied cotton operatives now in receipt of relief are numerous and have become continually more urgent', the Central Committee reported in April 1863, and H.B. Farnall stressed in a report to the Poor Law Board the need to provide unemployed hands with work for wages since they had no interest in work for parish relief or charitable aid.[79] 'The people must be either emigrated or occupied', Robert Baker told the Home Secretary.[80]

Both the Central Committee and the Poor Law Board were thus coming round to the belief that the only way out of the Lancashire crisis was the generation of some alternative form of employment for the cotton operatives. There remained the problem of how this was to be provided. Local landowners were unlikely to be willing or able to invest in estate development on a scale large enough to absorb the 90,000 unemployed operatives. Whilst many Lancashire towns were in urgent need of sanitary improvement, ratepayers were already hard pressed enough by the poor rates and were unlikely to approve plans by town councils or local boards of health which would involve expensive capital borrowing.[81] Increasingly the government found itself under pressure to provide the necessary finance, and, following a full scale Commons debate on the Lancashire distress, the Home Secretary sent the civil engineer, Robert Rawlinson, to the distressed areas to report on the possibilities of public works as a means of relieving unemployment.[82] 'The object for which all work which may be undertaken is instituted is the immediate employment of the distressed operatives for wages', Rawlinson was told, and the urgency of the matter was impressed upon him, 'as no time is to be lost you may reserve your detailed and minute reports, and give in the first instance a statement only of work which can be done without delay'.[83] Rawlinson in his early reports to C.P. Villiers, the President of the Poor Law Board, found that both the need and the enthusiasm for public works schemes existed in Lancashire. Unemployed men told him that they would 'far rather work than sit stewing in the schools', whilst local authorities were willing to proceed provided that they could obtain low cost finance and retain complete control over any schemes which were set on foot.[84] Throughout May and June 1863, Kay-Shuttleworth was in London, lobbying MPs, organising deputations from the Central Committee, and discussing with C.P. Villiers the drafting of a bill on the question of 'our Public Works for cotton workmen'.[85]

The Public Works (Manufacturing Districts) Bill which emerged from these discussions had a relatively easy passage through Parliament, and received the Royal Assent on 21 July 1863. Under its terms, local authorities were able to obtain loans at 3½ per cent over a period of thirty years from a £1.2m fund, made available to the Public Works Loan Commissioners for the purpose of carrying out works of public utility and sanitary improvement. Schemes for such works were to be submitted to the Poor Law Board who would then advise the Public Works Loan Commissioners as to whether or not a loan should be granted.[86]

It is generally accepted that the Act, in Henderson's words, 'failed to fulfil the sanguine expectations of its promoters'.[87] Rawlinson in his early reports to the Poor Law Board had hoped that 'work may be found for every able bodied distressed operative out of work', and the Central Committee had expressed the hope that the provisions of the Act would be sufficient to maintain between a fifth and a sixth of the indigent, or between 15,000 and 16,000 operatives.[88] In February 1864, however, H.B. Farnall expressed considerable disappointment that only 2,500 operatives had been set to work on schemes financed by the Act, instead of the 12,000 he had hoped for.[89] Two months later, Rawlinson reported that 3,435 operatives were employed in 49 places where improvement work was in progress, and that another 3,000 were indirectly employed in obtaining and conveying materials.[90]

This relative failure of the scheme was put down to a number of causes. Local authorities blamed the Poor Law Board for taking too long to approve schemes submitted to it and in some cases for rejecting them unfairly.[91] Some local authorities were accused of taking advantage of the scheme to obtain cheap finance and then of ignoring the provision that the major object of any scheme should be the employment of unemployed cotton workers.[92] Some of the works undertaken necessitated the employment of skilled navvies, and the unemployed, lacking experience of sewering or paving, could only be engaged in a subsidiary role. Nevertheless, the heavy demand for loans under the Act and the fact that relief committees were able to reduce the scale of their operations considerably after its passage may indicate that it had a greater impact on the relief problem than it has sometimes been credited with.[93]

For the purposes of this paper, however, what is perhaps more important than the actual operation of the Public Works Act is the principle involved in it. To a society still imbued with the ideal of *laissez-faire* individualism, and mindful of such dubious precedents for state inolvement in relief efforts as the Irish famine or the French *ateliers nationaux*, governmental involvement in the relief of distress outside the approved and limited channels of the poor law seemed fraught with danger. 'I feel the delicacy, and in some respects danger in exceptional legislation but do not know how it is to be avoided in this case', Rawlinson reported, whilst the *Economist* warned of the dangers of hasty legislation which might create work for work's sake as during the Irish famine.[94] Indeed, the extreme caution with which the Act was operated, Rawlinson's insistence for example that local authorities must be completely free to develop their own works schemes without central interference and the Central Committee's stern warning to local relief committees that they must on no account supplement the earnings of those employed under the Act, are indicative of the attitudes towards this piece of exceptional legislation.[95] Its passage reveals the extent to which the growing discontent of the Lancashire unemployed, dramatically illustrated by the Stalybridge riots, had persuaded public opinion that poor relief and private philanthropy had failed, and that some new policy was imperative if Lancashire was not to be pauperised.

By the time that the Public Works Bill reached the statute book, the numbers oñ relief were already falling and the winter of 1863-4 did not place relief agencies under such pressure as that of 1862-3 had done.[96] As early as October 1863, the Central Committee was asking local committees to consider the propriety of suspending operations, and a year later was pressing them to cease all joint operations with boards of guardians.[97] By the middle of 1865, the Central Committee had ceased to make any more grants and dissolved itself in December 1865 with a surplus of £97,000 still in its coffers.[98] Lancashire pauperism was back to its normally low level, and the attention of philanthropists shifted back to the more continuous problems of London. 'Notwithstanding the gloomy forebodings of those who, in the early part of the distress, expressed their opinion that the distribution of relief through exceptional channels would tend to a permanent increase of pauperism in the district, returns from twenty-eight unions prove that the pauperism of the cotton district had been reduced to the ordinary level', commented the Central Committee in its final report.[99]

This tone of self-satisfaction marked, as has been seen, most later accounts of the relief of distress during the cotton famine. The unemployed had borne their affliction nobly. The disciplined administration of relief and the cooperation of boards of guardians and relief committees had prevented the pauperising of the distressed operatives. Distance however lent enchantment to the view. At the onset of the famine, attitudes had been dominated by the almost pathological Victorian fear that the unemployed would be pauperised by unconditional relief. Thus controls had been devised to ensure that relief should be minimal in amount and disciplined and discriminating in nature. The growing volume of protest from the unemployed culminating in the Stalybridge outburst demonstrated the failure of this policy and forced the adoption of new and exceptional methods. The conversion of the English lion into the Lancashire lamb proved less easy than some accounts of the cotton famine have implied.

Notes

*I should like to thank Professor W. Ashworth and his graduate seminar at the University of Bristol and also the History Workshop seminar at Manchester Polytechnic for their helpful comments in discussing earlier versions of this paper.

1. *The Unemployed Operatives of Lancashire and the Lancashire Relief Committees,* printed pamphlet enclosed in HO 45/0.S. 7523.
2. G. Stedman Jones, *Outcast London* (Oxford, 1971), p.8.
3. Royden Harrison, *Before the Socialists* (London, 1965), pp.113,119.
4. 'And the manufacturing districts, were they not supposed even in our own time to be filled with a population, whose loyalty could only be insured by the material bribe of high wages, — by the constant company of light dragoons and by the continual indulgence of their self will and interest in the legislation of the country?', R.A. Arnold, *The History of the Cotton Famine* (London, 1864), p.51. *Vide* also: J. Kay-Shuttleworth, *Thoughts*

and Suggestions on Certain Social Problems (London, 1873), pp.22-3, 63-7; S.A. Nichols, *Darwen and the Cotton Famine* (Darwen, 1893), ch.I, pp.1-15.

5. 'The unemployed bore their affliction with the phlegm of the Saxon and the stoicism of the peasant'. D.A. Farnie, 'The Cotton Famine in Great Britain' in B.M. Ratcliffe (ed.), *Great Britain and Her World, 1750-1914* (Manchester, 1975), p.168. Henderson's own account, whilst noting contemporary praise of the operatives' conduct, also devotes a good deal of time to a discussion of disturbances during the cotton famine. W.O. Henderson, *The Lancashire Cotton Famine 1861-65* , 2nd edn., (Manchester, 1969), chap. V, pp.94-115.

6. The Board's miscellaneous correspondence for this period contains a number of handwritten transcripts from newspaper accounts of the distress. P.R.O. MH 25/14.

7. Poor Law Board, *15th Ann. Rep.*, 1862-3, p.14. Letter of Instructions From the President of the Poor Law Board to H.B. Farnall Esq., *PP* 1862, (413), XLIX, Part I, p.89. The poor law inspector in the area, J.L. Manwaring, continued to act in his normal capacity.

8. M.E. Rose, 'The New Poor Law in an Industrial Area' in R.M. Hartwell, (ed.), *The Industrial Revolution* (Oxford, 1970), pp.121-43.

9. Stedman Jones, op.cit., chap. XIII, pp.241-61. A report by Farnall on poor relief in London dated 26 Jan. 1861 was filed with some of his later correspondence relating to Lancashire. H.B. Farnall's Correspondence. P.R.O. MH 32/24.

10. S.C. Poor Relief (England), First Report, *PP* 1861 (180), IX, p.3.

11. Ibid., Index of Evidence, p.174.

12. C.L. Mowat, *The Charity Organisation Society 1869-1913* (London, 1961), p.70; M. Rooff, *A Hundred Years of Family Welfare* (London, 1972), p.47.

13. Wm. Heys to P.L.B., 24 Jan. 1862. P.R.O. MH12/1149. Several philanthropists engaged in relief work in London visited Lancashire during the cotton famine to view the arrangements for relief. E. Barlee, *A Visit to Lancashire in December 1862* (London, 1863); M. Bayly, *Lancashire Homes and What Ails Them,* 2nd edn. (London, 1863)

14. Poor Law Board, *5th Ann. Rep.,* 1852, Appendix No. 3.

15. M.E. Rose, *The English Poor Law, 1780-1930* (Newton Abbot, 1971), pp.146-50. D. Ashforth, 'The Urban Poor Law', in D. Fraser, (ed.), *The New Poor Law in the 19th Century* (London, 1976), pp.135-9.

16. A.B. Wimpenny to P.L.B., 22 Aug. 1862, P.R.O. MH 12/5421.

17. Union Clerk, Ashton to P.L.B., 8 Nov. 1861, P.R.O. MH 12/5421.

18. Union Clerk, Stockport to P.L.B., 22 March 1862, P.R.O. MH 12/1149.

19. J.L. Manwaring, Report to P.L.B., 28 Nov. 1861, P.R.O. MH 12/5421.

20. *Oldham Standard,* 8 March 1862.

21. Susan Liveing, *A 19th Century Teacher. John Henry Bridges, M.B., F.R.C.P.* (London, 1926), p.102. John Henry Bridges (1832-1906) was physician to Bradford Infirmary at the time of the cotton famine and became involved in a heated public debate with the Manchester board of guardians about their methods of relief administration. A friend of the Positivist thinkers Edward Beesly and Frederic Harrison, he was later appointed Medical Inspector of the Local Government Board.

22. P.L.B. reply to memorandum from Ashton board of guardians 17 July 1862, P.R.O. MH 12/5421. A similar reply was sent to the Rochdale board of guardians. See also, P.L.B. to Manchester board of guardians, 28 Oct. 1862, P.R.O. MH 12/6053.

23. Returns of numbers relieved outside Relief Regulation Order, Dec. 1862,

P.R.O. MH 12/5421. Return Relating to the Lancs. Unions, *PP* 1863, (199), LII, p.223.

24. *Ashton and Stalybridge Reporter,* 7 March 1863. Ashton guardians, as a general rule, gave 2s a week relief to an adult applicant and 1s per child. Recipients were allowed to supplement this sum up to a limit of 3s 6d per head a week. loc. cit. 7 February 1863.

25. H.B. Farnall estimated that on the current relief scales a family of five would receive 8s 9d a week, 'a fact which justifies me in assuming that the amount of parochial relief which they are now receiving is not calculated to demoralize them'. P.L.B., *15th Ann. Rep.* 1862-3, Appendix 9(c).

26. The Union Relief Aid Act (25 and 26 Vic. c. 160) allowed parishes in which the poor rate exceeded 3s in the £ to charge the relief of their poor to the common fund of the Union, thus sharing the cost amongst the other constituent parishes. Unions where the rate exceeded 5s in the £ might apply to the Poor Law Board for an order requiring other unions in the county to levy a rate in aid to relieve the hard pressed union. Unions with a rate exceeding 3s in the £ could also apply for government loans on the security of their rates. Sir G. Nicholls, *A History of the English Poor Law,* Vol. III by T. Mackay, new edn. (London, 1904), p.395; Arnold, op.cit., pp.529-32. In the Ashton Union in Dec. 1862, £40,000 of poor rates were outstanding and the guardians' account had twice been overdrawn. By Jan. 1863 one parish owed the guardians £20,000 in unpaid rates and the board were threatening legal action against the overseers for recovery of the sums owed. Whilst the Union Relief Aid Act provided some relief, only £2,000 of the £8,000 the Ashton guardians requested from other Unions in Cheshire was paid. *Ashton and Stalybridge Reporter,* 3 Jan., 28 March 1863. I.R. Coulthart to P.L.B., 27 Nov.,12 Dec. 1862, P.R.O. MH 12/5421. Return relating to the Lancashire Unions, *PP* 1863 (199), LII, p.223.

27. P.L.B., *15th Ann. Rep.* 1862-3, Appendix No. 9(e).

28. J. Watts, *The Facts of the Cotton Famine* (1866. New edn. London, 1968) chap. X pp.156-68.

29. Clergymen were particularly suspect as being careless in the administration of charity. The secretary of the Darwen Relief Committee found two of the clerical members of his committee were 'often too credulous', whilst Bury guardians held that 'the clergy were about the last persons into whose hands funds for the general relief of the poor should be entrusted'. S.A. Nichols, op.cit., p.60. *Bury Times,* 9 Aug. 1862. I am grateful to Mr J. Wierzbicki for this reference.

30. Arnold, op.cit., pp.122-3, 175-9.

31. Arnold, op.cit. pp.119-20.

32. F. Smith, *The Life and Work of Sir James Kay-Shuttleworth* (London, 1923).

33. 'Political liberty in its widest and most complete sense under the guidance of the educated intelligence and enlightened interest of the nation.' J. Kay-Shuttleworth to Ughtred Kay-Shuttleworth, 10 Jan. 1863. Kay-Shuttleworth papers, John Rylands University Library of Manchester.

34. Of the sums expended on relief up to Michaelmas, 1863, £263,000 had been raised locally and £893,000 came from central and general funds. Central Executive Committee, *Fund for the Relief of Distress in the Manufacturing Districts,* Manchester Cent. Ref. Political Tracts, p.3339.

35. *Ashton and Stalybridge Reporter,* 4 April 1863. Central Executive Committee *Address to the Secretaries of the General and Executive Local Committees of Relief,* 29 Sep. 1862.

36.　Medical Officer of the Committee of Council on Health, 5th Report *PP* 1863, XXC, Appendix V. T.C. Barker, D.J. Oddy and J. Yudkin, *The Dietary Surveys of Dr Edward Smith 1862-3,* Queen Elizabeth College, Occasional Paper no. 1 (London, 1970), pp.17-18.

37.　Bloom Street Relief Committee, Minute Book. Manchester Cent. Ref. Library, Archives Dept.

38.　Central Executive Committee, *Report,* 30 Sept. 1862, p. 1, Manchester Cent. Ref. Library Political Tracts, p.3339.

39.　Ibid., *Report,* 23 Feb. 1863, Appendix.

40.　Central Executive Committee, *Address to Boards of Guardians,* 8 Sept. 1862.

41.　Ibid.

42.　In Darwen, there was cordial cooperation between the relief committee and the guardians with Thomas Kenyon serving as a member of both bodies. S.A. Nichols, op.cit., p.62. In Bury the two bodies remained independent of one another, but after a meeting in October 1862 they resolved to work in unison, J. Wierzbicki, *Bury Poverty and the Cotton Famine 1861-5* (Manchester University Extra Mural Certificate Dissertation, 1976), p.47.
　　　A committee of the Manchester guardians stressed the desirability of providing educational facilities particularly for unemployed young persons 'left with little or no occupation or control'; and also recommended employers to set up their own schools as 'a means of keeping their workpeople together ready for the resumption of labour when trade revives'. Manchester Board of Guardians, Report of Office Committee, 27 Aug. 1862. P.R.O. MH 12/6053.

43.　*Ashton and Stalybridge Reporter,* 14 Feb. 1863.

44.　Poor Law Board, *22nd Ann. Rep.,* 1869-70, Appendix No. 4, Mowat, op.cit., p.7.

45.　Memorial of Stalybridge Unemployed to Home Office, 23 Feb. 1863, in P.R.O. HO 45/O.S. 7523. *Ashton and Stalybridge Reporter,* 28 Feb. 1863.

46.　Petition in Manchester Board of Guardians Correspondence, 16 March 1863. Leaflet in Manchester Cent. Ref. Political Tracts, P. 2200.

47.　*Ashton and Stalybridge Reporter,* 21 and 28 Feb. 1863.

48.　*Manchester Guardian,* 24 March 1863.

49.　Vide, e.g, *Ashton and Stalybridge Reporter,* 31 Jan. 1863.

50.　*Ashton and Stalybridge Reporter,* 14 March, 21 March 1863.

51.　*Ashton and Stalybridge Reporter,* 28 March, 4 April 1863. *Manchester Guardian,* 23 and 24 March 1863; Arnold, op.cit., pp.396-408; Watts, op.cit., chap. XIV, pp.262-82.

52.　*Ashton and Stalybridge Reporter,* 4 and 11 April 1863.

53.　Poor Law Board, *15th Ann. Rep.,* 1862-3, Appendix 9(c); Central Executive Committee, *Fund for the Relief of Distress in the Manufacturing Districts,* Manchester Cent. Ref. Political Tracts, P.3339.

54.　*Ashton'and Stalybridge Reporter,* 14 March 1863.

55.　Vide e.g. *Ashton and Stalybridge Reporter,* 3,10,17 Jan. 1863.

56.　F.C. Mather, 'The General Strike of 1842' in R. Quinault and J. Stevenson, *Popular Protest and Public Order* (London, 1974), pp.115-140.

57.　On Stephens, vide: J.T. Ward, 'Revolutionary Tory. The Life of J.R. Stephens of Ashton under Lyne,' *Trans. Lancs. and Cheshire Antiquarian Society,* LXVIII (1958), pp.93-116.

58.　R. Hopwood, J. Kirk, R. Bates to H.B. Farnall, 23 Feb. 1863. Copy in P.R.O. HO 45/O.S. 7523. Hopwood was Mayor of Stalybridge,and Bates was secretary of the relief committee.

59.　*Economist,* 28 March 1863; *The Times,* 23 March 1863; Chief Constable of Cheshire to Home Secretary, 25 March 1863, P.R.O., HO 45/O.S. 7523 A.A report of an earlier disturbance at Glossop contained phrases like 'the sons and daughters of Erin took a prominent part', and, 'the Hibernians taking the lead, both young men and young women'. *Ashton and Stalybridge Reporter,* 7 March 1863.

60.　Arnold, op.cit., pp.394-408; Watts, op.cit., pp.262-82.

61.　*The Times,* 23,24,25,26,27, 30 March 1863; *Manchester Guardian,* 23,24, 27,28,30 March 1863; *Ashton and Stalybridge Reporter,* 4 and 11 April 1863, contains extracts from a number of national newspapers and periodicals commenting on the Stalybridge riots.

62.　*The Times,* 24 and 26 March 1863; *Ashton and Stalybridge Reporter,* 28 March 1863; Watts, op.cit., pp.274-6.

63.　*The Times,* 30 March 1863.

64.　*Hansard,* Parl. Debates, 3rd Series, CLXX, 27 March 1863.

65.　Ughtred Kay-Shuttleworth to Sir James Kay-Shuttleworth, 25 March 1863. Kay-Shuttleworth papers.

66.　Sir James Kay-Shuttleworth to Ughtred Kay-Shuttleworth, 26 March 1863. Kay-Shuttleworth papers.

67.　*The Times,* 30 March 1863; *Economist,* 30 May 1863.

68.　Ughtred Kay-Shuttleworth to Sir James Kay-Shuttleworth, 25 March 1863. Kay-Shuttleworth papers.

69.　Mr Oram to Alexander Redgrave, 30 March 1863, P.R.O. HO 45/O.S. 7523A.

70.　Liveing, op.cit., p.97.

71.　Watts, op.cit., pp.214-16.

72.　Central Executive Committee, *Report,* 23 Feb. 1863, p.1, Manchester Cent. Ref. Political Tracts, P.3339

73.　Poor Law Board, *15th Ann. Rep.,* 1862-3, Appendix 9(b).

74.　'The candidates for emigration in these towns were fifteen or twenty times as numerous as passages we had to offer', wrote W. Murdoch of the Emigration Board to the Home Office, commenting on a letter from the Unemployed Operatives Emigration Society of Pendleton asking for advice and assistance. W. Murdoch to Home Office, 23 March 1863, P.R.O. HO 45/O.S. 7523.
　　　An Emigrants Aid Society was established in Manchester in April 1863. Watts, op.cit., p.213.

75.　*The Times,* 30 March 1863.

76.　*The Times,* 27 and 31 March 1863; F.E. Kingsley, *Charles Kingsley. His Letters and Memories of his Life* (London, 1899 edn.), p.248.

77.　S. and G. Checkland (eds), *The Poor Law Report of 1834* (Harmondsworth, 1974).

78.　Robert Baker to Home Secretary, 22 April 1863, P.R.O. HO 45/O.S. 7523; see also *PP* 1863 (288), LII, p. 43.

79.　Central Executive Committee, *Report,* 27 April 1863, p.1, Manchester Cent. Ref. Political Tracts, P. 3339; Poor Law Board, *15th Ann. Rep.,* 1862-3, Appendix 9(e).

80.　R. Baker to Home Secretary, 22 April 1863. op.cit.

81.　Central Executive Committee, *Report,* 27 April 1863, pp.1-2, Manchester Cent. Ref. Political Tracts, P. 3339.

82.　Memoranda to Home Secretary from Stockport Town Council, 16 May 1863, and Blackburn Town Council, 15 May 1863. P.R.O. HO/O.S. 7523; *Hansard,* Parl. Debates, 3rd Series, CLXX, 27 April 1863.

83.　Letter of Instruction to R.Rawlinson Esq., 28 April 1863, P.R.O. HO 45/O.S. 7523. Robert Rawlinson (1810-98) was the son of a Lancashire builder, and had held a number of civil engineering posts in the county before being appointed a government inspector under the 1848 Public Health Act.

84.   R. Rawlinson to C.P. Villiers, 4 and 8 May 1863 (293), LII , pp. 51, 6-7. Cotton Manufacturing Districs, *PP* 1863, (293), LII, p.51, pp.6-7.

85.   Kay-Shuttleworth papers, May-June 1863.

86.   26 and 27 Vic. c. 70, reprinted in Arnold, op.cit., pp.534-45.

87.   W.O. Henderson, 'The Public Works Act, 1863',*Economic History*, II (1931), pp.312-21.

88.   Rawlinson to Villiers, 4 May 1863, loc.cit.; Central Executive Committee, *Report,* 20 July 1863, p.3; Manchester Cent.Ref. Political Tracts, P.3339.

89.   H.B. Farnall, note on letter from Union Clerk, Ashton, to P.L.B., 26 Feb. 1864, P.R.O. MH 12/5422.

90.   R. Rawlinson to C.P. Villiers, 7 April 1864, *PP* 1864 (225), LII.

91.   Watts, op.cit., pp.319-20. Correspondence with P.L.B. in Ashton Union Correspondence, 1864. P.R.O. MH 12/5423

92.   Manchester City Council was strongly criticised on this score. Watts, op.cit., pp.320-26. Town Clerk, Manchester, to P.L.B., 2 April 1864, P.R.O. MH 12/6056; *Manchester Guardian,* 19 April 1864.

93.   The file of correspondence between the Ashton Union and the Poor Law Board for 1864 is full of requests from town councils and local boards of health for loans under the scheme. P.R.O. MH 12/5423. The numbers aided by relief committees fell from 235,741 in January 1863 to 69,657 in January 1864 and to 16,523 in July 1864. 'The Cost of the Cotton Famine in Relief to the Poor', *Journal of the Statistical Society (London),* (Dec. 1864), XXVII, p.600. There was a good deal of disagreement as to the total numbers supported by wages earned under the Public Works Act. Rawlinson held that every operative at work under the Act supported 3.5 dependents, and that as many as 38,000 people were by 1864 dependent on the scheme. The Central Committee regarded this as a gross over-estimate and reckoned each operative as supporting only 1.3 to 1.5 dependents. Watts, op.cit., p.327. A rough estimate based on returns from boards of guardians and relief committees would seem to show a ratio of about 1:3 between cases and persons relieved. The whole question of the effect of the Act would however benefit from further quantitative investigation.

94.   R. Rawlinson to C.P. Villiers, 8 May 1863, op.cit.; *Economist,* 30 May 1863.

95.   R. Rawlinson to C.P. Villiers, 8 May 1863, op.cit.; Central Executive Committee, *Report,* 25 January 1864, p.2, Manchester Cent.Ref. Political Tracts, P.3339.

96.   *Journal of Statistical Society (London),* op.cit., pp.596-602.

97.   Central Executive Committee, *Reports;* 19 Oct. 1863, 10 Oct.1864. Manchester Cent.Ref. Political Tracts, P. 3339.

98.   Watts, op.cit., p.451.

99.   Central Executive Committee, *Report,* 4 Dec. 1865, Manchester Cent.Ref. Political Tracts, P. 3339.

8 THE CHARITY ORGANISATION SOCIETY AND SOCIAL CASEWORK IN LONDON 1869-1900

Judith Fido

The Charity Organisation Society (COS) occupies an important place in the history of social work because of its pioneering of the practice of social casework.[1] Yet historians[2] of social welfare have generally felt ambivalent about the organisation. On the one hand, it has been argued, the techniques of social casework which the COS developed were durable and progressive. On the other, it was ferociously individualist in ideology, resisting until well into the twentieth century every important legislative measure of social welfare; from school meals to old age pensions. This was what Derek Fraser calls the 'paradoxical duality' of the COS; it was 'professionally pioneering but ideologically reactionary'.[3] The assertion of such a duality is reassuring to social workers. It is, after all, through the development of casework that social workers have acquired a professional status in modern society, and the assertion that it is possible to deny the integration of casework and social theory enables them to avoid the conclusion that casework is contingent on particular moral and social theories.

Yet such a view has been challenged from a number of directions. Within the COS, Bernard Bosanquet held that the ethical point of view is concrete. Similarly, COS caseworkers saw their work with individuals and families as principles translated into action. Modern critics of social work have also drawn attention to the uneasy relationship between social work and social control.[4] Once it is acknowledged that through the institutions of social work society expresses 'compassion for, and control of, certain forms of behaviour',[5] it becomes clear that casework represents ideas in operational terms. Finally, the historian Gareth Stedman Jones has suggested that to assert the separability of ideology and its expression 'does violence to the unity between the theory and practice of the Society'.[6] An examination of the ideology of the COS, the relationship to it of its organisation, and the practice of casework further illustrates the unitary nature of theory and practice.

It also shows the connection between both and the main body of nineteenth-century thinking on the moral 'problem' of the poor. The ideology and organisation of the Society may be seen as a late and sophisticated attempt to achieve what had become by the 1870s almost a traditional preoccupation: the remoralisation of the poor, maybe even the reimposition of 'social police'.[7] Perhaps even more important, from the point of view of this essay, social casework, developed initially as a *pis aller* by the COS, was not, so to speak, an exquisite and 'progressive' bloom thrown up in a bed of rank and 'reactionary' weeds. It was a logical development of earlier attempts to embody philanthropic ideology; the caseworkers' ancestors include curates and schoolteachers, even the policeman acting as 'domestic missionary'.[8]

I

The COS was founded for 'Organising Charitable Relief and Repressing Mendicity'. Concerned at the proliferation of philanthropic effort which was working randomly and independently of the poor law, a group of well-to-do individuals in London created a Society which, they fervently hoped, would put charity on a scientific basis and remoralise the poor degraded by indiscriminate donations of cash and gifts. In each poor law division, a local committee organised a charity office to coordinate the activities of all charities and the poor law in the district. Rather than helping individuals and families directly, the original aim was to act as an agency of referral, keeping a register of all cases relieved in the district and sending them on to the appropriate charity, church or to the relieving officer. In this way overlapping of cases would be prevented, fraud and imposture would be detected, and relief would take place in an orderly, rational and principled manner. The example of schemes tried out during the Lancashire cotton famine had shown how this could be done successfully.

Underlying its endeavours were a number of social beliefs common to most nineteenth-century thought on social policy. Thus, like earlier theorists they noted and deplored the separation of classes produced by industrialism. Helen Bosanquet, one of the most prolific and influential of COS writers, commented that

The separation between rich and poor in our large towns, and more especially in London, has often been pointed out as one of the most characteristic and threatening signs of the times. On the one hand, it is said, we have a large number of wealthy people, living an idle, luxurious life in their own quarter, and knowing or caring little about anything outside; on the other hand, we have a much larger number of poverty stricken people herded together at the opposite extreme of the town, with all their energies exhausted in the futile endeavour to secure a tolerable existence.[9]

The ideal, according to Bernard Bosanquet, was 'the citizen who lives at home and works among his neighbours'. Looking back to the organic society of the ancient Greeks where the actual existence of every citizen was bound up with his discharge of civic duty and nothing stood between a man and his fellows, he observed that in modern society, 'We have not their definite set of duties *on which the common good visibly depended*. . . the little drama of our own character and destiny plays itself out on its tiny little stage, but we do not see how our fate and character is the fate and character of our nation.'[10]

Thus Bosanquet recognised, in an almost Durkheimian phraseology, the importance of community, a community in which a shared value system might have currency. This was not a new preoccupation and, equally, the Society's solution was traditional. The inadequacies of industrialism could be remedied and a moral regeneration of the poor could be achieved through personal influence. The example of the work of Octavia Hill, who described herself as 'one, heart and soul, with the Society'[11] seemed to demonstrate the efficacy of the personal touch in social reform, for she accomplished the hard-headed business of housing management by the tender means of personal sympathy. C.S. Loch, Secretary and guiding spirit of the Society, was insistent on the importance of influence. 'The gift avails little', he wrote, 'the influence may avail much. . The reform does not depend on large schemes, but on the fulfilment of duty and the use of influence in the thousand and one relations of life.'[12]

Explaining what visitors could do for the poor, the COS appealed for volunteers to

visit those who have been helped, and to exercise a personal influence over them, so as to insure that the aid given may be really beneficial. To take charge of individual cases, seeing that the relief required for them, sometimes for a long period, is procured and carefully administered. . .By many of these means, not charitable but rather social, class distinctions may be partly effaced.[13]

This implied a sustained personal effort by the visitor. A paper on the potential of this kind of charitable work with the poor, even in times of exceptional distress, urged that

The true principle in dealing with them seens to be this: They may rightly be assisted by a sufficient allowance from charity, but only on one condition, namely, that charity shall not cease her action as soon as the period of want is past, but shall keep in touch with the man who has been so helped, and persuade him to save and join a club and in other ways to protect himself against the recurrence of distress.[14]

There was nothing new in any of these ideas, but their application to the question of charity had a uniquely systematic individualistic aspect, and novel too, was the organisational structure through which they were to be expressed in concrete action. The Society argued that the segregation of classes, the absence of personal contact, and the lack of an immediately visible organic community had, as Stedman Jones suggests,[15] robbed the charitable transaction of its force. 'In a great city', lamented Loch, 'the larger proportion of applications for relief are made from strangers to strangers.'[16] Consequently, the element of obligation inherent in the gift had gone. 'If we do not improve them by the gift, must we not do them [the poor] harm?' asked Octavia Hill.[17] In a London with 'large quarters of the town without the light which comes from brotherhood, and large masses of the people without the friendship of those better taught than themselves',[18] there was, in the opinion of the Society, widespread demoralisation of the poor, because of the ready availability of doles and the 'fatal facilities now offered at every turn for embracing a life with no true industrial basis rather than a life depending on definite organisable ability'.[19]

This problem could be resolved, the spirit of community reasserted, and the poor remoralised through personal influence exercised in a structured and responsible way. Thus COS workers were expected to develop an intimate knowledge of their district, so that they would be working within a locality 'not as a chaotic agglomeration of atoms, but as an organic whole'.[20] COS workers were confident that, even under the pressure of large-scale distress in hard winters, the machinery of close personal supervision could be applied, for a corps of professional workers could, if necessary, mobilise and direct temporary workers; each case could still be separately and thoroughly dealt with according to a definite plan of rehabilitation. This was 'the sort of organisation which the intricate conditions of modern city life demand'.[21] When people in a district could band together to improve the conditions of the poor by a definite and intelligent policy in the personal administration of charitable relief, the division between the classes in the city would be healed and 'the specialisation which is an indispensable feature of modern life shall not isolate us from the citizen spirit, the pulse-beat of the social heart'.[22] If those who wished to help the poor insisted on 'entering into the mind, habits, and feelings of the classes under consideration, and on comprehending their lives from the beginning to the end',[23] the moral and intellectual isolation of the classes could be broken down. But, it was not sufficient for the charitable transaction to take place in the context of a personal relationship between giver and recipient; it had to be thought out in terms of the effect of the gift on the community:

> What can do nothing but good is that a lady, who is exercising such a vocation, should have learned or should learn to appreciate the bearing of her work, not only on the immediate sufferer (and that, in the largest sense, including his future and that of the other members of his family), but also on the progress or retrogression in the whole condition of the poor, and consequently in the welfare and good life of society as a whole. Then, in the particular case, her trained wisdom will suggest to her what measures to adopt, and she will be an educating influence not only as regards the conditions of health, but as regards those of character.[24]

From time to time in COS publications, case histories were given to exemplify the effectiveness of personal influence in helping families to become self-reliant. A typical description was that of a family suffering from neglect, poverty and unhappiness; the man drank, the rooms were dirty, the children were neglected, the wife was hopeless. The man, a butcher's porter, earned plenty of money but never thought of saving anything. The family were constantly in debt, living from hand to mouth. Many visits were paid to his house before the man began to realise that by means of systematic saving he might transform his home and entirely change the position of himself and his family. Conviction dawned on him, he began to put by, and was eventually able to take a home and shop in a London suburb.[25]

As Loch pointed out, COS work was no 'playing at' reform of character. Its work aimed at thoroughness, perhaps even at character transformation. The question, thus, was not merely one of asking and giving: the more was given thoughtlessly, the more demands were made. He realised that the notion of organisation might seem to negate that of charity:

> At first sight the words Charity and Organisation seem to be a contradiction in terms. Charity is free, independent, fervent, impulsive. Organisation implies order and method, sacrifice for a

common end, self-restraint. There is a kind of wildness in the enthusiasm of charity. But organisation and its kindred words suggest the quietness of gradual growth, the social results of a circumspect sobriety, a balanced and temperate progress. The Charity Organisation Society represents an attempt to draw together and combine these opposite forces. . . The Society then aims at preserving and aiding the quickness and discretion and even the secretness of personal charity, and enabling it by union and cooperation to improve the condition of the poor.[26]

So organisation should be an integral part of the charitable impulse, one which substituted controlled and conditional help for the spontaneous and careless gift. The charitable donation thoughtlessly given and thoughtlessly received, distorted the proper relations between people; the rich man could heedlessly assuage his guilt, the poor man would come to live on the expectations of easy handouts instead of relying on his own labours for his subsistence. The charity of doles and patronage was 'mean and delusive';[27] intelligent casework was welcome after 'the dreary monotony of dole-giving or ticket-dispensing'.[28] The charitable impulse was not allowed to flow freely; it had to be scientifically harnessed in a regulated environment if it was not to degrade both recipient and giver. It was a view not always popular. One bystander noted

Rich people with tender hearts have been having a hard time of it lately in many ways. Never, surely, before were so many and such harrowing appeals made every day to their feelings on behalf of sufferers of every description. . . Schemes for alleviations and reforms meet us at every turn; but in our attempts to solace ourselves by giving alms, we are met by innumerable difficulties, and hampered and bewildered by unanswerable admonitions both from within and without, about the danger of pauperizing, till some of us scarcely dare offer a cup of beef-tea to a sick neighbour for fear of demoralizing him, and offending against the canons of political economy and the organization of charity. . . how one longs for some outpouring of comfortable, unhesitating, old-fashioned, joyous bounty — not judicious administration of charity, but a good hearty swing of generosity — if only it might be innocently indulged in.[29]

II

Organisation was, then, an integral part of charity, intimately linked with
with the Society's aims and ideology. Through it, 'scientific' approaches
to charity could be made, rationality and order replace impulsiveness
and disorder, and a serious impact be made in an area where so far
efforts had been unavailing. It was a characteristically late-Victorian
'businesslike' approach, similar to that underlying the contemporary
social investigations of Charles Booth. The Society sought to achieve the
end of 'Organising Charitable Relief and Repressing Mendicity' through
establishing an organisation which at district level would channel local
charitable contributions, and coordinate the work of voluntary
charitable organisations and the poor law. It thus aimed at control in a
number of areas. The behaviour of donors and of charity workers was
to be controlled, in the great interest of controlling the poor. This
latter aim, the crucial goal of the society, came to be attempted
primarily through the caseworkers, as we shall see.

The basis of the COS organisation was the district committee, which
corresponded to the poor law divisions. By 1872, under the direction of
Central Council, district offices had been set up in thirty-six poor law
districts. Although Loch and others lamented the fact, the committees
did not generally comprise working-class people; they consisted of
clergy, businessmen, doctors, civil servants, retired army officers and
later, well-to-do women. Though there was a considerable degree of
local variation coherent schemes were developed. The district
committees attempted to ensure that applications for assistance were
fully investigated to assess if and how they should be helped. In each
case they mobilised the resources for assistance from the family,
interested persons and charitable institutions.

The Society tried to bring together into cooperation the various
charitable agencies and individuals in each district, to prevent the
misapplication of relief and the evils of overlapping. The intention was
that by making the district committee representative of local charities
and a centre of reference for all interested in charitable work local
schemes for the aid of the poor could be promoted and COS ideas
could be disseminated. 'Clergy returns' were issued to local parsons so
that they could refer applicants to the Society for investigation. Local
individuals and organisations thus became accustomed to ask the office
for help and enquiry in particular cases. It is typical to find a letter
from a vicar to the effect that someone is 'a deserving case for the COS'
or a letter from the secretary of a trade society asking help for a man
who is 'out of work chiefly through the frost'. In some districts, with

varying success, a central register of cases was kept to prevent overlapping and to detect professional begging.

COS workers and committee members also involved themselves in matters concerning the poor by acting as guardians, school managers, vestrymen and so on. As Norman McCord has indicated,[30] in practice official and unofficial activity for the care of the poor were controlled by much the same people. Thus an attempt was made to infuse a district with COS ideas and methods. Mrs Leon, hon. secretary of St George's Committee, was a school manager of an elementary board school. Finding that free school dinners were being supplied wholesale, she set up a committee, including Loch, COS representatives and clergy to deal separately with each case along COS lines. Needy cases were referred to COS committees but it was impossible to keep up an intimate acquaintance with 500 children, though 'that is what is really wanted — an up-to-date knowledge of each family'.[31] A compromise was reached by giving nothing free on a regular basis.

The Society estimated the potential of district casework very highly; sub-committees were set up to deal with particular problems, for example to raise and administer old age pensions, in the hope of meeting the needs of all the aged poor in a district, thus obviating any necessity for state pensions.

The Society assumed a relationship of mutual responsibility with the poor law, an assumption encouraged by the Poor Law Board's Minute on 'The Relief of the Poor in the Metropolis' in 1869 shortly after the Society's foundation. The Goschen Minute defined the appropriate spheres of action of the poor law and charity, and advocated schemes of cooperation. No supplementation of outdoor relief was permitted. As the poor law was deterrent rather than reformatory, dealing with those who had become paupers, charity dealt with those in distress who could not or should not be relieved by the poor law. The poor law had no power to give tools or redeem pawns, but such activities could be undertaken by charity.

The COS believed in the principles of 1834, and according to Loch, shared with the poor law the duty not to meet the ordinary contingencies of life; charity could only meet these with 'the exercise of such influence on the part of the donor as will induce the person to provide for himself against similar contingencies in the future'.[32] Casework was for selected cases in which self-reliance could be recovered or maintained: 'Charity takes account of character, and selects those cases in which assistance will lead to self-support; the possession of some resources makes a case more suitable for charity'.[33] The threat of the poor law was used as a sanction in some cases, and sometimes casework dovetailed neatly with the poor law:

> A sick man in Holborn was sent to the Infirmary. He did not belong to a club so, out of anxiety for his family, he came out too soon. He was then sent to the COS by the Guardians and was prevailed upon to return to the Infirmary, while 10/- a week was given to the family by the Society. He was able to work again after convalescence and promised to join a savings club.[34]

In general, district offices failed to coordinate all the relief work of the poor law and local charities but what is significant from the stand-point of this paper is the way in which the shared philosophy of the poor law and the Society permeated the casework. Loch, Thomas MacKay and other COS supporters wrote extensively on poor law matters, served as guardians and allied themselves with it. In a sense, the existence of the poor law was necessary to the Charity Organisation Society. The poor law was less eligible than charity and charity was less eligible than the exertions of self-reliance. The poor law and charity came full circle; the condition of the independent labourer was more eligible than submission to the ministrations of either. The workhouse test could be applied to the undeserving, the 'casework test' could be applied to the deserving. Systematised charity imposed its own stigma on the poor.

The organisation aimed to control the donors of charity. From its inception, the COS encouraged people who had received appeals for help not to deal with them themselves but to pass them on to the Society to be handled systematically. If the applicants proved to be *bona fide* and worthy cases, the Society undertook to administer any fund which the donor chose to make available. The Society would have liked any gifts which the donors had not the time or inclination to apply personally and systematically to be put in the hands of organised charity. The charitable motives of the donor and his interest in the case were not set aside if the COS took it over; they were fostered and maintained. The Society was punctilious in reporting back to donors. Occasionally people were distressed by the zeal with which the COS investigated the cases which they had referred to them and by the stern judgements which were applied in the casework. In one instance a family was denied assistance because of the refusal by the father to allow the COS to make further enquiries about their circumstances. The parson who had referred the case was told of the decision and replied indignantly that he had understood that the COS had found the father to be a respectable man in great want: 'As you had already verified his character sufficiently to give him fourteen shillings to [redeem clothes in pawn] I should myself have thought it unnecessary to make any further enquiries before giving him the remainder of the two pounds I had sent to you.'[35] The gift thus had to be applied in an informed way. Unaided good nature should submit to the broader implications of the gift, implications which the layman might not appreciate.

Where conflict arose in attempts to control donors' behaviour, it was often over the harshness of the Society's judgements. Within the organisation itself, the same controls operated over members, sometimes with similar results. Canon Barnett[36] was only one of those who found increasing difficulty in accepting the stern criteria of the Society. But for its members, control was often two-edged, curbing impulses on the one hand, but on the other contributing, in Durkheim's sense, to its growth as a 'solidary' system. Thus, one worker wrote that as a young girl she had been in the habit of giving indiscriminately and had observed with despair that her actions had no real impact, the need of those she helped never grew less: 'I felt that alone I could not deal with these great needs; I had not experience, money or knowledge enough. I dreaded adopting the hopeless attitude of so many of our most earnest workers, who, standing alone, feel overwhelmed by the sin and sorrow around them.'[37] She wrote that she had wished to learn from the experiences of others and to benefit from training. To the argument that it might be difficult to combine in one person all the kinds of knowledge and experience which were needed, the answer lay in the collective decision-making of the Society and committee discussion of difficult cases (in modern parlance, the 'case conference'). As Young and Ashton remark: 'In the COS action was the result not of the unaided judgement of a single social worker, but the combined knowledge and wisdom of the group.'[38] The interaction of control and joint creativity was to be of importance not only to the COS, but in the continuing development of the social work profession.

III

Social casework was not the original or major objective of the COS and was not initially 'the part of its activity in which the Society takes most pride'.[39] Nevertheless, the logic of its ideology would probably have driven it to develop casework. As it was, the process was hastened by the failure of the Society in other areas. The objectives of charity organisation and repression of mendicity were difficult, if not impossible to achieve. The failure lay in the fact, noted by Beatrice Webb,[40] that churches, hospitals and other charities refused to cooperate with the COS, partly because of the harshness of its principles, and partly from the understandable preference of charities to choose their own beneficiaries. In addition, the poor law authorities were generally impervious to the Society's influence. Faced with these problems, the Society turned to social casework, which, far from being an unconsidered by-product of its work (and ideologically neutral) became the main instrument for forming and transmitting its ideology into action. By 1886, COS caseworkers in London were handling 25,000 cases a year.

Looking back on the history of the Society in 1914, Helen Bosanquet stated that casework came to absorb the bulk of the work done by it, and noted how, by 1895, the work itself had improved in quality to show a consideration of detail and carefulness of treatment in each individual case which was not there fifteen to twenty years before, and how home visiting, supervision and plans for treatment were more complete and thought out. It is not surprising, then, that an examination of the Society's social casework reveals its ideology in action.

Casework was undertaken according to a carefully specified procedure. The particulars of the case were taken down in the district office to which the application had been made. The agent, a paid official of the Society, or a voluntary worker then verified the facts of the case by writing to or by visiting the referees and other persons named in connection with the case. The applicant was interviewed at home by the agent or a voluntary worker. The information acquired was written up for 'the record should not be merely in the mind of a secretary or agent'.[41] He might go, the papers would remain. Full reports were asked for. The case was then presented to the Committee or a sub-committee, who made the decision whether or not to take on the case, and if so, what form assistance from the Society should take. (In the early years, applicants sometimes had to appear in person before the committee.) The immediate needs of the case were considered, but a definite plan had to be made for the future. The applicant was informed of the decision and if he was to be helped he was visited repeatedly and members of his family, neighbours and others would be interviewed or written to. Throughout, visits, interviews and action taken were recorded in the casepaper. Letters to the committee and copies of letters from the office and other relevant material, such as press cuttings, were kept in the file. The district secretary surveyed the work of the district office and saw that the casework was performed and the money spent in accordance with the committee's decision. Central Council of the Society had the responsibility of making sure that the casework of the districts was thorough and was carried out in accordance with COS principles: no help could be given without personal application, help was given on a personal level, it was undertaken on the basis of thorough knowledge of the individual applicant and any material aid had to be adequate and rehabilitative rather than palliative.

A COS casepaper is an awesome document. The front of the file abounds with headings designed to show the applicant's normal circumstances and the reason for his present difficulty at a glance. His trade and his normal earnings and those (if any) of his wife and his children who might be wage earners were recorded as was their trade and their place of employment, and their addresses if they lived away from the parental home. It was noted whether the applicant was in lodgings, or was a householder, the number of rooms he had, how long he had lived there and his previous addresses. Arrears of rent and details of other debts, pawn tickets and so on are also recorded. Whether the applicant belonged to a club, trade or benefit society was another crucial factor to be noted, for it indicated whether he had a record of thrift and that could help decide his eligibility for COS aid. Any relief from the poor law was also taken into consideration. By the 1890s it was recommended that a trained person should take down the application and that the applicant should be interviewed in a special room to help him disclose the facts about himself: 'the object of taking down a case is not merely to get a statement of the facts, but if possible to enter into the mind and thoughts of the applicant'.[42]

An examination of old COS casepapers shows how thorough the investigatory processes of their casework were. The referees which the applicant had to name were followed up. Often one COS office asked another district office to make enquiries on their behalf — for example, to obtain information from an applicant's previous address or to interview relatives who might be living in a different district from that of the applicant. Enquiries were made of clergy, relieving officers, landlords past and present, savings club secretaries and employers. It was not uncommon for social workers to question the applicant's neighbours and tradesmen in his locality about his circumstances and character. A casepaper of 1875, concerning Wood, an unemployed dock labourer reads: 'The neighbours and tradesmen in the immediate neighbourhood of the applicant's residence seem to have a good opinion of the family — the man is described as being sober and industrious but not of a strong constitution.'[43]

Some social workers felt that there was a problem when information was sought from people of the same social class as the applicant, for example, from a foreman 'who often is of no better class than the applicant himself, there is the danger of his being liable to underestimate the man's wages and also to let his mates know that he is applying for charity'.[44] Informants in a working-class neighbourhood might be unreliable. One suggestion was that a list of reliable people in various streets should be kept. No doubt some COS visitors saw the solidarity of working-class neighbourhoods as a possible obstacle to enquiries. In Wood's case, the Society's agent experienced difficulty in getting information from a rent collector whom he found 'very curt and reticent' and could not get him to say if the applicant was in arrears or not. The agent went on to report: 'I have no doubt from his manner that in the meantime he will acquaint Wood of the enquiry that has been made of him.' The district committee reported to central council that they

> were unanimously of the opinion that it w^d be impolitic in their agent to make any further inquiries as suspicion seems to be already aroused, and the Committee are anxious that nothing sh^d take place by the direct action of their agent which w^d prevent his obtaining in future information which has hitherto been given without reserve — the Committee think that this is one of those special cases which should be dealt with by some officer of the Society, who is unconnected with the district.[45]

The Society decided, after making enquiries, that the case was not deserving of assistance. The opinion of the vicar was recorded: 'He thinks the man is lazy and improvident — Mr. Walton would be glad to get them out of his parish.'

An Occasional Paper of 1893 indicates the direction and principles of investigation in COS casework. In the case of a widow, the kind of questions to be borne in mind were: 'Is she energetic and willing to take advice — a good manager with a tidy home? Will her relations second her efforts?' In the case of a sick person:

> *Serious illness* is an evil against which the working class can insure themselves by membership of a sound benefit society. Every effort should be made to induce them to do so in time of health. Men who

have not neglected the opportunities of thrift should be supported. . . In less satisfactory cases help on a first application may be justified if it is made conditional on the exercise of greater forethought in the future.

An example is given of a case of sickness successfully dealt with:

> the family was in distress because the father, a copperworker, suffered from chest disease. Two boys in the family earned a few shillings through odd jobs and there were three younger children. This was 'a most respectable family'. At first efforts were concentrated on the father's health in the way of diet, hospital and convalescent help. Finally 'an excellent mangle with a good connection' was obtained and the family were making 12/- a week by it. In this way the family was 'saved from pauperism'.[46]

Any assistance which the COS rendered was conditional on the applicant's submitting to the processes of investigation on which the Society insisted. Failure to comply could mean refusal to help. In 1898 the father of a young girl was denied assistance for his daughter's convalescence because 'he refuses the usual questions'.[47] From the case-papers it is evident that applicants sometimes became disturbed at the range and intensity of the enquiries which the COS set in motion:

> In 1887 Mr Webb, an unemployed insurance agent, asked for money to redeem clothes which had been pawned so that he could be interviewed for a job. The visitor reported that the applicant had not realised that his first caller was an agent of the COS and only realised it when he was visited a second time by someone with a casepaper and was asked questions: 'He was particularly anxious to know who had written to us about him — I could not tell him as I did not know — he will not have his uncle or brother written to or any further enquiries made from any relations. . . in fact he wishes no further enquiries made at all. It would be simply ruin to him if it were known in business circles that he had been helped by charity.' Later the applicant wrote objecting to the COS approaching his landlord 'With the idea, as it seemed to me, of making enquiries of him. As I certainly wish to keep a roof over my head, and am not in the habit of confiding in a man of his position, nor desirous of bandying words, I felt that enquiries had gone quite far enough, especially as the letter to my father's friend (which had been

forwarded on to the COS) was a *private* one and which I think the
recipient should have treated in that light.' He also wanted to know
if any communication had been made with his employer about him
'as it will do me incalculable injury, in fact I shall have to throw up
the appointment I have obtained if it has been done.' The
Secretary replied 'as you decline to allow us to make any further
enquiry, we must consider your application to be withdrawn'.
However, the COS visitor, moved by the suffering of the applicant's
wife and children, visited again and noted the poor condition of the
family, who by this time had pawned virtually all their possessions
so that they had all (with the exception of a fourteen year old child)
been unable to go out for six to seven weeks because they had no
shoes. She immediately gave them £1.[48]

It is clear from a case like this that permission was not always sought
before enquiries were made. However, as time went on, social workers
became uneasy about this kind of practice and by the 1890s it was being
recommended that the permission of applicants should be gained before
making enquiries of employers. But, if permission was refused, the
Society could always turn down the application.

An essential element in investigation was the home visit. The practice
of visiting the applicant in his own home was always followed; he had
to be seen in his domestic surroundings where his character and
circumstances could be accurately assessed. More subtly, if the social
worker was to influence him in a deep and lasting way the office
interview was insufficient. That a home visit might be construed by the
applicant as an intrusive act was only appreciated much later by the
Society. Helen Bosanquet noted that among East Enders 'Anything, for
instance, of the nature of inquisitiveness into another person's affairs,
and especially intrusion into their home unbidden, is a great offence
against social etiquette',[49] and the Society was certainly against the sort
of wholesale visiting that the visiting societies practised. But Helen
Bosanquet's knowledge of East End working-class life did not prevent
her assuming that the very fact of a person applying to the COS gave
them *carte blanche* to visit him at home. In a vivid phrase, Fraser refers
to the practice of home visiting as 'in effect a cultural assault on the
working-clsss way of life'.[50] H.V. Toynbee, reflecting on the necessity
to use trained workers and volunteers rather than agents or enquiry
officers for this delicate work, wrote that the home visit 'enables them
to form a much better judgement of the case as a whole, for the
conditions and surroundings of the home are among some of the best

indications of character'.[51] On being visited, applicants were asked to produce rent books, pawn tickets, and the like for the attention of the visitor. On the one hand the condition of the home was used as an indication of the respectability of the applicant, on the other hand it allowed an accurate assessment of the real needs of the case. Though remarks were made on the furniture, number of rooms and sleeping arrangements as well as the tidiness and cleanliness of the home as a basis for making rather subjective judgements about the character of the applicants, a home visit could also be the occasion for appreciating the urgency and extent of need. Thus, during the course of a particularly intractable case, a worker was able, by seeing the man and his family at home at frequent intervals, to respond sensitively to the fluctuating needs of the family. At various times, clothes and blankets were obtained for them, clothes were redeemed from pawn and bills were paid. The circumstances of wives and children were also noted in a way that might not otherwise have been possible.

But applicants were not always content to be visited at home. In one instance, described below, the son-in-law of an old lady for whom the Society were trying to arrange a pension, hid from the Society's agent when the family was visited at home. Noel Timms has also indicated that the home visit has positive and negative features for casework.[52] He maintains that during a home visit it is easier for the client to manipulate the worker, who is by no means always in control as she is more likely to be in an office. Sometimes this is apparent from the casepapers; thus one worker reported that when she visited an applicant at home he 'talked so fast he rather bewildered me. . . His attitude was such that I could not make any enquiries as to bedding etc. . . as he made me feel they would be an impertinence.'[53]

The casework of the Charity Organisation Society rested on a model of human behaviour that was based on the notion of 'character'. 'Character' determined whether or not an applicant would be assisted and what form of help he would get. The character of the applicant was embodied in his past history, as recorded in the casepaper. Material aid was conditional on evidence of character; old age pensions, for example, were reserved for those in whose cases there were some special points of merit, who had shown that they valued their independence by having made some tangible effort to provide for the future, according to their means. A kind of 'thrift test' was applied.

The ideal of character was related to those attributes which ensure the smooth operation of market forces in an industrialising economy. Thus the values of economic independence, foresight, self-control and sustained effort were stressed. What the ideal of character is emerges most clearly from the sensational descriptions of the working-class 'residuum' by COS writers like Helen and Bernard Bosanquet. In place of foresight, a member of the residuum displayed a feckless Micawber-like belief that something will turn up; instead of self-control he exhibited an impulsive restlessness:

> The true type of this class lives in the present moment only; not only is he without foresight, — he is almost without memory, in the sense that his past is so completely past that he has no more organised experience to refer to than a child. Hence his life is one incoherent jumble from beginning to end; it would be impossible to make even a connected story out of it, for every day merely repeats the mistakes, the follies and mishaps of yesterday; there is no development in it; all is aimless and drifting.[54]

The life of one in the residuum was marked by a more or less permanent failure to maintain himself and his family by honest toil; often his family ties were loose and feelings of mutual responsibility between parents and children and brothers and sisters were weak. His work was intermittent and low grade, not because of the exigencies of the economy but because of his abhorrence of regular work. Stedman Jones has convincingly suggested that the COS as a new urban gentry were particularly hard on what they saw as fecklessness in the poor, because they had attained their own social position by means of 'austere virtues'.[55] So economic success and failure came to be associated with virtue and vice respectively. The assumption was that the applicant was a wholly rational being who could choose whether or not to be virtuous. Uncontrolled giving helped him to make the wrong choice. Casework helped a man to make the right choice. This harsh view of the world was imbued with ideas of natural selection. The natural consequences of sin and vice had to be allowed to operate without interference; any attempt to break the connection between moral failings and their natural punishment would retard social progress. In the view of the Society, casework allowed this to happen because, unlike wholesale and non-selective measures, it was applied only in accordance with certain principles which aimed at ensuring that the social fabric was not damaged by unthinking charity.

A distinction was made between those who possessed 'the industrial character' and the chronic unemployed; the 'provident poor' and idle 'social wrecks'. Somewhere between were the respectable but not provident poor: 'They do not save, or join clubs, or in any way look forward to the future; they simply spend their earnings as they come; but they are on the whole industrious and sober and possessed of tidy homes'.[56] The vigour natural to the true working class had to be fostered through casework. Just as modern caseworkers extol the middle-class ideal of 'deferred gratification', Charity Organisation Society workers extolled thrift:

> Thrift is the characteristic of the steadfast mind, reflecting the unity and necessity of life and the universe, and exercising self-control in the present for the sake of ensuring that the future shall at any rate approximate to it in value.[57]

The growth of working-class thrift through friendly societies, the cooperative movement, the national Penny Bank and the like, seemed to Loch and other members of the COS a vindication of their philosophy. Loch went so far as to hope that in melting away class distinctions, charity could 'create what in a sense might be called a great friendly society'.[58]

This notion of character infused the casework of the COS, but it could not be neatly and stringently applied in practice. It is true that a considerable number of people were refused assistance because they were unable to produce evidence of character but others were helped although they would seem to display to a marked degree just those defects of character outlined above. Thus when Webb, the unemployed insurance agent, was helped by the Society he was described by the visitor as

> a genuine case to be accounted for by the character of the man — He strikes me as utterly without the smallest idea of providence or thrift and with a cork like lightness of heart that prevents his suffering much where most people would be in despair. He thinks now he has got one piece of work he shall 'pull through' and cares very little whether we help him further or not. . .I think he is a sort of man who would lend his own last guinea or borrow his friend's with an equally light heart.[59]

It is possible that in this case, as in others which are similar, the COS decided to help because the man was a clerical worker and because he initially displayed the frankness and communicativeness which they valued.

Character was associated with the exercise of responsibility within the family. It is no accident that the Charity Organisation Society became the Family Welfare Association. The moral education which casework entailed was related to the nurturing of the material and moral responsibility of the extended family for its members. The case-paper was a family casepaper. The members of the family recorded in it represented liabilities to be met but also resources to be tapped in a plan of rehabilitation. The category 'Relations Able to Assist' appears as a section on the case front. COS workers tended to coax the children and grandchildren of applicants to contribute to their support, or if necessary to coerce them into doing so. The way in which they dealt with applications for financial help to old people illustrates their approach.

A casepaper of 1894 shows what happened in the case of Mrs Finch, a widow of seventy-three. According to their usual custom the Society decided to persuade her children (and other interested individuals) to subscribe to a pension for her, which they would administer personally. The record indicates the poverty of the children themselves; several had families of their own to support, and one had nine children. The workers on the case were prepared to go to considerable lengths in their attempts to ensure that the family supported the old lady:

A daughter in service is visited at her employer's and the visitor reports that 'she expresses her willingness to assist in keeping her mother but will see her first and talk the matter over with her and tell her what she will give'. The old lady is interviewed at home and says that she had thought there would be no trouble about getting a pension and 'had she known that matters would have come to what they have, she would not have troubled the Society'. Wilfred, a son who lives with her, hides from the COS Agent and this refusal to co-operate leads the Committee to close the case. Two months later Wilfrid calls at the COS office and is told that the family can probably arrange between themselves to help the mother. But, prompted by Loch, the Committee resume work with the family. The visitor proposes to see if members of the family will contribute weekly to the widow's support, and to persuade her to do without Jane (a 14 year old grand-daughter living with her) who could possibly go into service. During the subsequent visit the old lady says that 'the original application was a mistake on the part of the son-in-law who thought the COS would provide a pension without applying to the family at all. Her family and especially the son with whom she lives did not like the idea of being interfered with and Mrs Finch herself thought it would be better to leave them to settle things among themselves. She feels very ill and does not think she can live long. . .Jane's mother (a deserted wife) sends all she can for Jane's support so that it is a benefit and not a drag to her grand-mother to have her.[60]

It is undoubtedly true that many families benefited from the very considerable skills of COS workers, some of whom were very resource-ful in mobilising help (financial, medical and educational). But their concern to maintain family obligations according to their own ideas of what these should be meant that their handling of cases was often crude and insensitive, because they allowed this concern to override the delicate balance of family relationships. In COS ideology the family was predominantly an economic rather than a psychical entity. The family was an agent of selection in the Darwinian sense, and to support a family that would not or could not support themselves was in conflict with the postulates of natural selection. The policy of the COS towards deserted wives, for example, was not to give assistance; in such cases the workhouse was recommended. During the winter of 1880-81, in cooperation with the poor law in the East End, the Society applied a modified workhouse test by offering 12s. or 15s. a week to the families of seasonally unemployed workers on condition that they themselves went into the workhouse.

A central tenet of casework is that help is given through a personal relationship between caseworker and client. COS caseworkers often got to know a particular family over a number of years and some of the surviving casepapers reveal the ambiguities of such a relationship, where sympathy, control and manipulation by social worker or client came into play. From 1874-84, the Society tried to help a man of 'superior' position who had lost his job and got into debt:

The Committee decided to raise a fund of £15 to give Mr. Blake a fresh start in life and to deprive him of all occasion for continuing to write begging letters. He will be able to get his books out of pawn and to study for a qualification. On the visitor's recommendation money is given to free the family (there is a wife and nine children) from some of their most pressing liabilities, though the Committee stipulate that it must not be spent 'unless there is a fair prospect of a successful result'. The family is visited many times, and the case-worker notes that with so many to keep it is not easy for them to

get on without great care and economy. Mr. Blake writes thanking
the Society for their help and telling her of his hopes for a better
situation: 'I have for some little time past been feeling most unwell
and little able to attend to even the most trivial duties, for the
mental distraction to which I have been subjected for so long a time
seems to have brought me terribly low'. He feels ashamed at his
inability to pay his rent, and replies to a letter from the worker
'although your letter has been haunting me day and night I have
been forced to postpone writing to you and I must beg of you not
to think unkindly of my delay'. By 1881 Mr. Blake is writing
begging letters again, and Loch comments that he 'had hoped
that Miss Carling (the caseworker) had satisfactorily disposed of the
case'. In 1884 another begging letter appears and the final comment
in the file reads 'judging from the result of our former efforts it
seems a difficult case to treat with success'.[61]

In this case, the applicant's middle-class origins allowed him to
communicate articulately with the worker and is therefore of considerable interest. Evidently he accepted her as an authority because she
controlled money and resources and knew that his access to them was
conditional on his behaviour and his ability to show that he was making
efforts to better his position. Because he was, as one of the recipients
of his begging letters commented, 'one of those unhappy people whose
affairs are doomed to be always in a muddle', he was overwhelmed by
his problems and unable to meet the expectations of the worker and
the Society. His letters to her reveal his efforts to remain in control of
his own affairs while recognising her control and his depression and
anxiety at his inadequacies.

It would be wrong to assume that casework was always applied by
the COS in a consistent manner. A great deal of the work was *ad hoc*
and spasmodic. The treatment of a case might well consist of a number
of discrete proceedings rather than a coordinated and cohesive course
of action. Barbara Wootton has pointed out[62] that the ways in which
social workers theorise about casework do not necessarily match the
work they actually do every day. So caution is needed in making
assumptions about the casework that was practised in London by the
COS in the nineteenth century. The COS districts varied to some extent
in their practice and much was dependent on the quality of the
individual worker. However, she was subject to the control of the
Society's organisation. The committee made the crucial decisions in the
case, and, as Loch observed, was 'a check on the individual almoner'.

The Society 'educated' her and monitored the work which she had to record for the Committee. By setting up a structure to control the administration of social assistance, the COS began to create a 'professional culture' for social work. They constructed a rational organisation for the exchange of ideas, attitudes and methods and for the transmission of these to new members of the organisation and to workers in other organisations, statutory and voluntary. A social work literature began to accumulate, in the form of the Charity Organisation Review, various Charity Organisation Papers and Special Reports and conferences on social issues. From the mid-1890s training for social workers began to be stressed.Increasingly, the work of investigation and visiting passed out of the hands of working-class agents of the Society into the hands of middle-class visitors and volunteers.

The Society enjoyed a period of success during the 1870s before the 'crisis' of the 1880s and the subsequent reappraisal of the nature of poverty. The Society's belief that organised charity and the poor law could between them deal with the mass of poverty of a whole society was discredited (though they were handling as many as 14,000 cases in 1901). Yet it will not do to claim that COS ideology disappeared while casework methods endured. The concept of personalised social welfare, as a specialist quasi-professional activity, had a potency which suggests that it answered a deep need in industrial societies. In 1895 a COS worker was appointed as the first hospital almoner. In an expanding and improving medical service the caseworker was to deal sensitively with the individual patient's needs, but, by discriminating between individuals she was also to check demand.[63] COS resistance to collective social welfare paralleled their earlier opposition to un-regulated philanthropy. In both cases the personal element, so essential for social control, seemed to be absent. Yet, though the worst fears of the COS materialised in the form of state provided social services, the personalised welfare relationship in which they so passionately believed has flourished in the Welfare State. Through this relationship, the social worker reminds the applicant of his dependency and his social obligations.

Notes

1.   There is considerable debate about the definition of social casework. Caseworkers today would no doubt argue that the nature of contemporary casework is rather different from that of the nineteenth century. However, then and now casework can be said to be a specialised *personal* service

provided in a disciplined manner by a social welfare organisation for families and individuals who require help, both material and emotional, with problems of social adjustment. Debate centres round the moral and political implications of such help.

2. A.F. Young and E.T. Ashton, *British Social Work in the Nineteenth Century* (London, 1956), pp.92-114; C.L. Mowat, *The Charity Organisation Society 1869-1913* (London,1961); K. Woodroofe, *From Charity to Social Work* (London, 1962), pp.25-55; Melvin Richter, *The Politics of Conscience: T.H. Green and His Age* (London, 1964), pp.330-9; D. Owen, *English Philanthropy 1660-1960* (Cambridge, Mass., 1965), pp.215-46; M. Rooff, *A Hundred Years of Family Welfare* (London, 1972). For a valuable analysis of different approaches to the ideas of the COS see C.S. Yeo's introduction to Helen Bosanquet, *Social Work in London 1869-1912,* 2nd edn. (Brighton 1973).

3. D. Fraser, *The Evolution of the British Welfare State* (London, 1974) p.121.

4. Notably B.J. Heraud, *Sociology and Social Work* (Oxford, 1970), pp.182-99; and P. Leonard, 'Social Control, Class Values and Social Work Practice', *Social Work,* XXII 4 (Oct. 1965), pp.9-13.

5. N. Timms, 'Social Work in Action – A Historical Study (1887-1937)', *Case Conference,* VIII, 1 (May 1961), p.7.

6. G. Stedman Jones, *Outcast London* (Harmondsworth, 1976), p.257.

7. See above, the essays of A.P. Donajgrodzki and R. Storch.

8. R. Storch, 'The Policeman as Domestic Missionary: Urban Discipline and Popular Culture in Northern England, 1850-80', *Journal of Social History,* IV (1976), pp.492-3.

9. Mrs Bernard Bosanquet, *Rich and Poor,* 2nd edn. (London, 1898), p.3.

10. Bernard Bosanquet, 'The Duties of Citizenship', in B. Bosanquet (ed.), *Aspects of the Social Problem* (London, 1895), p.6.

11. Octavia Hill, 'The Charity Organisation Society', *COS Occasional Papers* (hereafter *COSOP*), First Series, no. 20 (1891), p.37. For other influences on the COS especially the work of Chalmers and the Elberfeld system, see Young and Ashton, *British Social Work,* pp.67-80.

12. C.S. Loch, *Charity Organisation* (London, 1890), pp.35, 41.

13. Anon. 'What Workers can do for the Poor in connection with the Charity Organisation Society', *COSOP,* 1st Ser. 9 (1893), pp.7-8.

14. Anon., 'Winter Distress', *COSOP,* 1st Ser. 53 (1896), p.230.

15. G.S. Jones, *Outcast London,* pp.241-61.

16. C.S. Loch, *Charity Organisation,* pp.61-2.

17. Octavia Hill, 'The Charity Organisation Society', *COSOP,* 1st Ser. 15 (1889), p.17.

18. Rev. and Mrs Samuel A. Barnett, *Practicable Socialism* (London, 1888), p.41.

19. B. Bosanquet, 'Character and its Bearing on Social Causation', *Aspects of the Social Problem,* p.113.

20. Mrs B. Bosanquet, *Rich and Poor,* p.6.

21. Anon., 'Winter Distress', p.232.

22. B. Bosanquet, 'The Duties of Citizenship', *Aspects of the Social Problem,* p.26.

23. B. Bosanquet, *Aspects of the Social Problem,* p.vi.

24. B. Bosanquet, 'The Duties of Citizenship', ibid., pp.22-3.

25. Anon., 'The Collecting Savings Bank', *COSOP,* 1st Ser. 36 (1894), p.121.

26. C.S. Loch, 'Charity Organisation', *COSOP,* 1st Ser. 40 (1893), p.153.

27. C.S. Loch, 'Charity Organisation', p.156.

28.   H. Dendy (later Bosanquet), 'The Meaning and Methods of True Charity'
      in B. Bosanquet, *Aspects of the Social Problem,* p.178.
29.   Caroline Emilia Stephen quoted in M. Goodwin (ed.), *Nineteenth
      Century Opinion* (Harmondsworth, 1951), pp.70-71.
30.   N. McCord, 'The Poor Law and Philanthropy', in D. Fraser (ed.), *The
      New Poor Law in the Nineteenth Century* (London, 1975), p.100.
31.   Mrs Leon, 'The Assistance of School Children', *COSOP,* 1st Ser.
      45 (1894), p.180.
32.   C.S. Loch, *Charity Organisation,* p.19.
33.   Anon., 'Why is it Wrong to Supplement Outdoor Relief?', *COSOP,*
      1st Ser. 31, (1893), p.99.
34.   Anon., 'Why is it Wrong. . .', p.104.
35.   COS Area 1, Case No.4995 (1887-1900), Greater London Council,
      Charity Organisation Society Casepapers(hereafter *Casepapers*). I am
      grateful to the Greater London Council and to the Family Welfare
      Association for permission to refer to these casepapers. In the passages
      which subsequently appear, names and other details are suitably disguised
      in order to respect the confidentiality of the papers.
36.   For an account of the Barnetts' alienation from the COS and Canon
      Barnett's quarrel with Loch in 1895 see Henrietta O. Barnett, *Canon
      Barnett: His Life, Work and Friends* (London, 1919), II, pp.5-7, 26,
      and Mowat, *Charity Organisation Society,* pp.126-9.
37.   Anon., 'Why I joined the Charity Organisation Society'. *COSOP,*
      1st Ser. 11 (n.d.), p.9.
38.   Young and Ashton, *British Social Work,* p.103.
39.   B. Kirkman Gray, *Philanthropy and the State* (London, 1908), p.113.
40.   Beatrice Webb, *My Apprenticeship* (London, 1926), p.203.
41.   H.L. Woolcombe, 'Enquiry and Office Work', *COSOP,* 1st Ser. 54
      (1893), p.238.
42.   H.L. Woolcombe, 'Enquiry and Office Work', p.234.
43.   COS, Central Case No. 1030 (1875-94), *Casepapers.*
44.   H.L. Woolcombe, 'Enquiry and Office Work', p.236.
45.   COS Central Case No. 1030, *Casepapers.*
46.   Anon., 'Why is it Wrong. . .', pp.101-4.
47.   Quoted in N.Timms, 'Social Work in Action – A Historical Study', *Case
      Conference,* VII 10 (April 1961), p.260.
48.   COS Area 1, Case No. 4995 (1887-1900), *Casepapers.*
49.   Mrs B. Bosanquet, *Rich and Poor,* p.120.
50.   D. Fraser, *British Welfare State,* p.119.
51.   H.V. Toynbee, 'The Employment of Volunteers' *COSOP.,* 1st Ser. 55
      (1893), p.245.
52.   N. Timms, *Social Casework* (London, 1964), p.196.
53.   COS Area 1, Case No. 4995, *Casepapers.*
54.   H. Bosanquet, *The Standard of Life,* 2nd edn. (London, 1906), p.169.
55.   G.S. Jones, *Outcast London,* p.270.
56.   Anon., 'Winter Distress', p.230.
57.   Mrs B. Bosanquet, *Rich and Poor,* p.99.
58.   C.S. Loch, 'Charity Organization', p.156.
59.   COS Area 1, Case No. 4995, *Casepapers.*
60.   COS Area 1, Case No. 10196 (1894-1911), *Casepapers.*
61.   COS Central Case No. 2489 (1874-84), *Casepapers.*
62.   Barbara Wootton, *Social Science and Social Pathology* (London, 1959),
      p.279.
63.   R. Pinker, *Social Theory and Social Policy* (London, 1971), p.186.

9 SALVATION ARMY RIOTS, THE 'SKELETON ARMY' AND LEGAL AUTHORITY IN THE PROVINCIAL TOWN*

Victor Bailey

There was a meeting of the Councillors yesterday and from reliable information that has reached me the Mayor has promised to hold aloof. The leading business men of the Town, with few exceptions are members of the Skeleton Army who have notices printed inviting members to join the Skeleton Army. Their programme on Sunday next, at a given signal is to cut open the drum end and put in the drummer, cover the processionists with red ruddle and flour and keep us from the Barracks.Oh! Hallelujah, the town is on a blaze from end to end, and much spiritual awakening in every chapel, glory be to Jesus! His name shall be praised! Bless Him! The employers promise their people that if they get saved they will not employ them any longer. But Hallelujah they are getting saved in spite of the Devil. The Superintendent has flatly refused either protection outside or inside. The Sergt. but grins and indirectly encourages them. On Sunday last when I got knocked down a policeman was by my side. He simply grinned and walked on. 30 Barrels of Beer were given to the roughs to prime them. A great many of these Dear misguided men have withdrawn and there will be grand results shortly Hallelujah! here we have clearly established our right of processioning. The publicans grind their teeth at me, their trade here is shaken to its very foundation. It is a fact that about 6 p.m. on Sunday last there were not 6 men in 23 public houses. The week-night services are well attended. The offerings are better & if the police would only do their duty, all would be well, as the dear people are just beginning to understand us.

'Captain' Lomas, 23 November 1882, Swan Temperance Hotel,
Honiton, Devon

I

In the late Victorian period the British economy underwent a major transition in response to the international challenge to its industrial and commercial supremacy. At the same time, the outlook and demeanour of the workforce pointed to the break-up of working-class liberalism and to

231

a revival of labour's own political aspirations. But throughout these years, there was a marked absence of the social disorder of a widespread, semi-revolutionary nature, characteristic of earlier economic and social transitions. With the onset of economic depression in the 1880s, London's propertied classes suspected the emergence of a revolutionary threat, but it was fired by a city-bred 'residuum', not an organised and rebellious working class.[1] Only the outlying rural areas in the Celtic fringe were at all affected by extensive social protest: the tithe riots in Wales and the crofting riots in Scotland, in the 1880s. In late Victorian England, the threat to public order came only from transient outbreaks of election, anti-Catholic and labour disturbances.[2] It was evident that the governmental acquiescence in alternative ways of 'handling' protest, notably trade unions and political associations, and the development of a system of preventive policing had done what was required of them. Riots no longer performed a crucial role in the articulation of social and economic grievances.

One effect of this undoubted decline of social protest from the mid-nineteenth century has been that historians have neglected the isolated outbreaks of riot in the late Victorian period.[3] The present study of the riots against the Salvation Army, between 1878 and 1890, is intended partially to correct that neglect. It alters in no way the overall view of the depleted role of social protest: indeed, it sustains the argument that riots in this period posed no substantial threat to the social order. But the riots of the late Victorian period can tell us a great deal about legal authority, and the use of discretionary legal powers — in this instance, by the local authorities of the smaller provincial towns of the southern counties. Previous references to the Salvation Army riots have come from the hands of criminal lawyers, but have said nothing about the administration of the law by local magistrates, even though the majority of offences relating to public order were tried summarily. Instead, the emphasis has been on the Queen's Bench judgements (regarding the law of public meeting and processioning) which have formed precedents in the warehouse of case law.[4] If much greater generosity is shown to the historical context in which the Salvation Army riots occurred, it becomes possible to reach behind these abstract legal decisions to the husbandry of the law by the local authorities. This examination reveals, above all, the unreality of the venerable notion of 'good law' which is seen as wholly autonomous in relation to human interests, and entirely independent of all social agencies.

II

The Christian faith has often confronted hostility, 'mobbing' and violent persecution. Opposition to an alien faith affected the growth and recruitment of early Methodism, Primitive Methodism and the Bible Christians. Persecution only strengthened the incipient movements. Anti-Methodist mobs were confirmation that at least the religious message was not ignored, and that the breakaway sect was reaching the large section of the ungodly who were excluded by the increasing respectability of the established congregations.[5] Formed in 1878, the Salvation Army similarly provoked physical opposition from organised 'Skeleton Armies' who tried to drive it out of the towns, just as protestant 'mobs' evicted newly-established Catholic missions.[6] The attitude of the Salvationists to the 'Skeleton Armies' was inevitably ambiguous. The 'Skeletons' were their harshest critics, but also testimony that the missionaries were reaching the 'social residuum'. 'It was very hard', said Mrs Booth, 'when the members of the Army were facing these dangerous classes. They had no other motive but to save them.'[7]

The earliest incidents which revealed an organised resistance to the Salvation Army were in East London. In the summer of 1880 'Captain' Payne of the Whitechapel corps told the *War Cry* of an opposition army entitled, 'The unconverted Salvation Army', which held open-air meetings and processions in imitation. But the 'real, original, first skeleton army', according to George Railton (first Commissioner of the Salvation Army) was organised in Weston-super-Mare (Somerset) in 1881.[8] As a term, 'Skeleton Army' was quickly taken up and used in other towns where the Salvationists were attacked.[9] Not all of the incidents in which the term was used, however, involved an organised 'Skeleton Army'. In Sheffield in January 1882 the Salvationists were attacked by irregular crowds of working men.[10] More strictly, the 'Skeleton Armies' were a social phenomenon of the Southern and Home Counties. The term itself seems to have derived from groups like the 'Skull and Crossbones Boys', organisations which celebrated Guy Fawkes' night.[11] Recruits came mainly from the working-class quarters of towns; predominantly young labourers, shop assistants or semi-skilled workers.[12] In most towns the public houses had a hand in the recruitment. Surrounding villages often contributed to the opposition army, as in Honiton (Devon) in 1882. Occasionally, 'Skeleton Armies' supported each other, as between towns along the Sussex coast in 1884.[13] The 'Skeletons' often wore elaborate costumes, and their processions were executed with care, incorporating parodied elements of the

Salvationist parades. Through subscriptions from publicans, beersellers and other tradesmen, the 'Skeleton Armies' became a well-organised secular imitation, and a unique instrument of social pressure.[14]

The 'Skeleton Armies' used a variety of tactics to intimidate the preachers. In Folkestone (Kent) as the Salvation Army came out of its barracks, seven hundred 'roughs' formed up across the street, 'moving as slowly as it was possible for them to do without stopping altogether'. At Basingstoke 'rough music' was played alongside the Salvationist processions. The borough magistrates believed the aim was, 'by marching in front and at the sides of the [Salvation] Army, making discordant noises, beating old kettles, trays, etc., and blowing horns, to bring that body into odium and disrepute'.[15] Most commonly, the 'Skeletons' indulged in rough 'horse-play', hustling the preachers as they marched through the streets, pelting them with lime dust and refuse. At times, brutal assaults were inflicted on the 'soldiers',[16] but the intimidation was meant to insult more than injure. In 1886, the 'Hallelujah Lasses' visited Ryde (Isle of Wight) where 'liquid manure and sewer contents were freely thrown at them'. At Honiton when the Salvationists left a prayer meeting, they were showered with turnips; and the female evangelists 'not only had their clothes smeared with cow dung but their faces covered with mud'. In St Albans (Herts.) 'officers' were ducked in a water-trough. In Eastbourne (Sussex) the Salvationists had bullocks driven into their procession, and they were also nearly forced into the sea by a crowd.[17] The 'Skeleton Armies' were artists in devising intimidating and humiliating sanctions, emphatically telling the Salvation Army to take its religious excesses out of the borough.

Salvation Army riots affected at least sixty towns and cities between 1878 and 1891. There was a rough correspondence in time between the direction of Salvation Army expansion and the riots.[18] North and North-western England, the Midlands and South Wales experienced riots between 1879 and 1882. There were disturbances in the Home Counties, Hampshire, Wiltshire, Somerset and Devon between 1881 and 1883; whilst the Southern counties of Sussex and Kent were affected between 1883 and 1885. Most of the riots, approximately one half, occurred in the years of greatest growth of the Salvation Army: 1882 and 1883. In relation to the distribution of 'Army' corps, the riots were over-represented in southern England. Disturbances broke out in Basingstoke (Hants., 1881); Salisbury (Wilts., 1881); Exeter and Honiton (Devon, 1881-2); Poole (Dorset, 1882); Weston-super-Mare and Yeovil (Somerset, 1882); Guildford (Surrey, 1882); Maidstone,

Folkestone and Gravesend (Kent, 1883); and Worthing and Hastings (Sussex, 1884). In contrast, the Midlands, Yorkshire, Northumberland and Lancashire were much less affected by the disturbances.[19] A variety of urban environments experienced riots, but one half of the outbreaks occurred in towns of between 3,000 and 20,000 population: in seaside resort towns like Worthing, Ryde and Weston-super-Mare; in declining manufacturing towns like Honiton and Frome; and in old provincial capitals like Salisbury.[20]

Salvationist riots did break out in larger towns above 50,000 population, in industrial cities like Sheffield (Yorks., 1881), Oldham (Lancs., 1882) and Birkenhead (Cheshire, 1882), and in some regions of London (between 1879 and 1883).[21] But in absolute numbers the riots were a product of small and medium-sized towns, especially in the South. Even in the 1880s, these towns were a vital proportion of urban England, and only gradually adjusting to nineteenth-century patterns of industrial and urban expansion.[22] Interpretation of the disturbances must especially admit such townships, where a large number of Salvation Army riots took place, and where, significantly, the legal authorities were implicated in the religious disorder.

There follows an examination of the different forms the impetus to riot could take — the conduct of the brewery trade; popular resentment against the social content of Salvationism; and community disapproval of an organisation extraneous to the local society. This assessment has the virtue of depicting the setting in which the legal authorities of the provincial southern towns acted. But it is useful, first, to highlight those features of the Salvation Army which assist in elucidating the intense opposition which emerged in these towns.

III

The Salvation Army was one variant of late Methodist revivalism. As with earlier schisms, there had been a charismatic preacher straining under the old discipline, eager to return to the outcast and their purity of heart. William Booth had originally intended creating a 'bridge' between the 'unchurched' and the nonconformist Church, but this adjusted to the formation of a separate religious organisation.[23] To attract what Booth termed the 'submerged tenth', the Nonconformists were too conventional. His work was a continuous protest against the religious sects which remained remote from the lives of the poor, and which stressed man's intellect above his soul.

Salvationism was defined by the emphasis upon a personal relationship with a personal God; and by an intense congregational participation in the service. There was no intellectualism and little theology. Nor was there confirmation, communion or other festivals, preparatory to salvation. The sacraments and the implication of a priesthood were thought to interfere with the essential transition from 'sinner' to 'saved'. The all-important theological tenet of Salvationism was complete faith in the atoning work of Christ, a faith which would lead to conversion, to an instant flight from the terror of hell to the assurance of heaven. In their meetings emotional appeals were repeatedly made for an immediate 'Closing with Christ'. In the 'closing' appeared the intense fervour characteristic of revivalist sessions.[24] Following conversion, the Salvationist dedicated himself to the spiritual welfare of other sinners. He was asked to adapt his religious message to the requirements of his own deprived inheritance; to call upon his own personal experience rather than upon authorised or established learning. He was thrust forward to testify to the effects of salvation in his indigenous language and style. The public confessional arrayed 'Blood Washed Colliers' and 'Hallelujah Fishmongers' with the 'Milkman who has not watered his milk since he was saved'. The Army's success, albeit limited, was due to this employment of all converts in the subsequent work, and to the recognition of the value of personal testimony presented on a popular cultural level, in vivacious language 'understanded of the people'.[25] Essential ingredients of any popular religion thus lay at the centre of Salvationism: the interleaving of religious and vernacular effect, and a trust in the flexible, anarchic quality of revivalist meetings.

In 1878 the Christian Mission transformed itself into the 'Salvation Army', with a centralised system of organisation and government, and with the full 'military' trappings of uniforms, bands and official titles.[26] The application of this military form to the 'Army's' evangelistic work took place amid a wave of Imperialist feeling at the time of the Russian-Turkish war; and it was an opportunist extension of this mood.[27] As befitted an 'Army' of Christian Soldiers, it concentrated on the 'war' to be waged against the 'dangerous classes' of urban society — 'men as essentially heathen', declared Mrs Booth, 'as any in the centre of Africa'.[28]. Salvationist publications emphasised that the ruffianism met by the 'soldiers' and 'officers' indicated the existence of an outlying 'continent' of evil, where irreligious masses were drowning in a sea of drunkenness and crime. It was a national benefit to civilise such people, 'to preserve the country from mob-violence and revolution'.[29] It all represented a belief that along with missionary activity in the outskirts of the Empire (and the Salvation Army became the most advanced exponent of religious colonisation),

the civilising mission against all sinners had also to be carried on at home.
As a great empire required an imperial race, so a Christian empire
required a Christian populace.[30]

The adjustment of the Salvation Army's organisation and style to
the military form enhanced the dichotomy of piety and aggression
which distinguished its work. A spiritual offensive was to be waged
against the 'Devil's Kingdom' — that great mass of urban demoralised
held captive by the publican, the brewer and other satanic subordinates.
A comprehensive code of directions was quickly available to field officers
on how to bombard, capture and hold fresh territory.[31] It was
recommended that the Army's 'invasion' of new towns and cities be
publicised in the most elaborate and antagonistic manner, luridly
dramatised as an imminent contest between Sin and Redemption.[32]
This militant evangelism was to rely on regular street meetings and
processions to reach the depressed strata of urban districts. A procession
through the working-class streets of the town and an open-air meeting
was held on most work-day evenings, varied by lunchtime meetings at
the gates of factories and workshops. On Sundays, when the urban poor
were at their leisure, the Salvationists went into the streets on two or
even three separate occasions, singing hymns adapted for their audience
— 'Out of the Gutter we pick them up' — led by officers in red guernseys
ornamented with religious texts. 'Open-airs' always ended with an
invitation to the audience to return to the barracks for an indoor service.
Alternatively, the procession alone was used as a 'beat-up' for recruits,
collecting a crowd of people 'with whom', the Queen's Bench judges
were told, 'attended by much shouting and singing, uproar and noise,
they eventually return to the hall, where a meeting is then held'.[33]

The overall aim was not merely to hold a temporary mission, or
conduct a few revival services. 'We desire', proclaimed a Salvationist
pamphlet, 'to make a permanent lodgement, and to raise up a force
that shall continue the war. . .To make a raid, and capture a few
prisoners, is a far less difficult task than the establishment and maintenance of a fort in the enemy's territory.'[34] This required carrying an
aggressive Christianity into the slums and working-class quarters of
towns. In this drive to become, in Booth's phrase, 'a great Hallelujah
press-gang', opposition was inevitably provoked. The 'Army' gave
notice to the Gravesend police in October 1884 that they would 'enter
and occupy'. *The Times* observed: 'A portion of the inhabitants have
intimated their intention of banding themselves together to oppose
the invasion.'[35]

IV

'My work', William Booth promised, 'is to make war on the hosts that keep the underworld submerged.'[36] The Salvation Army's militant, evangelistic campaign centred particularly on the cultural distractions to a truly religious life. All symbols of spiritual degeneration — theatres, boxing booths, pubs and music halls — were attacked in print and on the platform. They were also 'invaded', like St Giles' Fair in Oxford, the racecourse at Northampton, or the new havens of cheap recreation, the seaside resort towns, where the entertainments of the music hall were repeated on the seashore.[37] General Booth was convinced that the 'Worthings' and 'Hastings' contained their own social residuum, contaminated by drink and the popular amusements, and were the weekend nurseries of London's thriftless pauperism. He was determined that the Salvation Army should pit its own literature, songs and recreations against the attractions of the tavern and music hall. Accordingly, the Salvationists sang outside public houses; touted the *War Cry* around tap rooms and music halls; and arranged religious 'free-and-easies'. Poverty, they largely attributed to drunkenness; spiritual and moral weakness, they laid at the door of the public house. They preached total abstinence from alcohol, and took as a major test of their success (celebrated in the reports sent into the *War Cry* each week) the estimated decline in public house patronage.[38] In numerous towns, theatres or halls of entertainment were purchased, and loudly proclaimed as a victory for Salvationism. In London the best-known attack on popular amusements took place around the Eagle Tavern in City Road, with its Grecian theatre and dancing gardens.[39] A moral imperialism looked to colonise spaces in which 'savage' entertainments were performed. In all, the Salvationists reinforced the Nonconformist 'social gospel' which traced human evils to drink, gambling and low music halls.[40]

This determined onslaught against public houses and forms of cheap entertainment like the music hall (commonly extensions of public houses), led to a recreational or cultural rivalry between the representatives of the brewery trade and the Salvation Army. Publicans immediately set about remunerating local 'roughs' for attacking the Salvationist processions. No explanation of the anti-Salvationist 'mobbing' was more commonly endorsed than the financing of 'Skeleton Armies' through the public houses.

The Salvation Army always held the 'trade' responsible for the organised opposition. A memorandum was prepared for the Home Secretary in 1881 in which it was claimed that:

. . .in nearly every town where there has been any opposition we have been able to trace it more or less, to the direct instigation, and often open leadership of either individual Brewers or Publicans, or their *employes* [sic].

The plan adopted is by treating and otherwise inciting gangs of roughs. . . to hustle and pelt, and mob the people.[41]

The document was based on the reports sent into 'Army' headquarters by 'officers' in the field. It was validated by a good deal more evidence in the next few years. Local Salvationists accused the 'trade' of instigating riots in Chester, Salisbury, Stamford, Maidstone, Gravesend, Honiton, Basingstoke, Luton and Eastbourne.[42] In Honiton, judging from court depositions, the publicans and leading shopkeepers were employing men from miles around. George Wood (a local farmer, who had allowed the Salvationists to meet in his cottage in 1882) deposed that the 'Skeleton Army' was 'supported strongly by the publicans. They have issued papers ridiculing the Salvation Army and by their papers as well as by words declare their intention of driving the Salvation Army from Honiton.'[43] It was not only the Salvationists and their sympathisers who blamed the 'trade' for the disturbances. The Basingstoke magistrates explained to the Home Secretary that once the Salvationists began to empty the public houses and diminish drunkenness, 'roughs' from the town and surrounding villages were organised through the pubs into a 'Skeleton Army', and paid by the main brewers in the town.[44]

It is unlikely that even the Salvationists anticipated the degree to which the brewers and publicans would go to stifle their campaign. The 'trade', however, was well-versed in organising intimidation, whether against harmful licensing legislation or on behalf of political patrons in election campaigns.[45] In the early 1880s the brewers mobilised their lower-class 'rowdies' to silence a religion which challenged their profits and their prestige.

Like other temperance reformers, the Salvation Army sought not only to free the 'unchurched' from the grips of the publican, but also to modify indigenous working-class mores. Implicit in the Salvationist crusade against the public houses and music halls was an arrogant attack on popular leisure habits and life-styles. The opposition to the Salvation Army included, in consequence, the so-called 'rough' working class who were determined to defend their entertainments, and who were hostile to the self-righteous cult of respectability.[46]

Contempt for particular working-class mores and behaviour patterns was an integral facet of the Salvationist creed. Dramatic conversions were claimed, conversions which were said to involve an instant switch in life-style from drunkard to preacher, and occasion an improvement in work and self-discipline. Abstention from working-class sports and pastimes, from theatre entertainment, and from drinking, swearing and smoking were all announced to be the results of 'finding the Lord'. In Sheffield there was the 'man who when converted hardly knew himself'.[47] The penitent seat, itself, placed in front of the platform, not only tested the sincerity of the 'calling', but also (as Bramwell Booth recognised) 'is conspicuous enough to register a distinct break in a man's life'.[48] Outspoken confession on the public platform, before other companions, was arranged to serve the same purpose. The major emphasis of Salvationism was on moral improvement, but the effects of being 'born again' were expected to leaven social as well as moral careers. Salvationists were not so conscious of the need to be industrious and to progress as previous generations of Methodists had been, but the conversion was promised to lead, in every case, to a 'self help' which offset poverty and engendered social respectability.[49]

No sooner was a good convert found than he was turned into a recruiting officer and sent into his native street to drum up fresh recruits. At open-air meetings, the new moral and social outlook was conceitedly advanced. In an unerring evocation of the earnest convert in close association with old friends, William Pett-Ridge in *Mord Em'ly* had Miss Gilliken testify to her recent criminal past:

> Many a time 'ave I with my ongodly companions, roamed about
> these streets, seeking what I might devour . . . thank the Lord, I
> 'ave been washed whiter than SNOW, and purified of my sins. . .
> and I do so want all you other sinful people to come and do likewise
> and not to 'old back, becos' you think you're too black, or too
> wicked, or too sinful; for b'lieve me, my friends, BAD as you may
> be, and no doubt are. . .[50]

It was this self-righteous unction, the arrogation of a new-found respectability which provoked stern resistance from the working-class communities which the Salvationists persistently entered. Many Salvationists were 'tin kettled' and otherwise intimidated by workmates alarmed at their 'going over'. Salvationist hymns and proceedings were ridiculed, according to Charles Booth, the social investigator, at public houses and in the music halls. And in London and other towns defensive barriers were erected at the ends of working-class streets to prevent the Salvationists' entry.[51]

An articulate working-class response to the Salvation Army was a feature of urban areas like London where working people, impervious to the evangelical crusade, clung to fixed drinking habits and leisure patterns.[52] Yet I would argue that working-class 'mobbing' of the Salvationists was most typical of the small southern towns. In these urban areas there was no radical working-class culture which had strongly adopted certain values of social respectability. This description would better fit the politically conscious strongholds of Lancashire and the West Riding, which were resistant to the Salvation Army, and which also showed few disturbances. Instead, there was an 'old culture' which in some ways was less inhibited and 'non-respectable', rudely rejecting the values of temperance and respectability, but which was equally often deferential and jingoist. It is beyond the scope of this essay, but the plebeian response to the Salvation Army reveals, at least in part, a confrontation *within* working-class culture.[53]

The Chief Constable of West Sussex, in correspondence with William Booth in 1884, admitted that, besides the opposition from 'the rougher portion of the inhabitants', the Worthing tradesmen and residents objected to the disruption of 'the customary quiet of the town'. The result was that 'the persons who form the 'Skeleton Army' have received and do receive considerable encouragement from those in a higher social position'.[54] In other middle-class watering places the complicity of more senior townsmen in the opposition to the Salvation Army was based on the anxiety that noisy bands and processions would ruin the fashionable season.[55] But something larger was involved than the reputations of seaside resorts. Behind the 'Skeleton Armies' there was a wider community sanction against an intruding religious organisation which disturbed customary religious and social patterns. In safely Conservative boroughs like Guildford and Eastbourne, in declining towns like Honiton and Frome, or in cathedral towns like Salisbury and Exeter, the pattern of social relationships retained a deferential character. Social ties sustained local rather than national loyalties. It was in such towns, portrayed so authentically by Robert Tressell in his 'Mugsborough' (based on Hastings), that the Salvation Army's entrance could release a wider outbreak of enraged traditionalism.[56]

Salvationist street processions and open-air meetings were thought to coarsen religion, and offended respectable townsmen.[57] Community hostility was intensified by stories of strange ceremonials and revivalist excesses inside the Salvationist barracks. Sexual rumours were rife, sustained by the evening revivalist meetings, and the ritual, 'Creeping for Jesus' when the lights were turned low and kneeling men and women groped with their hands in the darkness.[58] Imagination and guilt fed the community's fears for established morality. The Salvationists also intensified a number of fundamental strains in the local society. They challenged traditional views of the woman's role in the church and family by refusing distinctions in rank, authority and duty between men and women preachers. In their campaign to forge a new cultural identity for the young, they defied parental authority.[59] Work relationships in the local society were also strained when employees were sent packing for joining the Salvationist processions. Tradesmen who supported the 'Army' were boycotted and put out of business.[60] Religious ill-feeling could develop, as in Basingstoke in 1881 when church and chapel took opposing sides. In other towns, the Salvationists rekindled the political rivalry between Tory and Liberal factions, an integral facet of which could be the respective allegiance to the drink trade and the temperance cause.[61] In all, there was the realistic anxiety that the Salvationists would divide families and the community.

Many of the 'Skeleton Armies' were embodiments of these fears of change and disruption in the traditional structure and control of the community.[62] Once established, social legitimacy was imparted to the 'Skeleton Army' in a number of ways. Pulpit speeches gave clerical sanction to mob violence in Basingstoke (1881) and in Eastbourne (1892). Local newspapers were believed to have incited disturbances in Gravesend (1883) and Worthing (1884). Special constables recruited from the tradesmen of Basingstoke refused to act against a 'Skeleton Army' which took the Union Jack as its colours.[63] If the 'Skeletons' were encouraged to evict the Salvation Army, they were also directed against those people in the community who welcomed or assisted the 'Army'.[64]

Whilst working men and 'roughs' constituted the 'Skeleton Armies', the wider community approved of them. The 'Skeletons' assisted the collective defence against anticipated religious and social change. In these towns there was a strong 'parochial consciousness', defined by a network of personal relations, and by a physically limited neighbourhood. It produced an insularity which inspired a xenophobic outburst against as well-defined a body of outsiders as the Salvation Army. In the anti-Salvationist riots in the southern towns there was a demonstration of fidelity to customary national values (which found another outlet for expression in the jingo riots against the pro-Boers at the end of the century).

In time, the Salvation Army was counted among the churches of most towns, and carried on its work without arousing physical opposition.[65] Its advance between 1878 and 1885, however, was met with sustained and organised 'mobbing', impeding, yet also firing its religious 'war' against the urban 'submerged'. The existence of fully-organised 'Skeleton Armies' in the provincial towns of the southern counties was, in part, an expression of the hostility of the brewery trade to an assault on popular entertainments which it provided. The opposition was also a lower-class reflex to an arrogant religiosity which lauded the social and moral values of 'respectability'. But these separate strands were often constituents of a larger community disquiet at the social and religious alterations which the 'Army' induced. It was in this context of the southern provincial town that the performance of the legal authorities was notoriously unsatisfactory. By May 1882 it led John Bright to regret 'the foolish and unjust magistrates to whom in some districts the administration of the law is unfortunately committed'.[66]

V

A crucial dimension to the Salvation Army riots was the role of the authorities who were responsible for the maintenance of public order. From a large number of towns affected by riots, the Home Secretary received complaints about the reluctance of the police and the magistracy to act firmly against the 'mobbing'. Most criticism was levelled at the authorities of the small towns of the southern counties, where the religious disorder was most extensive.[67] In these provincial towns, law enforcement policy had the same character. The 'Skeleton Army' was officially endorsed in the hope that the Salvationists would tire of being rabbled; and more permanent prohibition of Salvationist meetings and processions was improvised through administrative action. Above all, the authorities seemed determined to curb the disorders without having either to repress the 'Skeleton Army' or to protect the Salvationists in their provocative missionary work.

Judicial and police behaviour in the towns of the southern counties clearly encouraged the mobbing of the Salvationists. Legitimacy was imparted to the 'Skeleton Armies' of Poole and Eastbourne by police court magistrates delivering public and abusive attacks on the beliefs and practices of the evangelists.[68] Magistrates at Worthing refused to issue summonses applied for by the Salvationists against members of the 'Skeleton Army', making comments, attested William Booth, 'calculated to encourage the mob, and to assure them of immunity from penal consequences'.[69] Well-publicised refusals by the Ryde and Salisbury magistrates to grant police protection to Salvationist processions similarly incited disturbances. In Exeter, Guildford, Gravesend and Folkestone, police constables openly refused to interfere to prevent the assaults, and declined to summons rioters whom they obviously recognised.[70] In Honiton at the end of 1882, the 'Skeleton Army' was even more evidently endorsed by the magistracy and police authority. After another day of disrupted meetings and processions in November, 'Captain' Lomas went to see Honiton's Mayor, an *ex officio* magistrate. The latter stated that 'he would not protect [the Salvationists] any more than he would the Skeleton Army'. Further, according to Lomas: 'He [the Mayor] said that it would be always like that while the Salvation Army remained, and he, with the Superintendent of Police would like to see us out of the town.' A week later, Lomas alleged in a sworn deposition that the ex-Mayor, also an *ex officio* magistrate, had recently informed the town council that 'if a hundred cases were brought before him by the Salvation Army he would dismiss them all'.[71] After court appearances in which the ex-Mayor deliberately refused to convict a number of rioters in spite of sufficient evidence, the Home Secretary notified the Lord Chancellor, who agreed that the Mayor and ex-Mayor were justly charged 'with having practically encouraged, and afforded impunity to these disturbances'.[72]

In many of the provincial towns where official licence was extended to the 'Skeleton Army', the legal authorities also looked to more effective administrative means of suppressing the outdoor work of the Salvationists. In the nineteenth century there was no nationwide statutory power to prohibit public meetings and processions. There were, however, statutory enactments applicable to a large number of individual towns which could be adapted to allow the suppression of street meetings and processions.[73] In particular, there were borough bye-laws and provisions in Local Acts. In response to the disorders, numerous Watch Committees and Local Boards utilised the discretionary powers afforded by this array of local enactments.

At the beginning of the 1880s, however, borough authorities attempted first to impose a *common law* power of prohibition over processioning. If there were disturbances as a result of Salvation Army processions, magistrates simply announced that no more processions could be held because they would lead to breaches of the peace. The Salvation officers, if they persisted, were fined and imprisoned. In so far as the prohibitory proclamation was dependent on the threat of disorder, it even made possible the direct exploitation of the 'Skeleton

Army' by the authorities. The magistrates of Basingstoke, William
Booth claimed, were party to a conspiracy 'to encourage the mob in the
creation of a state of things which can then be used as an excuse for
attempting by law to stop our work in the streets'.[74] In March, 1881,
when the 'Skeleton Army' assaulted a Sunday procession, the Mayor
read the Riot Act, and called out a battery of artillery billeted in the
town. In his report to the War Office, Major Curson maintained that,
whilst met by large crowds in the streets, 'I did not see any rioting,
and the mob seemed to me to be remarkably good tempered.' But the
day's proceedings were to validate the proclamation, issued in April,
which forbade the Salvation Army from holding processions or open-
air meetings.[75]

In April, 1882, however, the Salvation Army succeeded in getting
a high court judgement on the validity of these proclamations. At
Weston-super-Mare, where the magistrates had likewise prohibited
processioning, the Salvation Army officer refused to disperse his
procession on the orders of the police, and submitted to arrest. The
magistrates convicted him of unlawful assembly, and bound him over
to keep the peace for twelve months. On appeal to the Divisional
Court, this conviction was reversed, the court stating that no crime
had been committed since the disturbances were caused by other
people whom the 'Army' did not incite.[76] This decision, in *Beatty* v.
Gillbanks, which effectively denied any nationwide common law
power to prohibit processions, forced the Home Office to issue
different directions to the magistracy.[77] By no means all local
authorities acted in accordance with this advice. Guildford's Mayor
told 'Captain' Bryan in September, 1882, that the bench had decided
to give no police protection 'adding that he knew the Salvation Army
had a legal right to procession in the streets, which they could exercise
if they liked, but if they did so it would be on their own risk and
responsibility'.[78] Other authorities pressed the Home Secretary for
amendments to the Town Police Clauses Act to give justices the general
discretionary power to prohibit processions.[79] Nevertheless, after 1882,
this avenue was largely abandoned, especially as subsequent legal
judgements gave confirmation to *Beatty* v. *Gillbanks.*[80] Instead, the
authorities turned to the remedies available through local enactments.

Between 1883 and 1891, bye-laws and Local Acts were used by a
number of provincial authorities in an attempt to repress the outdoor
work of the Salvation Army. In Ryde and Truro, bye-laws which
prohibited singing and the playing of music, under certain conditions,
were enforced by the authorities against the 'Army's' processions. To

give body to the Ryde enactment, all police protection of street parades was withdrawn, and the Salvationists were left to the mercy of the 'Skeleton Army'.[81] At the end of 1884, when the Sussex watering places came under attack from the Salvation Army, a conference of coastal towns approved the inclusion of clauses prohibiting Sunday processions in the Local Acts of Hastings and Eastbourne.[82] In 1886, the Torquay authorities inserted a similar clause in their Improvement Act. This led to protracted struggles between the Salvationists and the local authorities in Torquay (1888) and Eastbourne (1891). For a period of two months in 1891, Eastbourne's Watch Committee prosecuted Sunday processionists; leading councillors called upon the 'Skeleton Army' to champion this administrative policy; whilst the magistrates refused to suppress the attacks made by the 'Skeleton Army' on the street processions and meetings.[83]

In conjunction with officially endorsed 'mobbing', then, a series of administrative powers was exploited by a large number of provincial authorities to put down the activities of the Salvation Army.[84] The 'Army' soon learned to expect and resist the authorities' opposition, the upshot being a fierce and varied legal battle during the 1880s in which the Salvationists earned a place alongside the Socialist groups as the defenders of the rights of processioning and meeting. Their struggle in the smaller provincial towns was the counterpart to the London fight to retain similar freedoms. But the struggle was not merely over the abstract legal rights of processioning and meeting, anymore than was the fight in London in the mid-1880s. The provincial authorities were resisting a larger challenge to social order and to legal prestige, which requires closer assessment.

VI

The particular character of the authorities' response to the disturbances was a result, in part, of magistrates joining, or being exhorted to join, with other businessmen and tradesmen to defend the special economic interests of the town. Official indulgence of 'mobbing', along with legal prevention of processioning, seemed directly related to the defence of the brewery trade in towns where the latter had representatives in authority.[85] In seaside towns, the authorities were more pressed to defend local interests in the tourist trade.[86] But the avoidance of damage to town economies was only part of the explanation. The authorities' actions were also determined by the difficulties of restoring public order once it was broken in these smaller provincial settings.

Small-town police forces were generally unprepared to deal with disturbances which raged around the street meetings and parades, held each evening and throughout the weekend.[87] Rather than overwork their police forces, or go to the expense and inconvenience of borrowing outside police or enrolling special constables, the authorities, in the first instance, often struck an informal bargain with the 'Skeleton Army' in the hope that the Salvationists would be forced by the 'mobbing' to restrict their work to indoor meetings.[88] For the same reason of maintaining public order, the authorities sought to prevent the Salvationists' outdoor work by taking premature administrative action against their meetings and processions. Fears that serious riots would result in Weston-super-Mare in March 1882, led the magistracy to prohibit the Salvationist processions.[89] A year later, at Folkestone, the authorities displayed a similar urgency to stop the disorders by acting against the Salvation Army. The clerk to the justices informed the Home Secretary that it was generally understood that 'if the Salvation Army will cease to parade the public streets the Skeleton Army will also discontinue their processions'. Therefore, despite the decision in *Beatty* v. *Gillbanks*, the clerk urged the government to give the justices discretionary power to prohibit processions.[90] In all, the authorities in many provincial towns agreed with the ex-Mayor at Honiton, who refused to act against the 'Skeleton Army', 'as he considered the Salvation Army were to blame and caused all the disturbances in the Town'.[91]

There was a more significant reason for the attitude and behaviour of the legal authorities to the Salvation Army. Salvationism challenged their social and legal influence. In its early years the Salvation Army must have appeared an awesome organisation: a body with effective national coordination, despatching, replacing and rearing disciplined cadres who spoke directly to the poor, who were unamenable to the local patterns of social discipline. Field officers stubbornly maintained their incessant missionary work in the streets, despite the disturbances it caused. They took unfavourable summary decisions to the higher courts; they refused to accept legal sanctions short of imprisonment.[92] Escorts were provided for convicted preachers on their way to prison; prisoners were welcomed home by a band and procession. And magisterial policy was denounced at indoor meetings and by way of public demonstrations.[93]

Moreover, just as the Salvation Army splintered religious and political communities, they could also divide, and thereby undermine the authorities in their administration of discretionary legal power. At Basingstoke in 1881, the magistrates initially employed both the

'Skeleton Army' and prohibitory proclamation to repress the
Salvationists. But after the appointment of new justices to the bench,
the Mayor lost control of magisterial policy. Thereafter, different
policies were enforced by the Mayor and Watch Committee (supported
by two more magistrates) on the one hand, and the rest of the bench
on the other. Whilst the Mayor tried to put down the 'Army's'
processions, the bench defended the preachers by imprisoning members
of the 'Skeleton Army'. For this firmness, the pro-Salvationist
magistrates were escorted to and from the police court by 'Skeletons'
playing 'rough music'.[94] Again in February 1882, when riots recurred,
the main bloc of magistrates used the county police to protect the
Salvation Army; the Mayor and Watch Committee reissued the
proclamation banning Salvationist processions.[95] This occasion
illustrates how the Salvation Army's entrance into one provincial
community led by stages from officially endorsed 'mobbing' and
administrative prohibition of the Salvationist processions, to public
dissension between the administrative and judicial arms of the law. At
the same time as the Salvation Army uncovered latent religious and
political rivalries, it provoked an associated conflict among the
Basingstoke authorities, which, in turn, engendered an inconsistent
policy of law enforcement. As in many other towns, the Salvation
Army's intransigence in the recruitment of the poor depreciated the
authority and standing of the law's representatives.

'The special sphere for the Salvation Army', explained Catherine Booth
in an address to London businessmen, 'is no doubt what are termed the
dangerous classes, and that there is great *need* for some such agency
recent events make but too manifest. The inability of the authorities
to cope with the ruffianly element. . .ought to awake everybody to the
necessity for something being done.'[96] The Salvation Army's assertion
that the organised 'Skeleton Armies' were a portent of the revolutionary
threat from the mass of urban demoralised, relied too heavily on
observation of metropolitan conditions. It did not accord with the
social configuration of the southern provincial towns. Fashionable
watering places and old provincial centres concealed aggregations of
badly housed, severely impoverished urban workers. But the poor were
still enclosed in social structures where personal influence and social
ties retarded class solidarities. The 'Skeleton Armies' were manifestations of these integrated social communities, more than of socially
segregated cities. They were participants in 'reactionary' riots on behalf
of established moral and social codes, not in disorder which presaged
social insurrection. Moreover, the Salvationists' submission that their

work was required to strengthen the inadequate forces of social order did not accord with the attitude and behaviour of judicial authority in many of the provincial towns where the 'Army' disembarked. Indeed, an essential facet of the outbreak and continuation of the riots against the Salvation Army was the role of the authorities. Provincial towns were not controlled by the professional agents of a dispassionate legal system. The juridical system was incestuously recruited from townsmen possessed of social and economic influence in the community. This urban elite enjoyed unhindered discretionary power, administering peacekeeping measures according to its personal assessment of the threat to public order. Hence, unlike London's legal system, relatively distanced from the community it policed, provincial authority retained a more intimate understanding of the nature of different species of disorder.[97] The informed basis of the authorities' behaviour was evident in the 'reactionary' riots against the Salvation Army. The authorities handed towns over to organised 'Skeleton Armies', approving and encouraging 'mobbing' in the hope of deterring a revivalist sect which disturbed the social peace. They buttressed the 'mobbing' by discriminative legal prohibitions of religious processions and meetings. The magistracy and Watch Committees sought, in these irregular ways, to disable what they perceived as a challenge from the Salvation Army to the social influence and authority of their class. In the consequent riots, there was frequent illustration of how the provincial authorities could regulate disorder which served as a form of social control rather than a challenge to it.

Notes

*I am grateful to Professor Royden Harrison, Mr Edward Thompson, Dr Tony Mason and Dr Sheridan Gilley for their valuable criticisms of earlier drafts of this article.
  1. See G. Stedman Jones, *Outcast London* (Oxford, 1971), chap. XVI. For an estimate of the middle-class perspective on the urban 'dangerous classes' and the threat of social disturbance, over the longer period from 1840-90, see V. Bailey, 'The Dangerous Classes in Late Victorian England' (Univ. of Warwick, PhD thesis, 1975), chap. V.
  2. See J.P.D. Dunbabin, *Rural Discontent in Nineteenth-Century Britain* (London, 1974), chaps. IX, X, XII and XIII. For references to election and anti-Catholic riots in the late Victorian period, see V. Bailey, op.cit., chap. III. For labour riots, see e.g., Public Record Office (hereafter PRO), HO 144/73872 (Lancs. cotton riots, 1878); PRO, HO 144/X41472 (Hull dock riots, 1893).
  3. However, see Dr Richter, 'The Role of Mob Riot in Victorian Elections, 1865-1885', *Victorian Studies,* vol.15 (1971),pp.19-28; R. Price, *An Imperial War and the British Working Class* (London, 1972), Chap. IV.

4.   See D.G.T. Williams, *Keeping the Peace* (London, 1967), chap.II.
5.   See J. Walsh, 'Methodism and the mob in the eighteenth century', in *Studies in Church History*, no. 8, ed. G.J. Cuming and D. Baker (Cambridge, 1972), pp.213-27.
6.   See J.F. Ede, *History of Wednesbury* (Wednesbury, 1962), p.318.
7.   *Daily Telegraph*, 23 April 1883, p.3.
8.   R. Sandall and A.R. Wiggins, *The History of the Salvation Army* (London, 1950), vol.II, pp.194-5; *The Times*, 15 Nov. 1881, p.10.
9.   e.g., in Exeter: *The Times*, 21 Oct. 1881.
10. *The Times*, 17 Jan. 1882, p.6.
11. *Worthing Gazette*, 17 July 1884. Cf. E. Rowan, *Wilson Carlile and the Church Army*, 3rd edn. (London, 1928), pp.66-7. The latest known reference to a 'Skeleton Army' was in 1893 in Egham, Surrey: 4 *Hansard* 17, 21 Sept. 1893, col. 1780.
12. The occupational data is drawn from press reports of court cases, mainly of rioters in Basingstoke (1881) and Worthing (1884).
13. Honiton: PRO, HO 45/A22415/5; *Sussex Coast Mercury*, 27 Sept. 1884, p.4.
14. Honiton: PRO; HO 45/A22415/10; R. Sandall, op.cit., II, p.193.
15. H. Castle, 16 April 1883: PRO, HO 45/A23941/5; Return containing Copies of any Correspondence which has passed between the Home Office and the Local Authorities of Basingstoke or other Places, with reference to the Suppression of Disturbances, *Parliamentary Papers*, 1882 (Cd. 132), vol. 54, p.17 at pp.29-30.
16. Folkestone, Jan. 1883: PRO, HO 45/A23941/3.
17. *Ryde and Isle of Wight News*, 24 Sept. 1886; Honiton: Dec. 1882; PRO, HO 45/A22415/4; St Albans: *Pall Mall Gazette*, 4 June 1888; Eastbourne, 1891: PRO, HO 144/X32743.
18. The Salvation Army's development is examined in C. Ward, 'The Social Sources of the Salvation Army 1865-1890' (Univ. of London, M Phil thesis, 1970), chap.IV.
19. There were few disturbances, and no organised 'Skeleton Armies' in strong Nonconformist areas like the Black Country or West Yorks: see *The Advertiser* (South Staffs.), 23 Aug. 1884, p.4. I am indebted to Ms Sheila Bailey of the University College of Swansea for the information on the Black Country.
20. Additionally, one fifth of the riots occurred in urban districts of 20,000-50,000 population, e.g. Exeter, Hastings, Eastbourne, Maidstone and Reading.
21. In London, the major disturbances took place in Hounslow, Walworth, Clapham, Stoke Newington and in the Whitechapel and City Roads: PRO, MEPO 2/168; Metropolitan Board of Works Papers, MBW 1023.
22. As a percentage of total population in 1891, urban sanitary districts of under 20,000 population contributed 26.3 per cent: S.J. Low 'The Rise of the Suburbs', *Contemporary Review*, 60 (Oct. 1891), p.548.
23. I am not attempting, here, to provide a full assessment of the Salvation Army as a religious and social organisation. For the detailed history of the movement, there is the Army's official history by R. Sandall and A.R. Wiggins, *The History of the Salvation Army*, 4 vols. (London, 1947-65). These volumes are no substitute, however, for the required work of historical sociology. The best historical critique of the Army is K.S. Inglis, *Churches and the Working Classes in Victorian England* (London, 1963), chap. V. See also, R. Robertson, 'The Salvation Army; the Persistence of Sectarianism', in *Patterns of Sectarianism*, ed. B.R. Wilson (London, 1967), pp.49-105.

24.   See Bramwell Booth, 'Salvation Army', in *Encyclopaedia of Religion and Ethics*, XI, ed. J. Hastings (Edinburgh, 2nd impress., 1934), p.157; R.Robertson, op.cit., pp.58-68.

25.   Rev. Randall Davidson, *The Times*, 29 June 1882, p.5. Cf. G.B. Shaw, *Major Barbara* (London, 1958), p.89.

26.   See *The Doctrines and Discipline of the Salvation Army* (London, 1881), section 29; R. Sandall, op.cit., II, chaps. VI-XVII. Cf. O. Anderson, 'The Growth of Christian Militarism in Mid-Victorian Britain', *English Historical Review*, vol. 86 (1971), pp.66-7.

27.   See R. Sandall, op.cit., I, pp.226, 285-7; H. Cunningham, 'Jingoism in 1877-78', *Victorian Studies*, XIV (1971), pp.429-53.

28.   *The Times*, 26 May 1880, p.7.

29.   20 Oct. 1881, in PRO, HO 45/A9228/3. See also, Catherine Booth, *Aggressive Christianity* (London, 1880), pp.11-12; Ditto, *The Salvation Army in relation to the Church and State* (London, 1883), pp.1-4.

30.   A few years later, in its elaborate scheme of farm and overseas colonies, the Salvation Army became an important constituent of the social-imperial movement: W. Booth, *In Darkest England and the Way Out* (London, 1890), *passim;* J. Harris, *Unemployment and Politics. A Study in English Social Policy 1886-1914* (Oxford, 1972), pp. 124-35.

31.   *Orders and Regulations for Field Officers of the Salvation Army* (London, 1886; first published in 1878), p.302.

32.   R. Sandall, op.cit., II, Appendix I, pp.326-7.

33.   *Beatty* v. *Gillbanks, The Times*, 14 June 1882, p.4. See also, PRO, MEPO 2/168; Charles Booth, *Life and Labour of the People in London*, 3rd series (London, 1903), vol.7, p.328.

34.   *All About the Salvation Army* (London, 1882), p.25.

35.   *The Times*, 15 May 1882, p.8.

36.   Quoted in A.G. Gardiner, *Prophets, Priests and Kings* (London, 1914), p.192.

37.   See S. Alexander, *St Giles Fair, 1830-1914* (Oxford, 1970), p.30; *The Times*, 19 Nov. 1886, p.5.

38.   *Daily Telegraph*, 31 Oct. 1881, p.2; H.S. Hume, *The Temperance Movement and the Salvation Army* (London, 1883), *passim.*

39.   *The Times*, 30 June 1882, p.10; *Daily Chronicle*, 13 Aug. 1882. When the 'Army' took possession of the Eagle Tavern, they were mobbed by large crowds in the surrounding streets: *The Times*, 23 Sept. 1882, p.5.

40.   See B. Harrison, *Drink and the Victorians* (London, 1971), p.333.

41.   Enclosed in PRO, HO 45/A2886/13. And see Bramwell Booth, *Echoes and Memories* (London, 1925), pp.28-9.

42.   *Chester Chronicle*, 1 April 1882, p.6; Salisbury, 1881: PRO, HO 45/A1775/2; Gravesend, 1884: HO 45/A32518/4; Honiton, 1883: HO 45/A22415/3; Basingstoke, 1881: HO 45/A2886/1; Luton, 1883: HO 45/A30742/1; Eastbourne, 1891: PRO, HO 144/X32743/61. London publicans were also said to be financing the 'Skeleton Army' in Whitechapel (1879) and in City Road (1883): *Saturday Review*, 5 July 1879; PRO, HO 45/A9275/26 (Jan. 1883).

43.   PRO, HO 45/A22415/3. The paper referred to was a publication entitled 'The Skeleton', circulated in Honiton.

44.   18 Aug. 1881: *PP* 1882, vol. 54, p.17 at pp.29-30; *Hants. and Berks. Gazette*, 24 Sept. 1881; PRO, HO 45/A2886/23. Cf., Gravesend, 1883: PRO, HO 45/A32518/1.

45.   See B. Harrison, op.cit., p.276; B.L. Crapster, ' "Our Trade, Our Politics". A Study of the Political Activity of the British Liquor Industry, 1868-1910' (Univ. of Harvard, PhD thesis, 1949), chap. III.

46. For the traditional attack by social or religious philanthropists on popular culture and life styles, see R.W. Malcolmson, *Popular Recreations in English Society 1700-1850* (Cambridge, 1973), pp.100-7; I. Bradley, *The Call to Seriousness — the Evangelical Impact on the Victorians* (London, 1976), chap. V.
47. *The Times*, 5 April 1882, p.8.
48. B. Booth, 'Salvation Army', in J. Hastings, op.cit.
49. *The Salvation Army as a Money-Making Concern* (London, 1881).
50. W. Pett-Ridge, *Mord Em'ly* (London, 1898), pp.135-6.
51. *The Salvation War* (London, 1883), p.35; C. Booth, op.cit., VII, p.325; Folkestone: PRO, HO 45/A23941/3. Street barriers were put up in Birkenhead: *Birkenhead and Cheshire Advertiser*, 28 Oct. 1882; and Hounslow: *The Times*, 25 Sept. 1884. And for contemporary reference to a conflict between the 'rough' and 'respectable' working class, see *Pall Mall Gazette*, 29 March 1881, p.3; *Saturday Review*, 20 Oct. 1883; *The Month*, vol. 44 (1882), p.480.
52. Cf. G. Stedman Jones, 'Working-Class Culture and Working-Class Politics in London, 1870-1900; Notes on the Remaking of a Working Class', *Journal of Social History*, VII, (Summer, 1974), pp.472-9 and 491.
53. Working-class opposition to the Salvation Army occasionally derived from religious sentiment, especially in Lancs. and Cheshire. Irish Catholics were responsible for riots in Bolton, 1882: H. Begbie, *The Life of General William Booth* (London, 1920), II, p. 5; Chester, 1882: *Chester Chronicle*, 1 April 1882; Birkenhead, 1883: *Birkenhead and Cheshire Advertiser*, 6 Jan. 1883; and Tredegar, 1882: PRO, HO 144/A18355/27.
54. 11 Aug. 1884: PRO, HO 45/X2676/12.
55. May 1883, Folkestone: PRO, HO 45/A23941/9.
56. See H. Pelling, *Social Geography of British Elections 1885-1900* (London, 1967), pp.85-6, 172; R. Tressell, *The Ragged Trousered Philanthropists* (London, 1968; first published 1914), *passim*.
57. Folkestone, Jan. 1883: PRO, HO 45/A23941/1.
58. H. Begbie, op.cit., II, p.17.
59. See O. Anderson, 'Women Preachers in Mid-Victorian Britain: Some reflexions on Feminism, Popular Religion and Social Change', *Historical Journal*, XII (1969), pp.467-84; H. Begbie, op.cit., I, p.479; Anon., *The Salvation Army: Is it a Good or an Evil? The Question Calmly Considered* (London, 1882), p.8.
60. Basingstoke: *Hants. and Berks. Gazette*, 23 April 1881, p.5; Honiton, Nov. 1882: PRO, HO 45/A22415/1; Whitchurch, 1888: PRO, HO 45/X24164/21; Eastbourne, 1891: PRO, HO 144/X32743/123.
61. *PP*, 1882, vol. 54, p.17 at pp.27-29; PRO, HO 45/A2886/16; Guildford, 1882: PRO, HO 45/A19890/8.
62. Guildford, Sept. 1882: PRO, HO 45/A19890/4. Cf., Salisbury, 1881: PRO, HO 45/A1775/4. Wealthier inhabitants sometimes worked vicariously through the publicans, as at Honiton: PRO, HO 45/A22415/5.
63. *Hants. and Berks. Gazette*, 17 Sept. 1881, p.5; PRO, HO 144/X32743/121; PRO, HO 45/A32518/3; *Sussex Coast Mercury*, 20 Sept. 1884, p.4; *Worthing Intelligencer*, 6 Sept. 1884. In Poole and Basingstoke (1881), imprisoned 'Skeletons' were escorted back into town by bands and a procession: PRO HO 45/A2886/13.
64. Worthing, 1884: PRO, HO 45/X2676/21; Basingstoke: *Hants. and Berks. Gazette*, 18 June 1884, p.5.
65. I have no strong explanation for the cessation of riots against the Salvation Army, except to suggest that familiarity bred indifference, and that the Army's adoption of social work from the mid-1880s attracted the support of the middle classes.

66.   Quoted in R. Sandall, op.cit., II, p.171.
67.   *The Times*, 4 Oct. 1883.
68.   PRO, HO 45/A2886/13; PRO, HO 144/X32743/28
69.   16 July 1884: PRO, HO 45/X2676/1. Cf., Basingstoke, 2 April 1881:
       PP 1882, vol. 54, p.17 at p.25; Folkestone: PRO, HO 45/A23941/4.
70.   *Ryde and Isle of Wight News*, 24 Sept. 1886; PRO, HO 45/A1775/6;
       HO 45/A18238/1; HO 45/A19890/1; HO 45/A32518/3; HO 45/A23941/3.
71.   27 Nov. 1882: PRO, HO 45/A22415/3.
72.   28 Dec. 1882, Lord Selborne to Sir William Harcourt (Home Secretary):
       PRO, HO 45/A22415/8.
73.   A fuller assessment of the law of public meeting and processioning is in
       D.G.T. Williams, *Keeping the Peace* (London, 1967), *passim.*
74.   2 April 1881: PRO, HO 45/A2886/13.
75.   *PP* 1882, vol. 54, p.17 at pp.19-21; PRO, HO 45/A2886/10.
76.   *Beatty* v. *Gillbanks*, 1882, QBD, vol. 9, p.308.
77.   PRO, HO 45/A9275/17.
78.   8 Sept. 1882: PRO, HO 45/A19890/4.
79.   Worthing: PRO, HO 45/X2676/19; Folkestone: HO 45/A23941/2.
80.   See *M'Clenaghan and others* v. *Waters, The Times*, 18 July 1882, p.4;
       PRO, HO 45/A16004/8 (Whitchurch); *Stone's Justices Manual*, 25th edn.
       (London, 1889), p.824; *Justice of the Peace*, vol. 48 (1884), p.659.
81.   PRO, HO 45/X4230/1; *R.* v. *Powell*, 1884, *Law Times*, vol. 51, p.92.
82.   *The Times*, 18 Nov. 1884, p.10; G.F. Chambers, *Eastbourne Memories
       of the Victorian Period 1845-1901* (Eastbourne, 1910), pp.209-10.
83.   PRO, HO 45/X18313; PRO, HO 144/X32743; Eastbourne Improvement
       Act, 1885 (Prosecutions for Open-Air Services), *PP* 1892 (Cd. 103), vol.
       65, p.115.
84.   Additionally, some authorities exploited the Highway Act (1835) to
       repress Salvationist street meetings – Stamford: PRO, HO 45/A47490B;
       Whitchurch: PRO, HO 45/X24164.
85.   Basingstoke, 1881: PRO, HO 45/A2886/2.
86.   Worthing: PRO, HO 45/X2676/1; Folkestone: HO 45/A23941/9.
87.   Salisbury, July 1882: PRO, HO 45/A18238/5; Folkestone, Feb. 1883:
       HO 45/A23941/4.
88.   Worthing: *Sussex Daily News*, 15 July 1884. Cf., Honiton, Nov. 1882:
       PRO, HO 45/A22415/2.
89.   1 April 1882: PRO, HO 45/A15220/2.
90.   Feb. to May 1883: PRO, HO 45/A23941/2-9.
91.   PRO, HO 45/A22415/6.
92.   Worthing: *The Salvation War* (London, 1884), p.12
93.   Frome: *The Times*, 30 Aug. 1884, p.4; Whitchurch: PRO, HO 45/A2886/20.
94.   7 Sept. 1881: PRO, HO 45/A2886/20; *PP* 1882, vol. 54, p.17 at p.31.
95.   March 1882: PRO, HO 45/A2886/25 and 29.
96.   C. Booth, *The Salvation Army in Relation to the Church and State* (London
       1883), p.1 (emphasis in original).
97.   See, V. Bailey, op.cit., chap. I, 'The Magistracy and the Urban Elite'.

INDEX